The
Ford Fleet
(1923-1989)

To a Ford "affectionado" —
Carl Barucelli with
best wishes!
John Greenwood
10/11/03

by
Clare J. Snider
and
Michael W. R. Davis

(fp)

Published
FRESHWATER PRESS, INC.
Cleveland, Ohio

Copyright © 1994 Helen Joan Snider

Library of Congress Card Catalog # 94-061026

Printed & Manufactured in the United States of America

Published by Freshwater Press, Inc.
Suite 3 R-E
1700 E. 13th Street
Cleveland, Ohio U.S.A.

TABLE OF CONTENTS

FAMILY FORWARD

Our family would like to dedicate the publication of this book to the memory of Clare J. Snider, a loving husband, father and extremely devoted Ford Motor Company employee. This book is a direct result of his love for his work and his concern for the preservation of the history of the Ford Fleet.

We would like to thank Mike Davis for his expert assistance and hard work in helping get this book to print. Also, I would like to thank Leonard Schimm and Ruth Tenorio for their help in locating many important photographs.

Our family memories of spring sailing dates, summer passengers, fall storms, winter coal runs and late night ship-to-shore calls will never be forgotten.

Thomas A. Snider

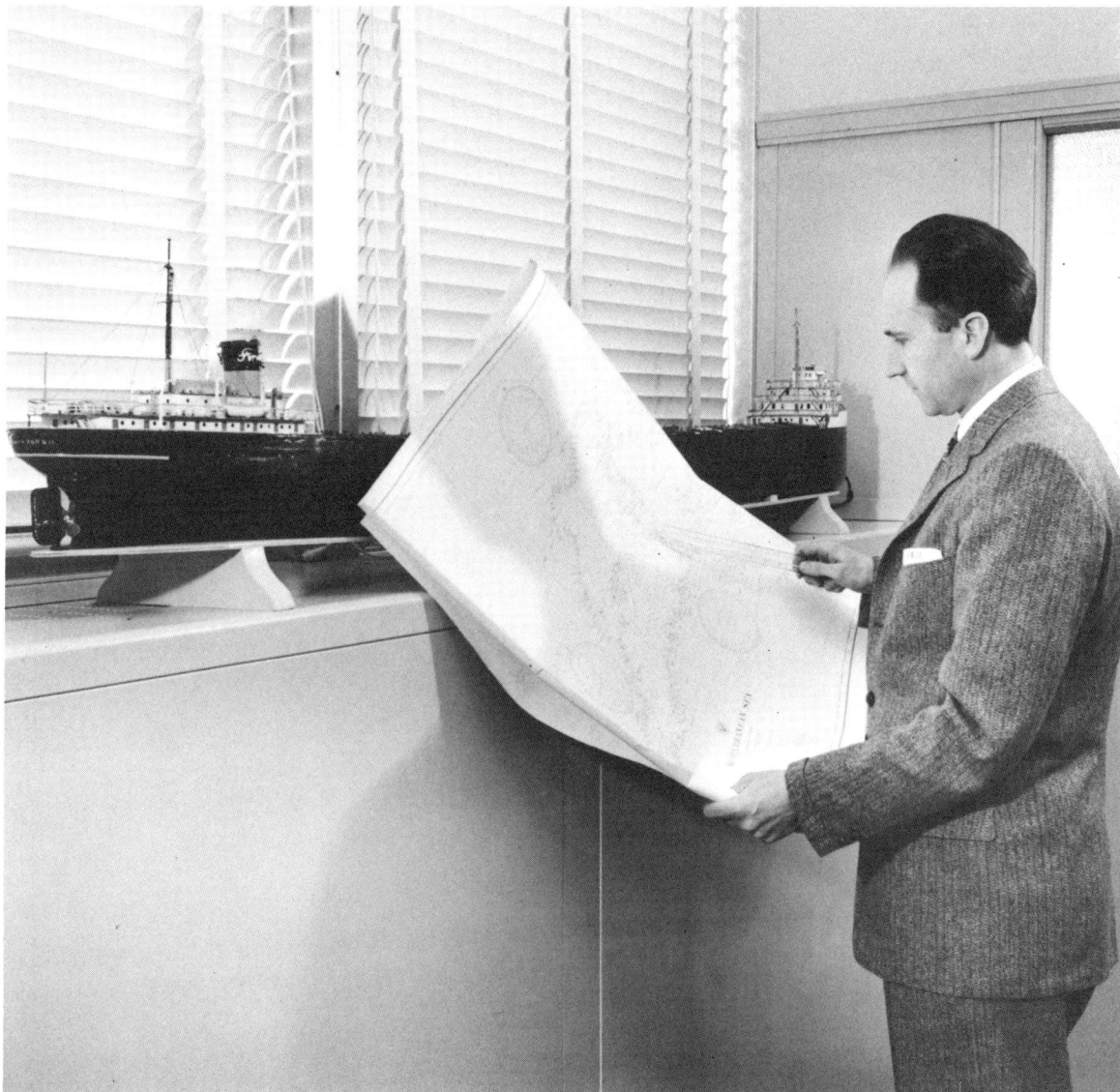

EDITOR'S NOTE

In January 1982, John G. Nye, then Marine Operations manager for Ford Motor Company's Steel Division, sent me a note asking that I respond to an attached inquiry letter from a woman in Florida. I was then Public Relations Services manager for Ford Motor Company's Public Affairs Staff and my PR responsibilities included Marine Operations. It was routine for Public Relations to handle inquiries from the public.

The letter surprised me with a little known facet of Ford's history — that the company had operated ocean–going ships, several of which were torpedoed and sunk by Nazi U–boats in World War II. Everyone along the Great Lakes seemed to know about Ford's ore carriers, which plied the inland waters between the western end of Lake Superior and Lake Erie. But ocean-going? Sunk by U-boats? My curiosity was immediately kindled.

Specifically, the inquiry letter (see Appendix IIB) asked for information about the woman's great uncle, John Sidney Kilpatrick, who had been chief engineer of Ford's LAKE OSWEYA. What information did we have on the ship's sinking and his death, she asked.

To help me respond, John had included in his transmittal "a section of Clare Snider's history of the Ford Marine Dept. that you may want to include in a reply to Miss Kilpatrick." The two-and- a-half-page enclosure — "Ford Marine Operations Goes To War" — was one of the most fascinating documents I'd seen in my more than 20 years with Ford.

A review of the definitive three-volume "official history" of Ford Motor Company by Columbia University Professors Allan Nevins and Frank Earnest Hill showed only a bare four paragraphs and a handful of references devoted to the "Ford Fleet" in more than 1900 pages of Ford history. Clare Snider's history clearly was a story that needed to be told.

I called John for more information: Who was Clare Snider? What did the rest of the history look like? Had it ever been published?

I learned that Clare had been the well-loved Marine Operations manager who had retired some years before, in 1975. I had not known him, as I had worked in quite different parts of the company in the years before 1975. John sent me a 50-page typed manuscript, which Clare had assembled before his retirement and from which the brief account of World War II events had been extracted, along with the further sad news that Clare had died suddenly only a few weeks earlier.

By itself, the manuscript had both a wealth of fascinating material and a shortage of the details necessary to constitute a publishable book, as opposed to a mere pamphlet. John told me, however, that Freshwater Press, which specialized in books about Great Lakes shipping, might be interested. Later he put me in touch with Clare's son, Tom. Itturned out, indeed, that Clare had continued working on the history after his retirement — but the family understandably was too distraught by his death to think about having it refined and updated for publication at that time.

Eventually, however, their grief diminished, I retired from Ford and subsequent activities, and this volume has resulted. Tom Snider brought me an expanded version of the manuscript, up from 50 to about 210 typewritten pages, which his father was actively working on at the time of his death. Most of this longer manuscript clearly had benefited from some erudite editing, which I subsequently determined was provided by a Roman Catholic cleric. The priest, one of several in Southeastern Michigan whose hobby is Great Lakes maritime history, is the Rev. Peter J. Van der Linden, assistant pastor of St. Joseph's parish in Port Huron, Michigan.

Freshwater Press and I have endeavored, where possible (especially for the post-World War II period), to maintain the language of Clare Snider's original account. Substantial additional information that has come to light, such as the sale of Ford's Fleet in 1989, or my interpretation of Clare's words, generally is indicated in footnotes, included in the appendix, or otherwise flagged.

Numerous persons have assisted in the research necessary to edit and augment Clare Snider's manuscript, and in its production. They include Darlene Flaherty, Robert Isom, Joel Pitcoff, Richard Routh and John Tome of Ford Motor Company; Tim Tigue of Rouge Steel Company; Dwight Vincent, a retired Navy Reserve captain and amateur marine historian; numerous personnel at the National Archives, Washington, D.C.; Kathy Lloyd and John Hodges of the Naval Historical Center; especially the Rev. Edward J. Dowling of the University of Detroit, always helpful with his library of facts and photos; and the reference librarians at the Birmingham (Michigan) Public Library.

Also Steve Mrozek, formerly of the Dossin Great Lakes Museum, and Robert Casey, of the Archives at Henry Ford Museum and Greenfield Village, both former colleagues from the Detroit Historical Museum; Robert W. Cosgrove, an amateur historian in several diverse fields; John Kelvin of Engineering Technology Publishing, Inc., and Barbara Kelvin and her daughter Wendy Hobart, who entered the original manuscript on a word processor; Bob Tera and fellow writer Doug Williams, word-processing counselors; Jack Kausch of Jack Kausch Photography; John Greenwood and Mike Dills of Freshwater Press; my daughter Betsy Davis; and fellow Ford retirees John Nye, former Marine Operations manager, and Captain Donald Erickson, long-time master of the S/S WILLIAM CLAY FORD. And finally, my wife Karen needs appreciation for her many hours of patience while this project was underway and for editing the final text.

To all, a hearty "thank you."

Michael W. R. Davis
Royal Oak, Michigan

INTRODUCTION

Many books have been written about the lore of the Great Lakes and many sea stories have been told to the thousands of "boat watchers" by those who have had an intimate connection with the sea, its ships and its people. Since water transportation was the superior way of travel for many decades even after modern land transportation was developed, there have been many pioneers in the maritime industry.

I found myself as one of those who, due to circumstances mostly beyond my control, was placed in a position where I became familiar with, and then responsible for, the operation of a Great Lakes fleet of ships, from its inception in the 1950s until after my retirement in 1975.

Because of this close connection with the Ford Motor Company Fleet and working for the men who originated and started the operation of the Fleet for Mr. Henry Ford when the Rouge Plant was being built, I now find myself in a unique position of being the only person still alive who has first-hand knowledge of both the day-to-day operation and historical background of this Fleet.

Therefore, I have written the following pages to describe and tell about what I know and remember about this small component of the company that was so good to me for the forty years I worked at Ford Motor Company.

Personal Notes: In 1934 when I graduated from high school in Remus, Michigan, in the central part of the state, our class motto was "Launched But Not Anchored." Maybe that motto has inspired me to take the time to write this pictorial and biographical history of the Ford Fleet.

Due to the 1929 depression the country was just recovering from at that time, it was necessary for most young men to go to work rather than on to higher education. I hitchhiked rides to Detroit several times looking for work and eventually got a job in a factory which was the ultimate place to work because of the high wages — 62.5 cents per hour. With no experience or college education, my employment with Ford started as a drill press operator in the Foundry Machine Shop at the Rouge Plant on February 28, 1935, when I was 18 years old.

As soon as I had saved enough money, I started night school, taking a secretarial course, and was fortunate enough to transfer to a job in the Rouge General Traffic Department in 1936. After working several years on the afternoon and midnight shifts, and with the help of a good friend of mine, I was given a clerk's job in the Marine Department in 1941.

Later, I became Vessel Dispatcher and then Marine Operations manager from 1958 until my retirement in 1975. Many people have asked me how I got a job like that and my only answer could be: "Be honest, work hard and be in the right place at the right time."

The following pages and illustrations will depict the history of the Ford Fleet, a history that is little known to many people, including many present company employees. To the best of my ability, I will present my experiences as accurately as possible, and I would like to give credit to all those Ford Marine employees I have worked with who helped to make this book possible. I also dedicate this book to the sailors of the past and present who crew the ships and have given me a chance to have the great experience of managing a fleet of Great Lakes ships.

In addition to the history of Ford's Marine Operations, I also have included a parallel history of the Ford Motor Company as I remembered the old timers telling their stories to me and from records that I had compiled or were made available to me. Mr. Ford built the Rouge Plant on the Rouge River so both the Fleet and the Plant were born at the same time and were never planned to be separated.[1]

Because this book is intended both for those who know a lot about the Ford Fleet and the members of the general public who have only seen our ships passing by, I have included a "Shipwatcher's Guide" so that some of the descriptions of shipboard positions and duties will make sense.

Clare J. Snider

EARLY HISTORY OF FORD MOTOR COMPANY

Henry Ford was a great man and the Ford Fleet was, relatively speaking, only a small but not insignificant part of his many adventures with the automobile industry. However, a fleet of ships was probably on his mind for a long time.

In 1902, after going through one failed automotive enterprise and withdrawing from another (which went on to become Cadillac) Henry Ford had decided he must have his own way with automobile manufacturing and further that he had to own a large stock interest, rather than a minor one as in the two past companies. He had set up a shop on Park Place, just north of Grand Circus Park in downtown Detroit, to build his "999" race car and develop a satisfactory "motorized family horse."

After winning an important race in October 1902, he attracted a new group of investors with the result the activity moved to a former wagon factory at Mack Avenue and the Belt Line railroad near the city's then eastern outskirts in April 1903. Incorporation of Ford Motor Company followed on June 16, 1903.

Production the first year totaled 1,700 cars, and the facility was quickly overwhelmed. So in 1905, the company moved to a newly built plant "ten times" larger at Piquette and Beaubien Streets, a few blocks southeast of Grand Boulevard and Woodward. It was probably about this time that his grand plan, which years later resulted in the Rouge Plant and Marine Operations, began to evolve.

Mr. Ford's ideal was to produce a standardized, inexpensive car for the masses. To do this, he had to gain clear control of the company from other stockholders who wanted to build expensive luxury cars. At the same time, he had to wrest control of manufacturing from suppliers like the Dodge brothers so he could reduce costs.

By 1907, a separate engine manufacturing plant had been created, sales had climbed to 8,423 cars and Mr. Ford had managed to become majority stockholder. The birth of the moving assembly line and mass production were on the horizon.

The Famous Model T

On October 1, 1908, the company introduced the famous Model T car, which was to remain in production, little changed, for 19 years. In 1910, Mr. Ford moved his operations northward three miles to the suburb of Highland Park, where a huge new plant included for the first time many manufacturing processes and even a test track. In a series of steps between 1912 and 1914, the moving assembly line was instituted and production rose to nearly a quarter million vehicles a year. He created a sensation in 1914 by announcing the five-dollar-a-day wage for his employees.

His success was so great that a further move was necessary and he began to acquire the Rouge property early in 1915. By this time he had already built one million Ford cars. Ford car production amounted to some 40 per cent of the whole industry's. Profits for reinvestment were huge.

Acquisition of the Rouge Property

The Rouge property Mr. Ford bought for his new plant was located on the east side of the Rouge River, five miles southwest of downtown Detroit. The river travelled from the farm lands northwest of Detroit through Dearborn and discharged into the Detroit River at the western edge of Detroit. It was shallow and carried its muddy water through swampy marshlands that were not navigable at that time. Mr. Ford selected a site for his new plant that was three miles from the river's mouth.

At the time, that stretch of the Rouge River was narrow and very winding and, to anyone but Mr. Ford, showed very little possibility for navigation by the large freighters that would eventually deliver raw materials to his new power plant and steelmaking facilities.

Mr. Ford originally envisaged the Rouge Plant as a supplement to Highland Park, to smelt iron, make coke for steel production, and especially as the location for a new farm tractor plant he had been wanting for some years.

Later his plans included making his own steel, glass, castings, stampings, etc., that were to be used in building Ford cars of the future. This required the construction of blast furnaces, coke ovens, a power house, open hearth furnaces, a rolling mill and glass plant, as well as many other large production buildings. All of these operations required huge amounts of iron ore, coal, limestone and sand to produce steel and glass. He also built a cement plant inside the complex that was to be used to construct the foundations and buildings.

During all of this planning, he intended to bring in these raw materials via the Rouge River, in ships that were the principal means of delivery at that time. Ultimately he wanted to control everything he could in the flow of production — raw materials, transportation and manufacture of all the components that went into car, truck and tractor assembly. Part of the transportation scene was creation of a new inland harbor. However, World War I, being fought with the Germans by that time, interfered.

World War I and the Eagle Boats
Mr. Ford had started out as an active pacifist, even leading an unsuccessful Peace Crusade in 1915. When continued German submarine warfare showed him that U. S. involvement was inevitable, he totally reversed his position and put the company's facilities at the disposal of the Allies, beginning with production of Dearborn-built Fordson farm tractors for the British in 1917.

Then, in addition to production of vehicles, helmets and Liberty aircraft engines at Highland Park for the U. S. war effort, in January 1918 Mr. Ford proposed to the U. S. Government that he could build up to 500 antisubmarine patrol boats on a Model T-like assembly line in a new plant to be constructed on the Rouge. The order came by telegram to produce 100 boats, the first to be delivered in five months, as Mr. Ford had somewhat optimistically proposed. Work started immediately (without a contract) to build what became known as "Eagle Boats."

First the Rouge had to be dredged and a launching platform, boat slip and dock built so that completed sub-chasers could be sailed out through the Great Lakes and New York Barge Canal or St. Lawrence River canal system to the Atlantic. Mr. Ford now had his inland harbor under way.

The Eagle Boats were to be built in the "A" and "B" Buildings under construction at the head of the Boat Slip. The A Building was 450 feet by 156 feet and was completed in 24 days. The B Building (today's Dearborn Assembly Plant) was 1,700 feet by 350 feet and was built between February 20 and May 25. According to Mr. Charles E. Sorensen, for many years head of production for Mr. Ford, the B Building "was high enough, with cranes the full length, to assemble the complete ship under its roof. It was designed so that we could add three floors the full width and use it for manufacturing and final assembly after we finished the Eagle boats."[2]

In order to complete the two buildings 4,150 tons of structural steel were used, two million board feet of wood flooring were laid and 56,000 panes of glass were set. To supply man power to work on this project, it was necessary for Mr. Ford to build a fleet of trucks and trailers to transport 8,000 employees from Detroit and Highland Park to the fields where this new plant was being built, because it was then so far from where they lived.

On the first of March — after the company had already expended millions of dollars — Mr. Ford received a contract signed by Franklin D. Roosevelt, then Assistant Secretary of the Navy. He signed and returned it to Washington along with a one-half-million-dollar personal bond. However, it was returned to Mr. Ford because he had failed to attach a 50-cent revenue stamp.[3]

The first keel was laid on May 7 before the buildings were finished, and the first Eagle Boat was launched into the new slip on July 10, less than six months after the proposal was made by Mr. Ford to Josephus Daniels, Secretary of the Navy.

After final assembly was completed, a hull was moved out of the B Building on a conveyor and the boat's pilot house installed. It was then placed in a cradle and moved west down the middle of the road to line up with the Boat Slip. Then the ship was placed on another set of tracks, over the property where the Marine Office Building now (1981) stands, and launched into the slip.

Before delivery of very many completed Eagle Boats could be made to the Government, the November 11, 1918, Armistice was signed, abruptly ending the war. At that time, 28 keels had been laid at the Rouge, 12 had been launched and seven had been commissioned by the Navy. It is doubtful if any of the boats ever saw combat service in World War I.

The production contract was soon amended to reduce the order to sixty of these 204-foot-long, 915-ton submarine pursuit vessels, and they all were commissioned by October 1919. They had been built from scratch in 21 months on an assembly line basis, when as many as 21 were in progress at one time.

Of the 60 built, a number were transferred by the U. S. to foreign fleets afterwards. Some became Coast Guard cutters. Some were sold as private yachts. The Navy used others for target ships. At the beginning of World War II in 1941, eight Eagles were still in Navy service. One, No. 56, was sunk, presumably by enemy action, on April 23, 1945.[4] The Eagles, you might say, were the beginning of the "FORD FLEET."

Model "T" Ford, 1920

CONSTRUCTION OF THE ROUGE PLANT

Work progressed on other facilities in the Rouge Plant and the city of Fordson grew up around the plant. The city of Dearborn was located several miles to the west of Fordson and Mr. Ford built a home out there. This home was known as "Fairlane," and was near his birthplace at Greenfield and Ford Roads. Later, Fordson and Dearborn merged into one city.

By the end of 1919, Mr. Ford was well on his way toward the original Rouge he had dreamed of. By August of that year, the B Building had been purchased from the Government and converted from Eagle Boat output to make Model T bodies. Two new coke ovens were put in production, miles of railways were laid and a sawmill was about to open.

In 1920, the "Henry" Blast Furnace was lighted and the Rouge Power House and the Dearborn Iron Foundry were put in operation. Mr. Ford purchased huge iron and lumber tracts in northern Michigan and coal mines in West Virginia and Kentucky. A railroad line was acquired which provided service to and from the plant, with connections to the port at Toledo and, further south, to main east-west rail lines (for easier distribution of cars and parts) and southern coal fields.

In 1921, Mr. Ford moved tractor production from the Dearborn plant near the present "Triple E" (Engine and Electrical Engineering) Building to the B Building and began operating a railroad within the plant. By this time he had built and sold 5,000,000 Ford cars. In 1922, he bought the Lincoln Motor Company, continued to produce Lincolns, and started making paper in a new paper mill. The "Benson" Blast Furnace was lighted in the same year.

Opening up the Rouge River

Just as earlier it had been necessary to dredge out the Rouge and build docks in order for the Eagle Boats to leave, the Rouge River now was made more navigable for big ships, such as ore carriers to bring in raw materials — ore, limestone, coal and sand — and freighters to carry out auto parts.

This project was largely undertaken by the U. S. Corps of Engineers as part of a larger scheme of improved inland navigation. A turning basin was dug at the south end of the Boat Slip. A deeper and straighter route to the Detroit River was carved out with a new channel opened between West Jefferson Avenue and the Detroit River. This was called the "Short Cut Canal" which, when completed, redefined the piece of property known as Zug Island by putting the main course of the river to the southwest rather than the north of the island. This canal was 3,000 feet long and about 400 feet wide at the Detroit River. Between the plant and the mouth, the Rouge was dredged and widened to have a bottom width of 200 feet and a depth of 21 feet.

Construction of drawbridges across the river was necessary, although the late Captain Frank Becker told me it was Mr. Ford's original idea to put rail and highway traffic under the river through a tunnel. However, he could never sell the idea to the Wayne County engineers and consequently three highway and three railway bridges were built across the Rouge between the Rouge Plant and the Detroit River.

The highway bridges were located at Dix, Fort and Jefferson Avenues. They were each 120 feet wide (broad for the time) and all at some elevation. New railway bridges for the Detroit Toledo and Ironton (DT&I), Pere Marquette and Wabash railroads also crossed the Rouge here, thus making six grade-level bridges that inbound and outbound ships had to pass through. This presented no navigation problems with the smaller ships that were in existence at that time.[5]

From July of 1922 until the opening of the new canal a year later, smaller vessels (550 to 900 tons) that could navigate the original course of the Rouge River were chartered to transfer raw materials from larger lake vessels to the plant complex. The first large ship to deliver a cargo of iron ore up the Rouge through the new Short Cut Canal was the 5500-gross-ton S/S CLETUS SCHNEIDER on July 11, 1923.

Altogether it took from 1917 to 1923 to complete this river navigation project and the cost (largely to the taxpayers and the railroads) was $10,000,000. Indeed, the DT&I was so short of money that it couldn't build its Rouge bridge. Mr. Ford ended up buying the railroad so that the bridge could get built and the navigation project go through. He then modernized the railroad according to exacting Ford standards, to serve the Rouge Plant and other company interests and then sold it at a considerable profit a few years later.

Mr. Ford also built many smaller plants in the outlying areas of southeastern Michigan to make parts for the Ford assembly lines. Nearly all of these plants were located on or near water, as was his home at Fairlane.

As the Rouge Plant began to need huge volumes of raw materials to feed the completed blast furnaces, coke ovens, power house, open hearth furnaces and glass plant, Mr. Ford made plans for his own fleet of ships.

Early view of Ford Rouge plant, c.1925

Eagle Boat keel in "B" building prior to launching, 1918

First completed Eagle Boat prior to launching, 1918

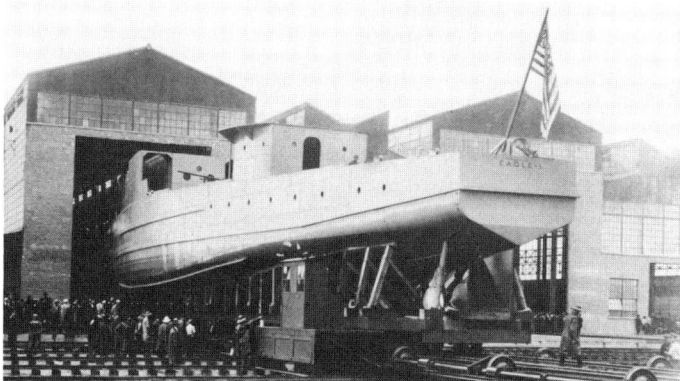

BEGINNING THE FORD FLEET

Mr. Ford followed two different paths to build his Fleet. First, in 1923, he ordered two 600-foot-long ore carriers to be built to company specifications, to bring raw materials into the Rouge Plant. Then, before these could be put into service, he began buying war-surplus freighters.

"Used" Ships

These "used" ships (although most were practically brand new) were first intended by Mr. Ford to be used as freighters carrying Ford cargo on the Great Lakes and as ocean-going freighters to carry Ford cars and parts overseas or along the Atlantic and Gulf seaboards. Later, as I will relate, other opportunities arose.

Following Mr. Ford's policy of adopting water transportation where possible, in early 1924 a large Ford dealer already was chartering a coastal freighter to carry new cars three times weekly from the Kearny, New Jersey, assembly plant to New Haven, Connecticut, and Providence, Rhode Island.[6]

The first Ford-owned ships to go into company service were two conventional small freighters, the S/S ONEIDA and the S/S ONONDAGA. These 261-foot-long, 2300-gross-ton freighters had been completed by Detroit Shipbuilding Company at Wyandotte, Michigan, in 1920. Ford bought them from the Independent Transportation Company for about $225,000 each. These two ships were of the "Laker" type, which will be discussed later. They made their first Ford trip on May 27, 1924, when together they left Toledo, Ohio, carrying coal to Ford facilities in Michigan's Upper Peninsula. On their return trip they carried lumber to the Rouge Plant.[7]

The HENRY and the BENSON

Far more important to this history of the Ford Fleet, however, was the launching of the two Ford ore carriers, because they remained in company service for more than 50 years and thus became very familiar to everyone along the waterways between western Lake Superior and Lake Erie.

Mr. Ford let contracts to the American Ship Building Company in Lorain, Ohio, to build the Motorship HENRY FORD II, launched March 1, 1924, and to Great Lakes Engineering Works in nearby Ecorse, Michigan, to build the Motorship BENSON FORD, launched April 26.[8] The BENSON actually was completed first and sailed on August 2, with the HENRY following on August 14, 1924. Six weeks before the HENRY was completed, a tornado struck Lorain, and the huge ship was broken loose from its moorings at the shipyard slip and crashed 50 yards away into the Nickel Plate Railroad bridge. Although the bridge was damaged, the ship fortunately was not.

The two new ships were named after Mr. Ford's two grandsons who were seven and five years old, respectively, at the time. Indeed, launch of the HENRY was accomplished by its young namesake via electrical remote control from Detroit. The HENRY and the BENSON were "put to work" instantly. By August 24, the HENRY had arrived at Duluth with 12,000 tons of coal from Ford mines in Kentucky, and the BENSON's initial voyage had been completed with iron ore delivered to the Rouge from Ford iron mines in the Upper Peninsula. The coal delivered upbound was for sale commercially in Minneapolis and St. Paul to "aid in maintaining reasonable prices and averting possible fuel shortages."[9]

From the very outset, these two ships were destined to be classics. Virtual twins, each had principal dimensions of 612' x 62', a moulded depth of 32 feet and a carrying capacity of 15,000 net tons at mid-summer draft.

When The HENRY and the BENSON were built, they were the most modern ships in the Great Lakes. To be the pride of the Lakes in 1924 meant they were competing with some 185 other

American ships that had been built since 1900. These were also considered great ships whey they were built. Most of them have now gone to the scrap yards.

The Sun-Doxford Engines: "Makin' Money, Makin' Money"

At Ford, innovation was not limited to the automotive products. These two new vessels took a departure from the usual coal-fired steam propulsion plant. The HENRY and the BENSON were each outfitted with a British-designed 3,000-hp Sun-Doxford diesel engine.

The patent right on these diesel engines was held by William Doxford & Sons Limited, Doxford, Sunderland, England. United States production rights for the Ford engines was granted to the Sun Shipbuilding & Drydock Company of Chester, Pennsylvania. The crankshafts were built at the Skoda Works, Pilsen, Czechoslovakia and approved for shipment on September 29, 1923.

Built for long and dependable service, the two "opposed-piston" Sun-Doxford engines were four–cylinder, two-cycle with a maximum horsepower rating of 3000 @ 85 rpm. As was the custom of the era, these engines were built with a long stroke — 91.2. As a consequence, they very efficiently pushed the HENRY and the BENSON through the water at a speed of 14.5 mph light and 13 mph loaded.

These were huge engines, yet they made very little noise for the 11-man engine room crew. However, the thump of the exhaust could be heard for miles. In fact, the steady "thump" of these engines was to become a matter of pride for the Ford Fleet. The shoreside sailors even joked that the engines' distinctive signature sounded like the words "makin' money, makin' money ..."

While it may have been a joke to some, it was no joke to Ford. These were engines for the long haul. Each burned a good grade of # 4 diesel oil to prevent wear to the cylinder walls and piston rings. They were started with compressed air and kept heated all during the shipping season to prevent expansion and contraction and leakage of water from the jackets. Additionally, each engine was completely overhauled each winter. They lasted the lifetime of the ships.

Of the first ten of the Sun-Doxford-built engines, Ford bought six. Two of the engines were 3,000-hp for the HENRY and BENSON. Two smaller 2,500-hp engines were installed in the M/S EAST INDIAN, a 461-foot former Government ocean freighter bought by Ford in 1925. Two 750-hp versions were installed in Henry Ford's personal yacht SIALIA. Later, a 1,000-hp Sun-Doxford was installed in another, smaller war–surplus ocean freighter, the 261-foot M/S LAKE OSWEYA.

As a matter of information, from the time Sun received its license from the Doxford company to build engines, many of its skilled technical personnel were brought over from the British Isles. In total, 64 Doxford engines of various sizes were built. The first three were installed in converted ocean steamers: BIDWELL, MILLER COUNTY and CHALLENGER. [10]

Mr. Ford and the HENRY

The M/S HENRY FORD II was Mr. Ford's favorite lake freighter. He took a personal interest in the ship and it was maintained in mint condition during his lifetime. Mr. Ford would spend many hours in the pilot house and engine room when he was on the ship and the crew could expect him to show up at any time during a voyage.

The handrails, switch gear, chadburns, steering wheel, etc., were all chrome-plated. Each winter these parts were removed from the ship and sent into the plant to be repaired and re-chromed. They were made in removable sections to make them easy to disassemble. The ship had teak-

M/S HENRY FORD II, c.1925

M/S BENSON FORD c. 1925

Henry Ford's yacht SIALIA

wood rails, doors and window sills that were continually refinished by experts from the plant. Stainless steel electric kitchens were installed, both forward and aft. The ship had the first electric winches and steering gears. Mr. Ford had electric heaters installed in each room of the forward cabins with individual thermostats. [12] (Other ships at that time were using steam to operate their equipment and to heat the living quarters.)

The HENRY had two master staterooms and two smaller staterooms on a lower deck, where guests or servants who travelled with Mr. Ford stayed. The rooms were furnished with Grand Rapids furniture of the finest quality. The original furniture remained on the ship until after his death in 1947.

Many advance plans had to be made by the Marine Department when Mr. Ford made his annual July trip to his summer home in the Huron Mountains near Marquette in northern Michigan. The HENRY would be completely repainted by the crew and shoreside workers. The trip schedule would be laid out in advance so that the Marine Office would know where the ship was at all times.

The BENSON was very similar to the HENRY but had only two master staterooms forward. She did have a forward galley, dining facilities and lounge. On the Texas deck there were two small staterooms. The staterooms and dining rooms on both ships were done with inlaid mahogany which, together with the candle wall lights and chandeliers, gave them an elegant appearance.

Yacht SIALIA
The SIALIA was also maintained by the Marine Department, as the operation was called in those days. As previously mentioned, Mr. Ford had installed two 750-hp Sun-Doxford diesel engines that were the 7th and 8th engines built by that company, and, inasmuch as these engines were similar to the ones in the HENRY and BENSON, the larger ships' engineers were familiar with their operation.

In one sense, you might call the SIALIA the first of Mr. Ford's Fleet. It started out as a twin-screw 1,200-hp steam yacht, 201 feet long with a 26-foot beam, displacing 726 tons, built at Wilmington, Delaware, in 1913 for a Chicago man, J. K. Stewart. Mr. Ford bought it from him in 1916, only to have it taken over by the Navy in June 1917 after U. S. entry into World War I.

Mr. Ford bought SIALIA back from the Government in 1920. Always interested in technological explorations in those days, it was natural for him to try the Sun-Doxfords in his own pleasure yacht. The vessel had to be lengthened 22 feet to accommodate the new engines, to a 223-foot overall length. But the conversion for the yacht did not work very well in that setting, and in disgust, he finally sold SIALIA about 1928. [13]

Mr. Ford had a boat house in the northwest corner of the Rouge Boat Slip where his son Edsel Ford also kept a yacht. The records show that in 1929, Mr. Edsel Ford owned two yachts, the 57-foot, 21-ton GREY HOUND and the 58-foot, 37-ton BUCKEYE, both powered by gasoline engines. A watchman was assigned to this boat house at all times and the yachts were maintained by the Ford Fleet crews off the ships. This boat house was dismantled following World War II.

The Ford Flag, Crew Uniforms and Other Tidbits
When Mr. Ford was aboard the HENRY, the "House" or "Owner's" flag would be flown. His own personal House Flag was called the "Bluebird of Happiness." It was designed for him and always flown on his Yacht SIALIA.

The Bluebird flag was enlarged to approximately four by seven feet and was flown from the flag staff of the HENRY to indicate when Mr. Ford was aboard. It had a blue bird with spread wings on a yellow background and blue borders. The same flag can now (1981) be seen flying from the forward flag staff of all the Ford ships. It has become a tradition for each fleet to fly its own House Flag at all times. However, at that time it was flown only when the owner was aboard a particular ship.

Also when Mr. Ford was aboard, the crew wore special "sailor suits" and the officers dressed in their navy blue officers' uniforms with the "Bluebird" ensign on their caps.

Both the HENRY and BENSON had the Ford insignia displayed in script on their stacks, white on a black background with the sign on the HENRY illuminated by hundreds of electric light bulbs that could be seen for miles. These were later replaced with signs that were easier and less costly to maintain. The old-fashioned stack on the BENSON was replaced in the 1960s with a new, modern, sloping stack.

The original colors for the two Ford vessels were black hulls, white superstructures, red decks and buff trim. In the mid-1960s, the new Company Corporate Design Policy required that the ships be trimmed in Corporate Blue and thus the buff was eliminated from the stacks and trim of the vessels.

Before our present modern communication systems were available, contact with the Ford ships was maintained through the use of Morse code radio telegraphy. In the late 1920s and early 30s, no other Great Lakes ships used or had communications with shoreside stations. This communication system was tied in with a radio station set up in Dearborn at the Ford Airport. It worked very successfully for many years.

Early Masters of the Ford Ships

When the BENSON was first put in service, Captain Stakes of Mr. Ford's Yacht SIALIA was named her master; he also functioned as the first head of Marine activities. When the HENRY was ready to sail, Captain Oscar A. Johnson, who was then master of a ship in the Tomlinson Fleet, was appointed master. He in turn brought John J. Pearce from the U. S. Steel Fleet as his first mate. When the BENSON's first captain damaged the ship on one of her first voyages, he was replaced by a Captain Daniels, then the steamboat inspector in Detroit. When Daniels also got into trouble, he too was replaced, in July 1925 by Pearce, who had been first mate of the sister ship only a year. Captain Pearce then sailed in the Ford Fleet as a master until his retirement in 1956.

By 1925, it was necessary to establish a Marine Department and Captain Johnson was brought ashore and appointed Marine superintendent. Captain Pearce was then transferred to the HENRY and Andy Pedersen was appointed master of the BENSON. He died aboard ship at the Soo in 1942, and was replaced by Captain John B. Martin.

When the BENSON under Captain Martin's command went aground in the St. Marys River, he resigned and was replaced by Captain Bernard Olsen. Likewise, Captain Sidney Inch gave up his command of the HENRY after striking the coal dock at Sandusky, Ohio. The ship encountered tornadic winds while trying to make the dock with tug assistance. He did, however, remain in the Fleet as a first mate until it was necessary for him to take medical retirement.

BUILDING FORD'S OCEAN & LAKE FLEET
1924-1941

As suggested earlier, following World War I many surplus ocean ships became available at bargain prices. During the war, shipbuilding contracts for many different types of vessels had been let, Eagle Boats being only one example. Three of these types later became part of the Ford Fleet: small 2300-ton freighters called "Lakers," designed narrow and short enough to pass through the Canadian canals and locks between the Great Lakes and the Atlantic; an 8000-ton ocean-going ship; and steel tugboats tough enough to operate in both the oceans and the Great Lakes.

World War I Lakers

The idea of the Lakers was to build small freighters on the Great Lakes which could carry supplies directly from Lake ports to England and France. These vessels were 247 to 261 feet long, no more than 43.5 feet wide, with gross tonnage ratings of 2300 to 2400, and 3200 to 4300-ton cargo capacities.

The Lakers had been built between 1917 and 1919 by such firms as Great Lakes Engineering Works (Ecorse, Michigan and Ashtabula, Ohio); Detroit Shipbuilding Company (Wyandotte, Michigan); American Ship Building Company (Cleveland and Lorain, Ohio; Superior, Wisconsin; Chicago, Illinois, and Buffalo, New York); Saginaw Shipbuilding Company (Saginaw, Michigan); Manitowoc Shipbuilding Company (Manitowoc, Wisconsin), and Toledo Shipbuilding Company (Toledo, Ohio).[14]

For many decades before World War I, large shipbuilding companies had sprung up around the Great Lakes. Prior to the introduction of the automobile, water transportation vied with railroads as the means for getting from one place to another. Shipbuilding on the Lakes boomed for many years. Today, few of these once great shipyards remain on the Lakes.

According to my friend and fellow marine historian Father Edward J. Dowling, S.J., retired professor of engineering graphics at the University of Detroit, the Lakers developed when the Canadian canal and lock systems were enlarged between 1884 and 1901. For the first time, shipbuilders in the Great Lakes could build vessels for the ocean trade, provided they were small enough to pass through the man-made waterways enroute to the Atlantic. In 1911, Great Lakes Engineering Works in Ecorse, Michigan, designed a new type of vessel specifically for this lake-to-ocean trade which became a prototype for the World War I freighters.

When the European war broke out in 1914, there was a rush of orders placed with shipyards in the Great Lakes for an "economical, medium-sized freighter known as the 'Fredrickstad' design." This design featured the "three island" profile so recognizable in the Lakers and was no longer than the 261 feet the Canadian locks would admit. When the U. S. entered the war in 1917, there were nearly a hundred Laker-type freighters being built in the Great Lakes for foreign nations. Almost all of these were taken over for American interests. Those which were being built for the British had two-word names, the first of which was "War." When they became U. S. ships, their names were generally changed to "Lake-something," and a number of them ended up in the Ford Fleet. For example, the WAR DRUM became Ford's LAKE LOUISE.

The United States Shipping Board then awarded war contracts for 346 additional merchant ships from Great Lakes yards, 307 of which were Lakers completed before cancellations at war's end, just as with the Eagle boats. "This program produced the largest number of standard type vessels built in the United States during World War I," Father Dowling wrote in his 1967 book, *The "Lakers" of World War I*. Only the Liberty ships and T-2 tankers built in World War II exceeded the number of Lakers; hence their familiar appearance on the oceans and, to a lesser extent, lakes earlier in this century.

Barge LAKE LOUISE in lay-up at L'Anse, Michigan

S/S ONONDAGA (2) loading lumber

Although the Lakers were similar in appearance and critical lock-clearing dimensions, there were several different designs spread among the shipyards listed above. These were known as the 1020A and B, 1042, 1044, 1074, 1093, 1099, 1143, 1144 and 1145. The Lakers in the Ford Fleet included 1020A and B, 1044, 1093 and 1144 designs. As examples of their original cost, the price paid by the Government to Great Lakes Engineering for Lakers increased from $455,000 each in November 1916, to $646,000 in March 1917, and $875,000 in April 1917.

The Lakers became almost the first types declared surplus by the U. S. Merchant Marine following the depression of 1921, when U. S. bottoms were undercut by foreign-flag pay scales. The Shipping Board had to put 800 of its 1,000 ships on inactive status by 1926. In April 1924, the Board decided to hold half of the 800 in reserve and sell or scrap the other 400.

Ford's First Lakers
Mr. Ford was quick to take advantage of the surplus ship windfall. By the end of May 1924, the 261-foot Lakers ONEIDA and ONONDAGA were already in Ford service on the Great Lakes. They had been quickly converted from coal to oil fuel and had been equipped with radio-telegraphs. (These two ships were what Father Dowling described as "post-Lakers," because they were built on speculation in 1920, along with a dozen-and-a-half others, from parts left over after the government war contracts expired.)

At the close of the 1924 Lakes shipping season that fall, the ONEIDA and the ONONDAGA went to sea for Ford. The latter ship departed from the Rouge November 7 as the first Ford Fleet vessel clearing from Detroit for a foreign port — Buenos Aires, Argentina. ONONDAGA's route took her down the Detroit River, across Lake Erie, through the Welland Canal to Lake Ontario, thence through the St. Lawrence canals and river to the Atlantic and straight to South America, reaching the destination on December 17 at the end of a 7,000-mile journey. The return voyage, with commercial cargo, ended at the Ford assembly plant in Norfolk, Virginia, where the ship was then to be based.

The ONEIDA's maiden ocean voyage for the company took her out of the Great Lakes the same way, then along the Atlantic and Gulf Coasts. She carried parts from the Rouge and Norfolk plants to Ford facilities at Jacksonville, New Orleans and Houston, reaching the last port on December 13, 1924. The cargo of parts for approximately 3,000 automobiles was the equivalent of 125 rail freight cars. Sugar was carried on the return trip to New York, arriving December 26.[15]

The company also was chartering vessels to carry its cargos from the Rouge to New York through the Barge Canal, from New York to Europe, and from Ford's Copenhagen, Denmark, plant to Scandinavian and Baltic Sea ports in Europe.

The M/S EAST INDIAN
Early in 1925, Mr. Ford continued to build an ocean fleet by purchasing the S/S EAST INDIAN from the reserve fleet of the U. S. Government for $80,000 with the provision she be converted from steam to diesel. At that time the Government was converting several other World War I-era steam freighters to diesel power, each with a different type and make of engine to determine which would be most suitable and economical for operation on different ocean trade routes. The 8200-ton EAST INDIAN was one of 20 ships ordered from Japanese shipyards by the U. S. Emergency Fleet Corporation in World War I. She was launched as the BEIKOKU MARU at Uraga in 1918, but like the smaller Lakers, became a member of the "mothball fleet" in 1920.

Inasmuch as the M/S HENRY FORD II and the M/S BENSON FORD were already in operation with new Sun-Doxford engines, Mr. Ford decided to install them in the EAST INDIAN also, as described earlier. At 461 feet, she was 200 feet too long to pass through the St. Lawrence River canal system and thus could only be used for ocean trade.[16]

M/S EAST INDIAN at an East Coast port

With her new engines totalling 3,000-hp and newly designated as "M/S" for Motor Ship (in place of "S/S" for Steam Ship), Ford Motor Company's EAST INDIAN became the most powerful merchant motorship then under the American flag.

Commander Beall's Account

In 1972, a former crewman aboard the EAST INDIAN on its maiden Ford voyage, retired Coast Guard Lieutenant Commander Irl V. Beall, wrote me his reminiscences of the voyage. I quote him at length because he describes in great firsthand detail Ford's Marine Operations more than 50 years ago and, also, because of the ship's eventual fate:

In the late Spring of 1925 EAST INDIAN was taken out of the mothball fleet and towed to Sun Shipbuilding, Chester, Pa., where everything in the engine and boiler rooms was removed, including the bulkhead between them. The steam steering engine and funnel were also removed, but all of the steam deck machinery was retained, such as cargo and anchor winches.

All Ford freighters on the lakes and ocean, and the land radio stations at Dearborn, Northville, L'Anse in Northern Michigan, and yacht SIALIA had radio operators. There was no opportunity for promotion in that field, so I decided to become a motorship engineer, since the Company's policy was, "We make our own marine engineers, we don't hire them." So Captain Stakes of SIALIA, who at that time was also Ford's marine superintendent, transferred me to the EAST INDIAN at Chester as a student engineer.

I arrived at Sun in late September 1925 and went to see the big ship which was to be my future home. The entire engine room area was as bare as Mother Hubbard's cupboard. I then contacted Mr. Fowler, Sun's engineer who had supervised tests on SIALIA's new engines in Detroit, and said to him, "I was told in Detroit that the ship was to sail in October." He replied, "Oh, she can sail in October all right, providing she can go without her engines. They are not finished yet."

16

Mr. Westley, former First Assistant Engineer of the HENRY, was there to supervise the conversion and to be Chief Engineer when completed. He assigned me to the machine shops several blocks from the shipyard where the engines were being built, working on various components, and later helping to install them in the ship. A young Scot machinist that I worked with said, "When I was serving my apprenticeship at the Doxford Works in England they called these kinds of engines 'Doxford's Cast Iron Monuments'." EAST INDIAN's 2,500 horsepower engines were 40 feet tall from bottom of bedplate to top of the upper piston guides, compared to SIALIA's smaller engines of 750 horsepower each which were 16 feet tall.

After all of the equipment had been installed in the engine room, the huge new funnel was put in place. It was oval in shape, 16 feet in diameter fore and aft, and painted in the usual Ford colors with Company name on the black band at the top. Floodlights were installed to illuminate the funnel, which were always turned on in port at night to show "FORD." The name and port of registry, San Francisco, were painted out on the stern, and big bronze letters, "EAST INDIAN / Detroit" were riveted on. One of the original boilers was modified and installed on a high platform amidships in the forward part of the engine room. Exhaust gases from the port main engine, when required, were passed through it to create sufficient steam pressure for heating the living areas when underway. In port, oil burners in the fire box (furnace) were used to generate a higher steam pressure for the cargo and anchor winches.

Electrical power was furnished by two 225-horsepower Worthington diesel engines connected to direct current generators, both located end-for-end on a raised platform on the port side of the lower engine room. A Hyde hydroelectric steering engine was installed to complete the big mechanical changes in the conversion. All staterooms were refurbished, and two new "Owner/ Guest" suites, one in light blue and the other in green, were built on the deck below the captain's quarters. Just as beautiful as on the SIALIA.

Upon close of navigation on the lakes, the three assistant engineers, two oilers, radio operator Humes and chief steward MacLean from the HENRY FORD II came down from River Rouge. Captain Hudgins and the three mates were all saltwater men from the ONEIDA and ONONDAGA, small lake-type ocean ships.

Henry Ford on the Rouge dock with Charles Sorenson

17

Loading of cargo began in mid-December, nearly three weeks before the ship was ready to leave the yard for trial runs off the Delaware Capes. This cargo consisted of complete Model T engines and hundreds of tons of metal parts brought down from Philadelphia by lighter, and consigned to the assembly plant in New Orleans.

We sailed from Chester on January 3, 1926, for the trial runs, and many notable men were on board as observers, among them J. N. Pew, president of Sun; Elmer Sperry of Sperry Gyroscope Company which built the navigation equipment including the "Metal Mike" for automatic steering, and William F. Gibbs of Gibbs & Cox naval architects, who in the early 1950's designed America's greatest liner, the UNITED STATES.

On full speed runs the ship made 16.5 knots with engines each running 96 revolutions per minute, with the ship partly loaded . The following day we returned to Philadelphia, loaded more parts and 600 complete Model T cars stowed in all the 'tween decks and in all available space on the top deck, and sailed for Tampa, Fla. on the 6th where the completed cars were discharged. Then to New Orleans where the parts were unloaded, and we made two trips more from there to Tampa with 600 cars each trip, thereby delivering 1,800 cars to Tampa at a time when the railroads running into Florida had placed an embargo on all automobile shipments into that state due to the severe congestion of building materials being shipped there.[17] So Ford got the jump on other car manufacturers with our big EAST INDIAN, unless they "caravanned" them into the state.

From Tampa we sailed to Weehawken, N.J., and loaded cars and parts for Europe. Evidently, the Company had decided to make its own stevedores, as it did its marine engineers, and it took three weeks to load the ship, working days and most nights with men brought over from the Kearny plant to run the winches, handle cargo, etc. Most of them had never worked on a ship before, and many of them did not return after one or two shifts. During the loading one man was killed and fifteen injured. After that experience the Company hired regular stevedoring firms to do the cargo handling. It was dangerous to even go on deck when those Kearny plant men were doing the loading.

Just before sailing from Weehawken the Company gave Captain Hudgins a schedule, giving time and date that the ship should arrive and depart at port in Europe. We departed that port on the Hudson opposite New York City on March 9th in a blinding snowstorm, when most other ships were at anchor or moored to piers, but a good pilot took us out to sea. Early one night mid-Atlantic a large liner was observed bound Westward and would pass us two or three miles away on our port side. EAST INDIAN's course was changed to pass the liner about a half mile off, and when almost abeam of us the floodlights that illuminated the funnel were turned on, thereby showing the big white letters "Ford" at the top. "It pays to advertise, even in the middle of the ocean," said First Assistant Engineer Atkinson.

The cargo consisted of 500 complete cars in individual boxes, with wheels removed and laid in each box, as Model Ts were not very large when so packed, all consigned to Trieste, Italy. We also carried 8,000 Model T engines, stacked in tiers in the 'tween decks; bundles of unpainted fenders and every kind of small metal parts for 8,000 cars to be assembled in the European plants, they furnishing all the tires, glass, wood, etc., for the cars. On deck we carried 100 complete Fordson tractors for Russia, which were unloaded at Trieste for transshipment by some foreign vessel to Odessa on the Black Sea.

The day after we arrived in Trieste right on schedule, the Italian motorship ALBERTA moored ahead of us with several hundred more Ford cars from New York. Two days later we got English language newspapers from Rome which contained big articles on the front page describing the uproar in the Italian senate about, "Why does Italy permit this dumping of cheap American cars in competition with our Fiat?"

Our next ports of call were Barcelona, Spain; Copenhagen, Denmark, and Antwerp, Belgium, having discharged car parts in all these ports, and so far, still on the Company's schedule given the Captain in New York.[18]

When empty, we began loading huge rails and other railroad equipment for the Company's

18

Detroit Toledo and Ironton Railroad, with stevedores working day and night. On the sixth morning at 6 a.m., with much cargo still on the dock and more arriving by rail and truck to fill the ship, orders were given to stop all loading and prepare to sail. Chief Officer Small said to Captain Hudgins, "We are not fully loaded and there is still cargo on the dock. Why can't we load it?" The Captain replied, "Our schedule says we must sail from Antwerp at 8 a.m. today. The ONEIDA or ONONDAGA can pick it up on their next trip. Secure for sea!"

Our next trip from Weehawken was to Northern Europe with car parts, then loaded wood pulp in Northern Sweden on the Gulf of Bothnia for the Scott Paper Company, Chester, Pa.

There I left the ship and returned to River Rouge where I was assigned to turbines in Power Plant No. 1. My one year as a junior engineer in connection with conversion and operation of the EAST INDIAN was not as easy, nor romantic, as I had anticipated. However, it was very interesting and educational, and soon thereafter I rejoined the Coast Guard.[19]

Ford Expansion Overseas

With the expansion of the company into Europe, Asia and South America, Mr. Ford used the EAST INDIAN and other surplus ships to carry knocked down autos and auto parts to his various foreign auto plants.

By the 1930s these plants had been located in Manchester and, later, Dagenham, England; Antwerp, Belgium; Copenhagen, Denmark; Berlin and, later, Cologne, Germany; Bordeaux and, later, Asnieres, Poissy and Strasbourg, France; Cork, Ireland; Amsterdam, Netherlands; Bucharest, Roumania; Constantinople, Turkey, and Barcelona, Spain. Also, Geelong, Sydney, Brisbane and Adelaide, Australia; Yokohama, Japan; Bombay, Calcutta and Madras, India; Singapore, Malaya; Colombo, Ceylon; Wellington, New Zealand; Johannesburg and Port Elizabeth, South Africa; Sao Paulo, Brazil; Montevideo, Uruguay; Buenos Aires, Argentina; Santiago, Chile; and Mexico City, Mexico.

Export plants were established in Chester, Pennsylvania, and Edgewater, New Jersey, where the Ford ships and others under charter would load their cargoes.

In essence, as this book illustrates, the ocean-going Ford Fleet functioned like "tramp steamers," carrying Ford cargo outbound and whatever they could rustle up for the voyage back to U. S. ports. Ford's Lakers and similar small freighters of other fleets indeed became the prototypical tramps of the world's seaways in the years between the wars.

The Mothball Fleet

While Mr. Ford was building up both his lake- and ocean-going fleets, the Government presented him with yet another opportunity. Early in 1925, a group of 200 surplus World War I merchant vessels were offered for sale, consisting of 150 Lakers and 50 larger "Subs" (so called because they were built by the Submarine Boat Company of Newark, N.J.).

Presented with the opportunity of bargain ships for sale, Mr. Ford pursued both his maritime and steelmaking interests. On August 18, 1925, his son Edsel B. Ford, president of Ford Motor Company, signed the papers to purchase 199 of these used ocean vessels from all over the East and Gulf Coasts for a total price of only $1,697,470 or about $8,530 each.

Twenty-one of the ships were tied up in the Delaware River near the Chester plant, 30 were on the Hudson, 10 at Staten Island, 109 on the James River near Norfolk, 18 at New Orleans, nine at Orange, Texas, and two at Mobile, Alabama. Most of these ended up being scrapped for the Rouge Plant's steel furnaces, but a baker's dozen were converted to barges and a handful reconditioned as conventional lake- and ocean-going freighters.

S/S LAKE GROGAN in old Welland Canal enroute to the Rouge plant for scrapping

For the most part, the Lakers were towed to the Rouge Plant in Dearborn between 1925 and 1927 by seven steel tugs, also purchased from the U. S. Shipping Board. The 50 "Subs" were too large (324 feet long) to pass through the canals and locks enroute to the Rouge and were cut up for scrap at Ford's eastern facilities. The scrap was loaded into the holds of the smaller ships being towed to Michigan. [20]

Three of the Lakers at New Orleans, LAKE BENBOW, LAKE GORIN and LAKE ORMOC, were immediately reconditioned to be used as towboats themselves. The Lakers were generally named after obscure small lakes all over the United States; for example, Benbow is a lake in northern California. All were ocean-type vessels and thus not too well suited for the Great Lakes trade. Their engine rooms were amidships and they had small cargo holds with 'tween decks and tail shaft tunnels in the after compartments. These deficiencies made them difficult to load and even more difficult to unload.

Nevertheless, after using them as towboats, Ford pressed the three ships from New Orleans into ocean-going freighter service. The LAKE GORIN and LAKE BENBOW were initially employed in the intercoastal trade. By the beginning of the 1929 shipping season, all three were in service between the Chester, Pennsylvania, plant and the Ford plant at Manchester, England. A fourth Laker from the mothball fleet, LAKE OSWEYA, was extensively reconditioned in 1930 with a Sun-Doxford 1,000-hp diesel and joined the other Ford ships on the high seas. Altogether, six Lakers became part of the ocean-going Ford Fleet as of 1930. [21]

Of the remaining 145 "mothballed" Lakers, 13 were converted for service in the Great Lakes as barges at the end of lines being towed by Ford's newly purchased surplus tugboats. The barge conversion process involved removal of engines, boilers and other equipment; cutting away of 'tween deck structures; and strengthening sides and decks by arch construction. The most obvious change was removal of the midship deck structure of pilot house, cabins and funnel.

The first Lakers made into barges were the LAKE ALLEN, LAKE CRYSTAL, LAKE FARGE, LAKE FRUMET, LAKE HEMLOCK, LAKE KYTTLE and LAKE LOUISE. As converted, the FARGE and the FRUMET had capacities of only 3200 tons each, down from their 4171-ton freighter ratings. The other five gained capacity, with ratings of 4300 tons, up from 3300 as freighters.

In 1929 and 1930, the last six barges from the mothball fleet - LAKE FOLCROFT, LAKE FREELAND, LAKE FRUGALITY, LAKE INAHA, LAKE PLEASANT and LAKE SAPOR - were lengthened from their original 261 feet to 323 feet by Great Lakes Engineering Works, at a cost of about $200,000 each. This increased their carrying capacities up to 5450 tons for all but the PLEASANT which went to 5900. The additional length restricted them from being taken through the Welland Canal into Lake Ontario and eastwards thereafter. (A table in Appendix III gives construction details of Ford's 19 Lakers.)

As can be seen from their photographs, after conversion all the barges looked more like conventional Great Lakes ore carriers than ocean ships, with their midship superstructure of pilot house, cabins and funnel removed to the stern area. These barges were put into service on the Lakes to haul coal, sand, limestone, lumber and iron ore to the Rouge Plant.

The Brazilian Rubber Plantation
Three of the Ford Fleet were key to the development, beginning in 1928, of Mr. Ford's rubber plantation in Brazil. Newly refurbished with a 1000-hp Busch Sulzer diesel, LAKE ORMOC departed the Rouge in August in the wake of the barge LAKE FARGE being towed by the tug BALLCAMP. All three were bound for a destination on an Amazon River tributary. On its deck,

21

S/S LAKE BENBOW

S/S ONEIDA (2) underway

S/S LAKE GORIN

Ship being scrapped at the Rouge Plant

Barge LAKE FARGE in River Rouge slip, 1928

Barge LAKE FOLCROFT upbound at the Soo Locks in tow of the tug BARRALLTON in the 1930's

Barge LAKE FRUGALITY on the Detroit River in the late 1930's

Barge LAKE FRUMET undergoing conversion at River Rouge in 1928

25

Barge LAKE INAHA under tow of the tug BUTTERCUP near the Soo Locks in the 1930's

Barge LAKE KYTTLE at an upper lakes lumber-loading port

Barge LAKE PLEASANT at River Rouge

Barge LAKE SAPOR in the Calumet River, Chicago, Illinois on May 15, 1938

27

M/V CHESTER in the Detroit River during 1940

M/V EDGEWATER loading bulk cargo on the East Coast

M/V GREEN ISLAND in the New York State Barge Canal

M/V NORFOLK approaching a lock in one of the canals

the FARGE also carried a small tug, the 45-foot, 60-hp SANTAREM, for river operations. [22]

The ORMOC had been completely refitted as a "base camp" for the plantation until shore facilities could be built. It was equipped with machine shop, hospital, chemistry laboratories, laundry, water distillation equipment, library-lounge and living quarters for plantation staff as well as seamen. The FARGE carried construction equipment down to Brazil and then became the river cargo carrier. The ORMOC's captain, Einard Oxholm, was named first manager of the rubber plantation although he knew nothing about agriculture. Later the ORMOC traveled back and forth between Brazil and the Rouge, where a tire plant was built in the 1930s.

Ford's Tugboats
The steel-hulled tugs bought from the Government in 1925 included the BALLCAMP, BARLOW, BARRALLTON, BATHALUM, BAYMEAD, BUTTERCUP and HUMRICK. Four of these, BALLCAMP, BARLOW, BARRALLTON and BUTTERCUP, were built in 1919 at Elizabeth, New Jersey. The BATHALUM and the BAYMEAD were built the same year in New York City, and the seventh, HUMRICK, was the 1919 product of a Superior, Wisconsin, shipyard.

Conversion of the tugs was easier than it had been for the 13 Lakers turned into barges. The tugs' coal-fired steam engines and coal storage areas were replaced with oil-fired mechanisms and fuel tanks, and radio equipment and direction finders were installed.

Initially, these tugs were used to tow the Lakers from their East and Gulf Coast anchorages to the Ford facilities for scrapping or conversion, and subsequently to tow the barges around the Lakes. One tug towed two of the barges at a time. The crew of the barges consisted of 10 to 13 men while a full crew of 20 men was assigned to the tug. The tug took one barge at a time out the Rouge River, assisted by the Harbor Tug DEARBORN. The crews anchored the one barge in the Detroit River and returned for the second. When both were ready, the two were made up into a Lake tow and departed. Inbound passages were made the same way. The DEARBORN was a small tug, not used for lake towing. Built in 1932 at Great Lakes Engineering in River Rouge, Michigan, it was only 85 feet long with 660 hp. The other tugs had 850 hp and were 142 feet long.

In addition Ford had bought from sources on the Lakes two old wooden tugs, JAY C. MORSE and DANIEL L. HEBARD, and they helped move the surplus ships into the Rouge for the scrapping operation. The 79-foot-long MORSE had been built in 1867 in Buffalo, New York, and the 98-foot HEBARD (formerly the P. L. JOHNSON) in 1875 at Cleveland. [23] The HEBARD was scrapped at the Rouge in July 1930 and the MORSE in August 1932, at the time the new DEARBORN was completed. Finding itself "over tugged," the company also sold off BALLCAMP, BAYMEAD and BATHALUM in the early Thirties. [24]

The BARLOW and the BARRALLTON swapped names and the new BARLOW was extensively reconstructed in 1931-32, being fitted out luxuriously for a tug. It was subsequently stationed until 1937 at the Ford facility at L'Anse in Michigan's Upper Peninsula for the personal use of Mr. Edsel Ford, who had been appointed to the Park Commission and used it for, among other things, traveling to Isle Royale.

Scrapping Process
The scrapping operation performed on the vast majority of the Lakers bought from the Government was massive. The first such scrapper reached the Rouge on December 17, 1925, under tow of the tug BALLCAMP, and the last arrived in August 1927. In total, some 145 ships were fetched from as far away as 4,332 miles.

The procedure involved Ford tugs pulling the Lakers up the Atlantic Coast and around

DANIEL L. HEBARD
at L'Anse, Michigan

JAY C. MORSE at River Rouge
on December 9, 1927

BALLCAMP at River Rouge
on December 6, 1927

BAYMEAD at River Rouge

BARLOW (1) at River Rouge

BARLOW (2) at River Rouge

BARRALLTON underway
on the Detroit River

BATHALUM

BUTTERCUP at River Rouge

DEARBORN

HUMRICK at River Rouge

into the St. Lawrence River as far as Montreal. There they were turned over to Canadian tug companies for the trip through what then amounted to 22 St. Lawrence Canal System locks and, after crossing Lake Ontario,[25] Welland Canal locks. In Lake Erie, Ford tugs again took over, sometimes towing as many as four Lakers at a time. There was a holding area in the Detroit River below the Rouge mouth where the Lakers could be moored until the cutting torch was ready for them. All this had to be accomplished in the months between lake freezes.

At the Rouge Plant, vessels to be scrapped were brought alongside the present West Dock, where as many as ten could be lined up without interfering with navigation to and from the East Dock on the other side of the Boat Slip.

At the Dock they were stripped for salvageable parts and then cut up into scrap, to be used to produce steel in the open hearth furnaces. A floating dry dock was purchased to lift the underwater portion of the ships out of water for final dismantling. Gantry cranes were installed on tracks that ran the full length of the dock to lift the dismantled parts from the ship and to place them on railroad cars. Inside and outside storage areas were provided to store the salvaged equipment for future use either as replacement parts for the remaining Lakers in the Ford Fleet, or in a myriad of ways in Ford plants. For example, ship steam engines were "recycled" as the power plants for assembly and manufacturing plants.

The scrapping operation continued on the West Dock where a large warehouse, built to store the salvageable parts removed from the ships, was filled to the rafters. Salvaged material such as deck winches, anchor windlasses, anchors, etc., was stored outside on the ground and remained there until the mid-1930s.

Then one day, according to the story I heard, Mr. Ford or one of his subordinates apparently decided that these spare parts were unnecessary, and overnight the parts were gathered up and dumped into the open hearth furnaces. The scrapping building was then torn down, leaving many men without a place to work. It was a common practice of the Gate 4 employment office at the Rouge to assign employees to work at the West Dock, but many times little was known of them or what they were supposed to be doing. Following the destruction of the scrapping facilities, several hundred men were laid off or reassigned.

The Special Ford Canal Vessels
With the development of the East Coast and overseas plants, Ford operations at Chester, Pennsylvania; Edgewater, New Jersey; Green Island, New York (near Albany), and Norfolk, Virginia, were expanded. It was decided to build specially designed canal vessels to carry auto parts to and from these plants.

The canal vessels S/S CHESTER and S/S EDGEWATER were built at Great Lakes Engineering Works, Ecorse, Michigan, and added to the Fleet in 1931. Ford paid $594,606 for the CHESTER and $592,903 for the EDGEWATER. They were 300 feet long and had a capacity of 2800 net tons at 12-foot draft. Each had 1600-hp steam engines and carried a crew of 22 men. These ships had retractable pilot houses, folding masts and funnels that could be lowered to permit them to pass under the bridges on the New York State Barge Canal. They were designed by Henry J. Gielow, Inc., naval architects of New York City. When the EDGEWATER made its maiden voyage through upstate New York in August 1931, the Schenectady newspaper headlined, "Biggest Cargo Ship on Canal Due Here Soon".

In 1937 the M/S GREEN ISLAND and M/S NORFOLK were built for Ford by Great Lakes Engineering Works at a cost of $491,921 and $493,924, respectively. When the GREEN ISLAND was launched, it was enthusiastically saluted. This was the first ship to be built on the U.

S. side of the Lakes in six years. These were similar ships in concept to the two earlier canal carriers but with considerably modified design as a result of experience with the 1931 vessels. For example, the pilot house was moved toward midship from the bow. They also had a larger capacity of 3,000 net tons each, and lower-powered, 1200-hp diesel engines. They were noted at that time for being the world's largest ships with welded hulls. All of the Ford canal carriers had long, low silhouettes, which led to at least one of them being mistaken for a submarine during World War II.

The canal ships operated between East Coast ports and Dearborn until 1941. They carried axles, springs, radiators and other finished auto parts to the Rouge and boxed export parts to the East Coast for shipment overseas. All four of these plants for which the canal vessels were named were located on water sites and the ships docked and transshipped their cargoes on plant property. In 1937, the Edgewater plant turned out 109,000 Ford V-8 cars and trucks, of which 40,800 were exported. It was Ford's largest branch plant with 3,500 employees and a production rate of 100 an hour. The Chester plant the same year produced 72,167 vehicles and shipped parts for 83,000 cars and trucks for overseas assembly.

At the tail end of the Ford Fleet were five lighters — flat-bottomed, un-powered barges used to load and unload larger ships — at the company's waterside East Coast plants. The first was a 194-ton, 123-foot-long unit named FORD NO. 1, bought in 1920 when only a year old, and sold in 1936. Three other lighters had been sold in 1933. By 1941, only NO. 5 was still in service. Based at the Edgewater plant across the Hudson River from mid-town Manhattan, the 100-foot-long, 400-ton capacity NO.5 had been built in 1913.

At the beginning of World War II and following the scrapping operation, the conversion of certain ships, sale of others, and the construction of five new units, the Ford Fleet consisted of 31 vessels. This 1941 Fleet consisted of thirteen barges converted from ocean-going ships, six tugs (the tiny one still in Brazil), five ocean-going ships, four canal carriers, the original two Great Lakes bulk carriers and the small lighter used at Edgewater.

Radio operator on Ford vessel

M/S HENRY FORD II officers in dress uniform on deck

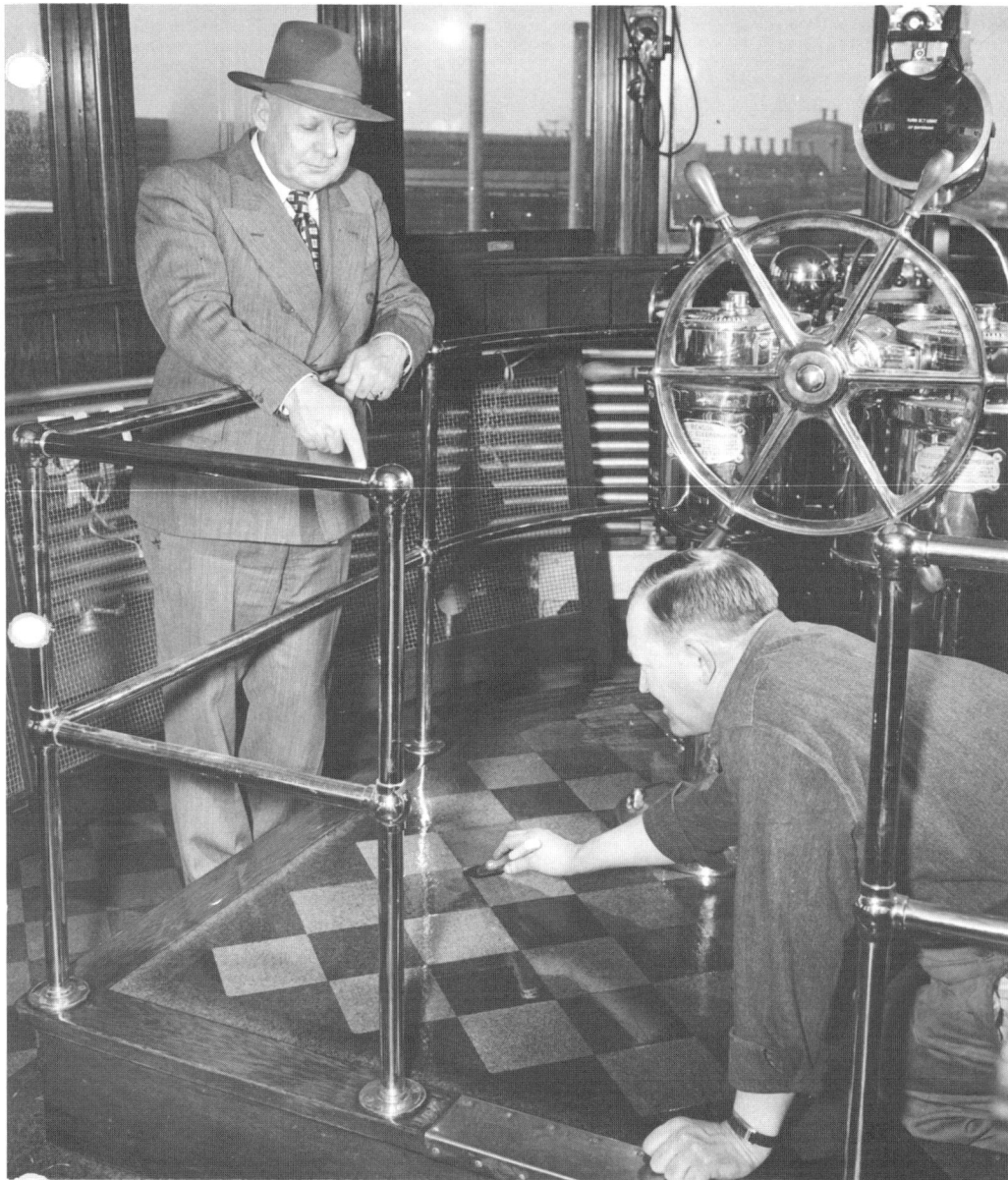

Captain John Pearce and Chief "Ike" on the HENRY FORD II, 1946

THE MARINE OFFICE

The Rouge Plant continued to grow with completion of the open hearth furnaces on June 21, 1926, and the opening of the Blueberry iron ore mine near Marquette, Michigan, on August 26, 1926. By 1927, 15,000,000 cars had been built and the change from the Model T to the Model A was made with the opening of the Rouge final assembly line on November 1st (thus transferring auto production from Highland Park).

About this time, however, world economics and trade policies changed radically. Protectionism of national interests soared. The big overseas automotive markets, Germany and England, both passed laws severely restricting production of American-type cars, in order to encourage local manufacture. As a consequence, the need for cargos of Ford parts from the U. S. to Europe was progressively reduced after about 1930. There was also the world-wide depression. The company sold two of its ocean-going ships in 1937, the same year it added two canal vessels strictly for the American market.

Industry production in the United States declined from 5,337,087 in 1929 to 3,588,889 in 1939, and worse, the Ford share of car sales plummeted from 34 per cent to 21 per cent. This meant our Fleet carried less iron ore and fewer finished products. Even so, "Ford's" Marine Operations kept very busy operating its Fleet. More than 30 vessels were actively engaged in delivering parts and materials to keep the assembly lines running. We were a very important part of the company and a very important result of Mr. Ford building the Rouge Plant.

In the 1930s, indeed up until Henry Ford II took over direction of Ford Motor Company in 1945, a few men with great authority — the "Old Guard" — ran each department or operation of the company. Names such as Harry Bennett, B. J. Craig, P. E. Martin, Arnold Miller, Ray Rausch, Charles E. Sorensen and our own Captain Oscar A. Johnson bring back memories of power and abuse of power.

When I joined the Marine Office in 1941, it was part of the General Traffic Department with offices in the old Administration Building at 3000 Schaefer Road in Dearborn, overlooking the Rouge Plant from the west. In this one office, located next to Captain Johnson's, were Marine Superintendent Norman J. Ahrens, John A. Fuhrman and myself. Mr. Fuhrman kept records and handled the personnel, the insurance coverage and related accidents and claims. I was the general clerk.

The company maintained its export operations in New Jersey and thus the Marine Traffic Department had its office at Edgewater, where the export paperwork was handled. The ships were dispatched from there but the New Jersey office reported directly to the central Marine Office in Dearborn.

Captain Johnson, who became Director of Traffic for the company in 1938, exercised complete control in decision-making policies of marine operations for the company. He would keep Harry Bennett advised, who in turn had the responsibility of keeping Mr. Henry Ford I informed. However, Captain Johnson's judgment was seldom questioned.

It was common knowledge in those days that anyone could tell a farm belonging to a "big boss at Ford's" by the color of paint on his barn. These men had the power to use company personnel, equipment and materials pretty much as they pleased. One of my duties as clerk in the Marine Office was to keep records on Captain Johnson's farm animals. I was never asked to work on the farm during haying or to fix fences, but many others were.

Despite this, for many years the company had been run by these men, who had certainly been of great assistance to Mr. Ford, because the company was not built by one man alone. These were the men who accomplished many of the successes of the Ford Motor Company from its founding through the Twenties and Thirties. They built the various manufacturing plants in the United States and around the world. They produced the Model T, the Model A and B, then the V-8 engine, etc. They built tractors, produced steel, cement, tires, many chemical products, fertilizer and paint. They built the largest industrial power house in the world, operated a fleet of ships, trucks, a railroad both inside and outside the plant and did hundreds of other things too numerous to mention.

This story is primarily about the Ford Fleet, but the company and its operations are mentioned here if only to emphasize the power and influence of one man, Captain O. A. Johnson, who contributed greatly to the success of the company during his working years as head of marine operations.

Operations During the Depression
According to what I heard, and records from the Marine office, the company had no sooner established its Fleet than business declined as the Great Depression of the 1930s came on. The Marine Department coped by cutting back on its lake shipping season and emphasizing non-Ford cargoes.

For example, in September 1931, only 8 of our 13 Laker barges were in operation. The new canal vessels were hauling sugar from the East Coast to Toronto, Buffalo, Cleveland, Toledo, Detroit and Milwaukee. Year-end return cargoes for the ocean vessels included coal, sulfate ammonia, wood pulp, nitrate soda, railroad ties and Quebrache wood. The IMAHA saw no service in 1930 or 1933, the FRUGALITY none in 1932, the SAPOR none in 1932, and the HEMLOCK none in 1933 or 1934.

Mr. Ford's proud big ore carriers likewise were cut back. The BENSON was idle during all of 1932 and 1933, and the HENRY's shipping seasons were cut short, from June 1 to November 13, 1932, from August 19 to November 30, 1933, from July 21 to November 30, 1934, and from May 6 to December 10, 1935. It was 1936 before our shipping got reasonably back to normal.

Winter Coal Run
Yet it was during this period that Ford Motor Company and Nicholson Transit Company of Ecorse, Michigan, pioneered the winter coal run, long before the present extended-season navigation program was formulated. The "regular" Great Lakes sailing season used to mean from mid-April to the end of November.

The run from Dearborn to Toledo included operation in the many shallow channels of the Rouge and Detroit Rivers and the Toledo Channel without the aid of buoys or range lights, although there were fixed lights in the Detroit River and Toledo Channel. Nevertheless, hundreds of trips were made long before the present "Winter Navigation" was begun. This emphasized the importance of qualified officers aboard the ships in order to operate them safely.

While tankers had been operating during the winter months on short runs and Ford had made some late-season trips with its tugs and barges, the first planned extended season was initiated when Ford contracted for operation of Nicholson Transit's Steamer E. C. POPE, starting on March 1, 1935. (That was the same day this writer reported to the company as a novice drill press operator for his first full day's work.)

On March 14, 1935, the Steamer FELLOWCRAFT was added to the coal run between Toledo and Dearborn. March operations continued in 1936 and in 1937, the winter operation was advanced to the month of February and the normal fall season was extended to December 29, when the Steamer JAMES WATT closed the season.

The regular April 15-November 30 sailing season was the period of normal insurance premiums. Any operations outside of those dates required sailing clearance from the underwriters and pre- or post-season insurance rates which were considerably higher than regular season rates. The reason for the insurance and operating concern was ice, as can be seen by the photo of the WATT caught in ice off Monroe, Michigan, about 1940. Soon after help arrived, the wind changed and relieved the ice pressure, rescue tugs freed the ship, and she proceeded to the Rouge Plant.

Mr. Ford's Cruises on the HENRY FORD II

I mentioned earlier how Mr. Ford considered the M/S HENRY FORD II his personal yacht. I remember spending hours preparing a huge chart of the Upper Great Lakes, showing the route and time schedule for his annual trip north. Mr. Ford would say when he wanted to leave and when he wanted to arrive. Usually it took about five days to make a "two-day" trip. The balance of the time would be spent cruising the Great Lakes. The ship might spend the night in Georgian Bay, then go through the Straits of Mackinaw and into upper Lake Michigan, then return to Lake Huron and up the St. Marys River and into Whitefish Bay. Then it would cruise Lake Superior before arriving at Marquette or L'Anse where the guests would disembark.

Mr. Ford was very proud of his ships, and this might be the reason for continuation of this tradition of pride even today in the Ford Fleet. Many of the frills and expensive furnishings and appliances have been eliminated due to their extreme costs to maintain. However, I know that I was proud of the ships, and this was true of the men who sailed them along with many other management people.

On these trips the menus would be planned in advance and the commissary at Highland Park would send down the required food supplies. Isaac Syria, the ship's cook, would prepare special pastries and baked goods. Mrs. Ford always liked his cookies. One time she was having a party at Fairlane and had "Ike" bake cookies on the way to the Soo. There they were taken off the ship, flown back to the Ford Airport and delivered to her in time for the party.

On some trips, Mr. Ford would take employees from Fairlane with him and they would stay in the lower staterooms. Another couple usually would share the other master stateroom with the Fords. In those days, when the forward galley was open, the ship's officers would eat in the forward officers' dining room and the guests would eat in the passengers' dining room. Both dining rooms had seatings for ten. A forward cook would prepare the meals for both dining rooms and a waiter would assist the steward in serving both the officers and guests. The Ford ships carried a steward for this purpose and only recently has this position been eliminated so that the galley is run and supervised by a steward-cook.

During the last years that Mr. Ford took his annual trip, it was necessary to lift him aboard from the dock to the passenger deck on a special elevator, built just for him . Imagine the preparation that would be necessary to make certain that this elevator would work safely for him to ride. Mr. Ford usually did not request all of this attention because he was very easy to please, but everyone was well trained and knew exactly what to do before he arrived. After the death of Henry Ford, Mrs. Ford continued to use this elevator when she made trips aboard the HENRY.

During the years that these trips were taken by Mr. Ford, Captain John J. Pearce was master of the HENRY. But Captain Johnson, first as Marine Superintendent and later as Director of Traffic, would also go along as advisor to make certain that everything was being handled properly. These trips occurred annually from the time the ship was built until Mr. Ford's death in 1947.

S/S LAKE OSWEYA sunk in collision, St. John's River, 1938

S/S LAKE OSWEYA - another view

Tug BARLOW (2) towing Barge LAKE FREELAND and an unidentified barge

S/S CLETUS SCHNEIDER being unloaded of iron ore July 12, 1923,
the first large vessel to arrive at Rouge Plant

It must be remembered that ships at this time did not have radar and radiotelephones. Navigation depended heavily on the knowledge and skills of the officers in charge. I cannot remember any difficulty or unusual delays during these trips. This attests to the great abilities of these men, particularly Captain Pearce.

Before all of the present-day navigation equipment and training of replacement officer personnel, it was a rare exception to have anyone aboard a ship who could replace the master. The master piloted the ship the entire length of the rivers and made all docks. The mate handled the ship only in the open lake. This procedure protected the jobs of the masters, but provided very little training for new men, unless the captain had some special person that he wanted to help.

I remember when Captain Andy Pedersen died aboard the BENSON in Lake Superior. The ship had to be anchored and Captain Johnson had to fly to the Soo and be put aboard to bring the ship down. Another time, when the BENSON struck a crib light in the Neebish Channel downbound in the St. Marys River and tied up hundreds of ships in Lake Superior, it was necessary to put a new skipper aboard to bring her down. This authoritarian attitude changed after the war.

The LAKE OSWEYA Incident

While the ore carriers, tugs and barges were operating on the Great Lakes, Ford also kept its ocean fleet busy around the world; not all were pleasant times. In April 1938, while on a round trip between Norfolk, Virginia, and Jacksonville, Florida, the LAKE OSWEYA had steering gear trouble and collided with the S/S SAN MATEO in the St. Johns River. As the accompanying photo shows, the OSWEYA went to the bottom of the fortunately shallow river between Jacksonville and the Atlantic. The ship had just off-loaded 177 cars and 7,677 feet of lumber and was outbound when the accident occurred.

A review of the ship's accounts from just after the accident provides some insight about operations in those pre-war years:
OSWEYA Captain Karl Prinz and Chief Engineer John Kilpatrick were being paid $375 and $350 a month, respectively. Capt. Prinz's expense report showed he was able to stay at Jacksonville's best hotel, the Roosevelt, for only $3.00 a night following the accident. Evidently, raising and repairing the OSWEYA was relatively simple, for within six weeks it was being reprovisioned at Norfolk.

The Steward's Department purchases daily in June 1938 for OSWEYA crew meals typically included 12 loaves of bread, 2 to 4 gallons of whole milk and a gallon of buttermilk. One grocery list included one-half bushel of string beans, 5 quarts of butter beans, 5 quarts of peas, a bunch of bananas, 12 pounds of white sugar, 12 pounds of brown sugar and 10 pounds of mackerel, all for $9.64. In re-provisioning staples, the steward ordered many still-familiar brand names: 4 cases of Super Suds, 2 cases of Lifebuoy, 2 cases of Lux, a case of Lava, 2 cases of Saniflush, a case of Dutch Cleanser, a case of Bon Ami and two gallons of Oxford Brass Polish, according to paid receipts in the OSWEYA file.

For the galley's refrigerator, the order was 30 dozen eggs, 36 pounds of Maxwell House coffee, a case of Aunt Jemima Pancake Flour, 14 pounds of ox tongue, 28 pounds of spring chicken, 10 pounds of salted pork rib, 72 pounds of loin beef, 42 pounds of rib beef, 24 pounds of side lamb, 49 pounds of saddle veal, 24 pounds of bacon, 11 pounds of fresh ham, 38 pounds of premium ham and 19 pounds of pork loin.

The Ford Crews

To man the tugs, barges and other ships, it was customary to take men out of the plant or

M/S LAKE OSWEYA in New York harbor

off the dock to fill the crews. The officers were moved from ship to ship, as they were needed, and when they were not sailing would spend time around the West Dock and Boat House. It would take several days to load and unload one of the cargo barges or ships. It was done with two large gantry cranes that ran on tracks the full length of the West Dock where the cargoes were stored. Because accumulation of these cargoes took considerable time to arrange and load or unload, this was a 24-hour-day operation.

Up until 1941, the crews did not come under the rules and regulations of the U. S. Coast Guard, as they do today. The men received their skills and knowledge by sailing on the ships, starting at the bottom and working their way up through the ranks. When they were qualified, they would write for their licenses. Engineers were trained in the Ford Power House and worked in both places.

Some idea of the wage scales in those days can be had by reference to the LAKE FREELAND's payroll, as recorded in 1942 when the Government was re-billed for the cost of transferring certain ships to Chicago. The master, or captain, was paid $275 per month; the engineer, $240; the mate, $215; the cook, $190, and the crewmen, from $120 to $160 depending on rating. The Social Security cost was only 80 cents a month per man. When compared to those officers' wages for the ocean-going LAKE OSWEYA in 1938 noted a few paragraphs back, it is obvious barge crewmen were at a lower scale. [25]

In February 1941, the Ford Navigation Company was incorporated to handle operations of the four canal boats and enable them to be qualified as "common carriers" by the Interstate Commerce Commission. Captain Johnson served as its chief executive as well as manager of the rest of the Marine Office. This was a bit of foresight by the company, as it saw declining demand for its ocean-going fleet with the war raging in Europe and increasingly on the Atlantic. Consequently there was an opportunity (and need) to sell Ford's cargo-carrying capacity to others. The Ford Navigation Company subsequently became the legal entity which the Government contracted with for Ford vessels in war service. The Navigation Company was dissolved in 1946.

S/S E.C. POPE with help from the tug ATOMIC on Ford's winter coal run

S/S JAMES WATT stuck in ice on winter coal run getting assistance
from the U.S. Coast Guard and tug ATOMIC

FORD FLEET GOES TO WAR

On December 8, 1941, the United States declared war on Japan following the attack on Pearl Harbor the day before. It is hard today to imagine the panic that the Japanese attack and their quickly following war successes at Guam, Wake Island, the Philippines and Malaya brought out in the American media and public. Yet in many ways, it was "business as usual." For example, Ford continued its civilian car production until February 10, and was the last of the auto manufacturers to be shut down.

In mid-December, after mutual declarations of war were exchanged between the U. S. and Nazi Germany, the German Navy ordered its "Operation Drumbeat" submarine warfare against American coastal shipping. The first sinkings took place unimpeded off the coast of Long Island in mid-January 1942, even though the British had managed to intercept Nazi radio traffic, and had warned Washington the attacks were coming.

Disorganized Defenses

Unfortunately the U. S. Navy and the Army Air Corps were so devastated by politics and the events in the Pacific that we Americans were unable to organize our Atlantic submarine defenses for many months. Truly, America was ill-prepared for war. In the fall of 1941, only weeks before Pearl Harbor, a bill in Congress to arm merchant ships had passed by a margin of only ten votes. Consequently, the Nazis had an incredibly easy time "pot-shotting" freighters and tankers literally within sight of eastern seaboard cities and resorts. There were no blackouts in the early days, and submarines could easily spot the silhouettes of ships against the lighted backdrops of the American coast.

Contrary to the impression left by countless movies, the U-boats' preferred battle technique in 1942 was on the surface at night, rather than submerged daylight attack. Indeed, when there was no threat of anti-submarine air attack, U-boat commanders sometimes would use deck guns rather than torpedoes to sink unarmed or weakly armed freighters. In that fashion they could stretch their war patrols, because the supply of fresh torpedoes was on the other side of the Atlantic. Although Americans were highly suspicious of Nazi subs having secret bases in Latin America, postwar investigations showed there had been none; nor were long-range German submarine "cows" or freighter supply vessels very successful in quartermastering the far-off submarines either.

The biggest advantage the U-boats had in the early days of the war was simply America's lack of preparation and slowness to respond. For example, in January 1942, the U. S. Navy had only 20 obsolete anti-submarine ships to protect 1500 miles of coastline in the Northeast, and for operational reasons, only three of those could be "on station" at once. The aircraft situation was not much better. The Navy had 103 airplanes between New England and Cape Hatteras, but most were trainers or utility planes. The Air Corps had 46 bombers stationed between Maine and Virginia, but operations permitted only two flights daily of three planes each, weather permitting. Moreover, none of the American flyers had much, if any, training in anti-submarine warfare.

To top that off, relations between the U. S. armed services (and with our British allies) were still plagued with jealousy and poor communications. If a Navy or Coast Guard coastwatcher thought he spotted a submarine off Key West, for instance, it was necessary to make a commercial long-distance telephone call 700 miles to the southeastern regional Air Corps Command at Charleston, S.C., requesting a bomber search; the Air Corps, in turn, had to telephone back to Miami, 160 miles northeast of Key West, ordering a flight off the ground.

Thus in the first six months of 1942, an astounding 500 ships were sunk by submarines in the Atlantic, most off the American coast, with casualties estimated at more than five thousand crewmen a far greater loss than at Pearl Harbor.[28] Ford ships and Marine Department employees paid heavily in this slaughter.

Requisition of Civilian Shipping

Beginning in 1939, the war closed down Ford's European passenger car (but not truck) production, and thus eliminated the need for much of the company's ocean-going Fleet. With no supplies to carry to Ford plants — most of which couldn't be reached anyway after mid-1940 because of the Nazi takeover and British blockade — the company's freighters had a hard time finding cargo.

The involvement of Ford ships in the war effort actually began months before Pearl Harbor. In the summer of 1941, the U. S. Government began compulsory charter of Ford vessels in the effort to supply Great Britain via North Atlantic convoy or to substitute in Caribbean use (mainly hauling sugar) for other ships now themselves in convoy service.

The first to be contracted for, incomprehensibly, was the canal vessel NORFOLK, recruited for Caribbean service in July 1941. Ford protested then and later that its canal vessels were designed for Great Lakes and New York Barge Canal use and only very limited, close-to-shore, coastal shipping. Ford's insurance company, for example, wouldn't insure the canal vessels against hurricane loss if they were operated south of Cape Hatteras, North Carolina, because of their deck and hatch design. But everyone was eager to help in the war effort, even before Pearl Harbor. LAKE OSWEYA was next to be drafted, for North Atlantic convoys on time charter beginning September 2, 1941. At first it carried no weapons, only a three-man U. S. Navy communications team.[29]

Third among Ford ships to go to war was the canal vessel GREEN ISLAND, put on U. S. Maritime Commission time charter in the Caribbean in November 1942. Ford also had received a summons in October for compulsory charter of the EAST INDIAN, but it then was at sea, headed for West Africa to pick up rubber.[30]

In January 1942, the U. S. Government began requisitioning all available vessel capacity to support the war effort and this included ships operating on the Great Lakes. At first the Government asked for an inventory of all ships over 300 feet in length, later for any of "1,000 gross tons or over which have not been previously chartered by us."

There was a time when telegrams or letters seemed to arrive almost daily in the Marine Office from the War Shipping Administration, successor to the Maritime Commission, directing the company to turn over certain ships, "no questions asked." They advised where and when the transfer of Ford vessels was to take place and under what conditions. The ships were either bought outright or taken over on time or "bareboat" charters. The company cooperated fully, even though it left the movement of its own materials to the Rouge Plant in doubt. You will recall that all of the tugs and barges were brought to Dearborn from deep sea and thus the Government wanted them returned to the same trade for which they were originally designed and used.

The Government also enlisted all of our seamen into the U. S. Merchant Marine and issued our officers regulation Naval uniforms. It was at this time that the U. S. Coast Guard began to regulate our ships, and required validated seaman's documents for security reasons. The Soo Locks were closed to visitors and military bases were set up to protect the facilities. Many new rules and regulations regarding the use of communications, lighting on the ships, etc., were instituted for security.

Ford's Baptism of Fire

Ford's East Coast-based ships were first to go to war. Curiously, the first of the Ford Fleet to suffer damage was an unlikely candidate, the five-year-old canal ship M/S GREEN ISLAND. Even though it was more a lake and canal freighter than an ocean ship, GREEN ISLAND had been recruited early for war service. On the night of January 26-27, 1942, the U. S. Navy Minesweeper HAMILTON was escorting a troop transport convoy bound from New York to the Panama Canal Zone (enemy attack on the Canal was greatly feared).

At 0500 hours, in the pre-dawn darkness, the escort sighted what she thought was a surfaced submarine and went immediately to general quarters. She fired a shot across the shape's bow and headed full speed on a collision course to ram the feared enemy. At the last moment the HAMILTON's skipper realized the "U-boat" was a darkened freighter, called for emergency "back full" and "rudder hard over." But it was too late. The Navy ship slammed into the GREEN ISLAND's port side. With its low silhouette due to the retractable pilothouse, masts and funnel, the vessel appeared to be a submarine in the dim light. What it was doing all alone, so far South and off the Florida coast, is unknown today. The GREEN ISLAND was soon repaired, perhaps too soon as events turned out.

Sinking of the M/S LAKE OSWEYA

The World War I Laker M/S LAKE OSWEYA, which had been refurbished in 1930 with a diesel engine, became the first Ford victim of the Nazi U-boats' Operation Drumbeat. After December 7 and its return from North Atlantic convoys, the Navy quickly converted OSWEYA to full war service at New York City (probably at the Brooklyn Navy Yard) by mounting two light machine guns and a three-inch cannon and installing Navy radio equipment, all by February 5.

Manned by a Ford (now Merchant Marine) crew of 30 under Captain Karl E. Prinz and carrying a Navy "armed guard" gun-and-communications crew consisting of an ensign and nine sailors, OSWEYA sailed from New York on February 17 loaded with a munitions cargo. Orders were to join a convoy off Halifax bound for Indiga, a Soviet port hundreds of miles east of Murmansk on the Barents Sea.

She never made the first rendezvous. Shortly before midnight February 19, 1942, at position 43°14' North - 64°45' West (roughly 250 miles east of Boston), a Nazi submarine nailed OSWEYA and she went down with all hands in the frigid Atlantic. The British ship EMPIRE SEAL was nearby and, fearful of further attacks, could report only that she saw and heard the explosion.[31]

The list of those lost on the OSWEYA reveals that the Boatswain, Herman Mathisen and his son, Herman Jr., an able seaman, both of New Orleans, went down together on the ship. In addition, Joseph Vealie, an oiler, was believed to be related to a Marine Department official at our Edgewater office.

The LAKE OSWEYA was then on bareboat charter to the Government and the insurance underwriters paid the company $500,000 for the loss. All ships were covered with war risk insurance during the war. At that time, the book value of the ship was $496,761. The original cost in 1930 had been $847,864.

The company was never involved with benefits ($5,000 each) paid to the families of lost crew members. This was handled by the War Shipping Administration. However, surviving crew members of ships sunk or next of kin were reimbursed for personal effects lost. Only two of the Ford crew lost on OSWEYA were from Michigan. Most were from the East Coast.[32]

As the winter's submarine campaign by the German Navy wore on, insurance rates soared astronomically. The rate for GREEN ISLAND and NORFOLK went from $40 a day each in January to $792 by the end of March, and over $1,000 daily by May. Captain Johnson had to explain to Company Vice President B. J. Craig why we were paying considerably more for insurance than receiving in charter fees of $760 a day. Of course, losses to submarines were kept officially secret, even though everyone in the shipping trade knew about the tragic losses being sustained along the coast.

In April the War Shipping Administration wired the Marine Office to requisition two more of Ford's ocean-going Lakers. The form telegraph message was brief:

```
                                                        APRIL 19, 1942
FROM: WAR SHIPPING ADMINISTRATION
TO:   FORD NAVIGATION COMPANY
      DETROIT, MICHIGAN


      THE ADMINISTRATOR WAR SHIPPING ADMINISTRATION HAS DETERMINED
TO AND DOES HEREBY REQUISITION POSSESSION AND USE ON TIME CHARTER
BASIS OF THE FOLLOWING VESSELS OWNED BY YOUR COMPANY EFFECTIVE AS
OF THE TIME OF TAKING POSSESSION THEREOF:
                              ONEIDA
                              ONONDAGA
```

As a result of this instruction and subsequent negotiations, the ONEIDA was officially handed over to the War Shipping Administration on June 13 at New Orleans, Louisiana, and the ONONDAGA on June 18 at Pensacola, Florida. In a separate transaction earlier, the Government purchased outright the small barges LAKE FRUMET and LAKE FARGE and the tug HUMRICK. These were turned over on April 24 to the Daniel C. Robinson company at the New York end of Lake Erie.

Sinking of the M/S GREEN ISLAND
In the meantime, it was the ill-fated canal vessel M/S GREEN ISLAND's turn to be the next victim of Nazi aggression.[33] On May 6, 1942, south of Grand Cayman Island between Cuba and Jamaica, she encountered a German submarine which surfaced and ordered the crew into lifeboats. After all were in the boats and safely away from the ship, the sub sent a torpedo into her hull and she went to the bottom of the ocean.[34] The entire crew was rescued later, the only Ford crew to be so fortunate when their ship was sunk.

The GREEN ISLAND had been hauling sugar from the southern coast of Cuba to the United States. For this ship the company collected $475,000 in insurance; the accounted original cost with improvements from 1937 was $515,000. The GREEN ISLAND carried a Ford crew and was on time charter at the time of her sinking. Symbolic of the ship and supply shortage in those early war months, carrying sugar was a strange assignment for a canal ship accustomed to hauling radiators from Green Island to Dearborn and engines from Dearborn to Edgewater. [35]

The Government would arrange for the cargoes to be carried, the schedules to be followed and convoys that the ships would be assigned. Most ships during the war travelled in convoys. However, this was not always the case especially early in hostilities when the ships were erroneously thought to be safe in the inter-coastal trade, such as to Cuba. [36]

Losses of ONEIDA and ONONDAGA
On July 13, 1942, only a month after being "federalized" and on her first Government voyage after being armed, the S/S ONEIDA on bareboat charter was sunk by a submarine off the east tip of Cuba. Six of the crew were lost. [37]

Official notification came in this letter:

```
                    War Shipping Administration
                            Washington


                                            July 16, 1942

               C O N F I D E N T I A L

Mr. W. C. Dierolf
Marine Export Manager
Ford Motor Company
Edgewater, New Jersey


                          S/S ONEIDA
Dear Mr. Dierolf:
     It is with regret we advise you of information received from the
Navy Department indicating the loss of the S/S ONEIDA as a result of
enemy action.
     We are advised the ONEIDA was torpedoed and sunk at 1610Z, July
13th, in position 20 degrees 17 minutes north - 74 degrees 06 minutes
west. Twenty-three survivors have been landed at Baracoa and it is re-
ported that six of the crew were drowned.
     When it is ascertained what loss of life occurred as a result of
this attack, Mr. C. W. Sanders of the Coast Guard will attend to noti-
fication of next of kin, and it is requested that you confine your no-
tification to cargo interests only.
     In notifying cargo interests please omit any reference as to
time, date and manner of the vessel's loss.


                    Very truly yours,
                         (s)
                    J. C. Outler
               Chief, Ship Movement and
               Communications Section
```

A copy of the U. S. Navy Official report on the ONEIDA sinking, in the files of the National Archives, also is interesting:

```
                            Op-16-B-5
                      C O N F I D E N T I A L
                         NAVY DEPARTMENT
              OFFICE OF THE CHIEF OF NAVAL OPERATIONS
                           WASHINGTON
                         July 24, 1942
                       MEMORANDUM FOR FILE
```
Subject: Summary of Statements by Survivors of S/S "ONEIDA",
U. S. Lake type freighter, 2309 G.T., owners: Ford Motor Co.,
Operated by U. S. Government.
     1.   The "ONEIDA" was torpedoed without warning at 1210 EWT,
July 13, 1942 at 20°17'N - 74°06'W, (1½ miles North of Cape Maisi,
Cuba), while en route from San Juan, P.R., to Punta Gorda, Cuba, in
ballast, drafts 13' aft, 6' forward. Ship sank by the stern within 3
minutes.
     2.   The freighter was on course 310° true, speed 10 knots,
not zigzagging, radio silent, 2 lookouts: 1 on the pilot house; one
on the port bridge. The weather was fine, sea moderate, a light
easterly wind, visibility good, daylight attack, no other ships in
sight.
     3.   The track of the torpedo was seen about 300 feet from
the ship and Captain ordered the wheel hard left; but the torpedo
struck on the starboard at the waterline before avoiding action
could be taken. The explosion breached 20 percent of the entire side
of the ship, resulting in immediate and complete flooding of the
ship and the ship quickly sank. It is estimated that the submarine
was one-half mile distant; bearing 220° at right angles to starboard
at the time of the attack. There was no time to send distress signals. Confidentials sank with the ship.
     4.   Of the 29 aboard, 23 were able to reach life rafts, and
6 are believed to have drowned. The 23 survivors reached the shore 5
miles N. W. of Cape Maisi, walked to the Cape, and then proceeded by
the Schooner "ZOILA" to Baracoa, arriving on July 13, 1942.
     5.   Sub surfaced after ship sank and was a 1200 ton motor
vessel, painted light grey, with low flat-topped conning tower, high
bow, low stern, appeared clean and undamaged, and was armed with 5"
gun forward, smaller gun aft, and 2 machine guns in conning tower. A
short mast was located forward. When last seen submarine was heading
N. E. at a fast speed.

                         E. D. Henderson
                       Ensign, U. S. N. R.

CC: ONI B-8, 16-A-4-d, F-9 (4 copies), F-10, Cominch, Cominch F-21-
22, F-252, F-353, F-37 (C & R), Op-23-L, Op-28, Op-30, Op-39,
BuShips, BuOrdnance (Ensign P. L. Vissat), BuOrdnance, Atlantic
Fleet Anti-Submarine Unit, BuPers-6.
```

Insurance paid the company $261,800 for the ONEIDA's loss; the book value of the ship at that time was $93,000, depreciated from an original cost of $221,815.
```

On July 23, 1942, the S/S ONONDAGA was also sunk by a German sub, off the northern coast of Cuba, about 200 miles west of where her sister vessel had gone down only a few days before. This ship was on a time charter and 14 of the crew were lost along with one passenger. Insurance paid the company $261,000 for the ship which had a book value of $95,000 and had originally cost the company $227,806.

The master of the vessel was Captain George D. Hodges, who was among the crew lost. Captain Hodges had been master of the EAST INDIAN for 11 years but had had to take leave because of illness. When he returned to duty, he was assigned as master of the ONONDAGA, replacing Captain F. C. Hudgins.

The July 28 notification letter from War Shipping's Outler to Ford's Dierolf indicated the ONONDAGA was sunk at "0030 GMT, July 24th, in position 22 degrees 37 minutes north - 79 degrees 00 minutes west." Outler added: "We have not as yet received information regarding disposition of the crew but we will advise you when further news is received."

The official report (reproduced in Appendix II D) from the survivors was filed at the Navy Department three weeks later and, while giving further details, also varied slightly in some respects from the initial report to Ford. It stated the ONONDAGA was carrying a full cargo of magnesium, enroute from Nuevitas to Havana when sunk at "1630 EWT, July 23, 1942, at 22°40' N - 78°44' W," a different date and location from Outler's July 28 letter.[38]

The report further said the ship was making 8.3 knots with two lookouts posted when an explosion took place amidships on the port side with "several small fishing boats in sight" during the late afternoon attack. Some survivors thought a second torpedo hit the starboard side, but no torpedo wakes or submarine were seen.[39] The vessel sank within one minute, so rapidly no lifeboats were launched. Fourteen crewmen survived by jumping overboard to two floating liferafts. They were picked up by the Cuban fishing boat LAVENTINA on July 24 and landed at Punta San Juan.

A postscript in the Navy report stated:

The U. S. Vice Consul at Nuevitas expresses the opinion that due to carelessness of the ship's crew during the 3 days shore leave, enjoyed prior to ship's departure, practically everyone in Nuevitas knew the ship's destination and time of departure.[40]

The Captain's Ring
Several months later, to the surprise of everyone in the Marine Office, a copy of the following letter was received:

'copy

CIA. AZUCARERA PUNTA ALEGRE, S. A.
Punta San Juan, Cuba

October 22, 1942

Mr. N. A. Alayeto, Admor.
LYKES BROS HAVANA AGENCY, S.A.
PO Box 788, Havana

Dear Mr. Alayeto:

I have come in touch with a matter which might be of great senti-mental value to some person and I will explain the matter to you thinking you might care to and be able to contact who might be the interested party.

In the vicinity of the Bahamas Channel where the S. S. ONONDAGA was torpedoed and several of its crew lost is a great shark fishing ground. Around there for years a family by the name of Carrillo have fished commercially for sharks.

A short time after the sinking of the ONONDAGA according to them as told to me by the one I think the most reliable, they caught a shark that had in its belly the flesh and bones of a human being. They say they took out and saved the bones from the hip to the ankle. Also at the same time they found with the rest two rings. They have shown me the rings and I have carefully examined them.

I thought they would be of interest mainly because the outside initials on the heavy gold signet ring are G. D. H. As it was my understanding that the Captain who went down with the ship was G. D. Hodges, it has occurred to me that this might be his ring. On the inside of this same ring it has engraved as follows: "E. R. G. '17". The bottom of the ring is broken.

The other ring seems to be made of some such material as bone and is of light yellow color with a large dark top imitating a stone of some kind.

If the widow of the good old man who went down with his ship knows this ring, I imagine it would be of great sentimental value to her.

I am giving you this information for you to do with as you think best.

Yours very truly,
(Sgd)
R. M. Jenkins
Manager

At a later date the two rings were received in the Marine Office. Mrs. Hodges was notified and identified the rings as belonging to her husband and they were presented to her.

Further Ship Requisition

In July the company received a letter (dated the same day as the ONEIDA's sinking) from War Shipping's Cleveland Office advising that the Government wished to charter Ford's four canal vessels for the war effort — even though one (GREEN ISLAND) already had been sunk and another (NORFOLK) had been in service for a year. Apparently there was additional confusion in War Shipping, as the purpose of the notification was "to remove them from the Lakes to salt water before freeze-up" and "enable vessel scheduling over the balance of the season."

With Ford's East Coast-based fleet elements put into war service — indeed, four out of nine sunk already — it was not long before the call came for most of the rest of those operated only on the Great Lakes. The Government requisition order arrived August 12, 1942. This time Ford protested. The next day Captain Johnson, Marine Department superintendent, wired D. F. Houlihan at War Shipping: *"Arriving Washington Monday morning 17th. Wish discuss with you requisitioning of our entire tug and barge fleet, per your wires 12th, as we feel this will have serious effect our War efforts."*

The appeal was to no avail. On the 18th, N. J. Ahrens of the Marine Department penned the following:

Capt. Johnson phoned from Washington that there was no possibility of our holding any of the six 315 ft. barges. Advised that we should get four of them out of the Rouge Plant, quickly as possible, for Chicago, where Government will take them over...

The Government is taking some old engines they have acquired and will place these engines in the hulls of the barges and float them down the Mississippi to the Gulf where engines and boilers and other equipment will be installed.

In the case of the small barges, it is the Government's plan to charter these along with the Tugs — Capt. Johnson further advised that he believed they might allow us to retain one of the towing tugs and one or two of the barges to handle our coal movement...

We are planning on getting two of the large barges out of here Wednesday night and two more Thursday or Friday, for Chicago.

Every little bit helped in those days. Enroute to Chicago under tow, Ford's large barges carried 4600 tons of limestone each from Calcite, Michigan, to be unloaded for the steel mills in South Chicago. Two barges were at L'Anse loading lumber for the Rouge when their numbers were called. So urgent was the summons that the FREELAND was brought down empty and the smaller LAKE CRYSTAL only half full.

As indicated in Ahrens' memo, the large barges LAKE FOLCROFT, LAKE FREELAND, LAKE FRUGALITY, LAKE INAHA, LAKE PLEASANT and LAKE SAPOR would be converted back into ocean cargo vessels for use in the war effort, moving materials for our fighting forces. None were lost to enemy action, although a couple had interesting adventures, as we shall relate.

The CHESTER was turned over to War Shipping at New York City on October 16, 1942. But there had been problems, due to wartime shortages, in obtaining enough of the right kind of fuel oil enroute from Dearborn. Ahrens also had to wire Edgewater to provide the crews with rail fares back to Detroit. The EDGEWATER likewise joined the war effort on October 21, and LAKE ORMOC, the last to be called, on bareboat charter at $2,625 per month beginning December 17.

Thus went the war effort. By the end of that year almost all the tugs, barges and ships were gone, leaving only the M/S HENRY FORD II, M/S BENSON FORD, the small barge LAKE KYTTLE, and the Harbor Tug DEARBORN in the Ford Fleet that had once consisted of more than 30 vessels. The KYTTLE was commandeered by the Government and moved to the East Coast in 1943.

Capt. George S. Hodges, master of the S/S ONONDAGA when it was sunk, with ring

53

Barge LAKE FREELAND being rebuilt for World War II service

S/S LAKE FOLCROFT after rebuilding

LOSS OF THE M/S EAST INDIAN

The fifth and last of the Ford vessels to be sunk by enemy action was the M/S EAST INDIAN, the pride of the company's ocean fleet. At the time of the disaster, she was on time charter to the War Shipping Administration and went down southwest of Capetown, South Africa.

MacLean's Account

When the ship was attacked and sinking, many members of the crew were able to get onto lifeboats or liferafts. Murdoch Stanley MacLean, then 57, of St. Petersburg, Florida, was one. He was Chief Steward aboard the EAST INDIAN on this fateful trip and had served in that capacity on other Ford ships. (You'll recall Commander Beall's account of MacLean joining the ship in 1925 directly from the HENRY FORD II.) Although badly injured in the attack, he survived and subsequently described his ordeal in a booklet published in 1943 entitled, 13 Days Adrift, the Experience of M. Stanley MacLean." He dedicated the book to his shipmates who had "paid the supreme sacrifice."

In his book MacLean described how many of the EAST INDIAN crew had premonitions in the spring of 1942 about the pending trip. At the time of Pearl Harbor, EAST INDIAN had been at Gambia on the West Africa coast to pick up a load of rubber. It remained trapped there for the winter, unarmed and fearing Nazi sub attacks. The original crew were greatly relieved the ship finally was able to dash across the Atlantic in April 1942 to Philadelphia and safety with its valuable shipment.

In New York for war fittings[41] and aware of the loss of their brother Ford sailors on the S/S LAKE OSWEYA two months earlier, some Ford crewmen declined to sign on the ship before it departed again on a voyage far away from home for so long.[42] One of those declining was the temporary captain, John M. Burke, who had earlier replaced Captain Hodges when he went on sick leave before the war began. So Captain O. L. Ste. Marie of Springfield, N.J., became master for the voyage.[43] Later, on what turned out to be this last voyage, MacLean and the rest of the crew (who had sailed with Captain Hodges for many years on the EAST INDIAN) learned of his fate on the ONONDAGA, increasing their misgivings.

Her Last Voyage

The Navy had installed seven anti-submarine and anti-aircraft guns on the EAST INDIAN and assigned a crew of 11 young Navy Gunners to man them. The vessel left New York City for the Persian Gulf[44] on May 8, 1942 (two days after the GREEN ISLAND sinking) and encountered further evidence of Nazi submarine warfare even before it reached Key West.

After refueling in Trinidad, she arrived three weeks later in South Africa. From there she continued uneventfully on schedule up through the Indian Ocean, supposedly infested with Japanese submarines, past Madagascar to the Persian Gulf. EAST INDIAN unaccountably spent 55 days in an Iranian port before sailing on to Colombo, Ceylon. The crew was shocked to see the harbor there still dotted with sunken ships, the result of a disastrous Japanese air raid on Easter Day.

Making several stops, including Calcutta, to discharge and pick up cargo, the EAST INDIAN finally completed loading her stateside-bound freight in southern India and proceeded toward South Africa. Her holds were filled with 3,500 tons of precious manganese ore, 500 tons of tea and 5,600 tons of general cargo including bamboo and jute bags. After three weeks of anxious sailing across the Indian Ocean, with many stops because of engine trouble, she reached Capetown for repairs and re-supplying which lasted ten days. It is easy to appreciate the crew's growing apprehension.

According to MacLean, the EAST INDIAN crew and passenger list then consisted of a total of 74 men.[45] They departed Capetown on November 2, 1942, on a route home that was to take about six weeks. An out-of-the-way course was planned to avoid German submarines: West-Southwest 4,600 miles across the South Atlantic, around Cape Horn into the Pacific, up the western side of South America and through the Panama Canal, there to join a protected convoy back to New York.

The Torpedo

Because of the hazards, Captain Ste. Marie gave orders for all crew members to sleep in their clothes. Unknown to them, the Nazi submarine U-181, enroute to the Indian Ocean to join up with the Japanese, had picked them up early on the morning of their second day out and was following, trying to get a shot at the relatively fast-moving ship traveling on a zig-zag course. It was about 5:00 o'clock in the afternoon of November 3 when a torpedo struck the ship. Within two minutes, the ship disappeared beneath the sea.

Here's how MacLean described it:

"Sitting in my stateroom, I was waiting for dinner when I heard that searing crash. Instantly I knew it was a torpedo, although I had never heard one before. A glance out the port revealed that the ship was rapidly settling. I remembered saying, perhaps aloud, "Oh my God," and I grabbed my life belt which was in the rack over the door.

Out in the hallway I found darkness and smoke and men filing up the stairs. My chef charged on some one ahead of him and knocked him down. The confusion and delay cost the chef his life. He went down with the ship.[46]

I reached the boat deck perfectly calm, not knowing what was ahead of me. To George, one of the boys of my department,[47] I said, "I think I'll run back and get my money." "Mac, look aft," he answered.

I looked, saw the deck was already submerged, and hurried to my lifeboat, number two. Alas, its lines were not freed before the pull of the rapidly sinking ship made it too late. Crowded with men, it submerged.

Instantly I was caught by the right shoulder as in some great vice with such tremendous weight bearing down on my right side I could not move. I was caught between the davit and the buoyant lifeboat as they were clamped together by the downward pull of the heavy ship.

Under water, I fought furiously to free myself. I was thinking, "This is the end; all will be over soon," when suddenly I was floating. The great weight had lifted — I was free! "Better kick and get to the surface," I thought, although naturally I was coming up all the time from the very instant of becoming free.

I shall always remember the white foam I beheld upon reaching the surface after having gone down 40 to 60 feet. My first glance around revealed that the ship had blown her farewell, had gone down dragging my lifeboat and its occupants with her. The ship standing on end and my struggle to free myself from the vice had evidently caused me to be thrown from the lifeboat.

I was the only one to come to the surface. The others, perhaps, had a death grip on something which they never turned loose. No doubt before they recovered from the initial shock of being pulled under, the swiftness of the descent had carried them past the 150 feet depth where the pressure crushes out consciousness...

I hooked my left arm through a life ring floating near my left hand. My right arm did not obey any impulse sent it. Although a part of me, it did not seem to be, as it floated strangely out in front of me. It was then I first realized I was seriously injured. Under the pressure of the salt water there had been no pain.

Looking about me, I observed Number Four Lifeboat and four rafts were afloat. Everywhere was swirling debris. I called to the boys on one of the rafts to come get me, for I was rapidly growing weak. George came and pulled me to a raft; he, Gillan, our second engineer, and Bernard lifted me on."[48]

The U-boat Surfaces

At that moment, MacLean related, the submarine surfaced, five officers came to the deck of the conning tower and their captain asked in good English with only slight accent if the EAST INDIAN survivors were "Limies."

When the third mate [49] replied, "No sir, we are Americans," the U-boat commander said, "Why are you helping the Limies and the Black Russians? We have nothing against you." Without waiting for an answer from his victims, the German officer continued: "I got a beam on you at nine this morning. Had we fired then, we would have saved you 100 miles. As it is you are now 300 miles from Capetown, and there is nothing for you to do but to row. I'm sorry, for you had a beautiful ship. However, this is war."

The commander wanted to talk to the EAST INDIAN's captain and chief engineer, but was told they had gone down with the ship. He wanted to know the ship's destination and cargo, why the course was so far South and whether an SOS had been sent.

The U-boat commander then offered the survivors food, water, cigarettes and first aid. All were refused in the heady defiance of wartime, a decision later much regretted. Finally he provided a compass heading to Capetown (treated suspiciously by the survivors), wished them "God Speed" and with the other officers, gave the Nazi salute. "As they sailed away into the dusk, the commander clasped both his hands in farewell," MacLean recalled. [50]

Separation of the Lifeboat from the Liferafts

All this time, Chief Mate Clayton Hammond[51] had been clinging to wreckage from the ship and now was taken into the one remaining lifeboat where he assumed command. "He told the boys in the four rafts to stay together and keep their heads," the chief steward related, because the lifeboat would head for Capetown "which it should reach in four to five days," and help would soon be speeded to those on the rafts. The lifeboat rowed away, and the last seen of the liferafts was about 7 p.m. on the 3rd, two hours after the sinking.

MacLean had been transferred from one of the rafts to the lifeboat because he was the only survivor injured. He was suffering terribly from a broken back, a fractured ankle, three broken ribs and fractures of the right wrist and right humerus, plus a dislocated and shattered right shoulder, all with not even one aspirin to dull the pain. (He had lost the medical kit that he carried as Steward when he fell into the water.)

After calling the roll, Chief Hammond determined that 23 had gone down with the ship, 34 were on the rafts and 17 were in the lifeboat.[52] According to MacLean, had it not been for the quick thinking of the third officer and the bos'n[53] in cutting the lifeboat loose from the ship, no one would have been heard from again.

As MacLean lay pain-stricken in the lifeboat, he pondered about the reaction of the other men from EAST INDIAN: "A young Finn, of upper Michigan,[54] caught the shrouds and hung on as she went down. O'Brien stood on deck, laughing and disappeared in the smoke.[55] Mr. Doyle, our chief engineer, could not comprehend what had happened. He stood wringing his hands; this confusion cost his life." [56]

As the lifeboat pulled away from the others, "I can still see Archie McHugh, our purser[57] and a great sport, as he sat on the raft calmly fixing the canvas around for a windbreaker," he wrote. "Young Jack Riggons from Carolina[58] stood on the raft, his hands in his pockets calmly surveying."

Lifeboat of the ill-fated EAST INDIAN

Ten EAST INDIAN survivors at Cape Town, South Africa

58

Murdock Stanley in a cast

Ensign Howard A. Axtell, Jr., in charge of
EAST INDIAN gun crew

The radio operator, "Sparks," worried about not getting off an SOS. This was "freezing" him inside, MacLean surmised, and "on the second day his mind gave way." Sparks gradually grew worse until he sank into a coma that for days necessitated his being tied to the boat to prevent his falling overboard.[59]

Ordeal in the Lifeboat

At times, the weather was calm but on the second day it rained. Whenever the weather was quiet enough to permit, the crew in the lifeboat steadily rowed, relieving each other every two hours. Once in a while the porpoises were with them and the sailors were fond of their company as they considered them a good omen. One night they were surrounded by huge whales and they feared that one of them might come up underneath the lifeboat and upset it.

Occasionally the survivors would get on each other's nerves so much that they would stand up and fight until the mate called a halt. His main purpose was to reach shore to get help for the men left behind on the rafts. For any who failed to accept his command, he claimed he had a Forty-Five which he would not hesitate to use. Whether or not he really had a pistol was not known, but the men could see he had a holster under his coat and the threat kept them in line.

Several days of strong winds caught their lifeboat and carried it far off course around the Cape of Good Hope and out into the Indian Ocean. Strong winds and currents also added to their difficulties when rain clouds filled with desperately sought water would be blown away from them. Night and day, in storms and calm, they flew their yellow distress flag from the mast. Weakened by hunger and thirst and the continuous rowing, the men began to show exhaustion. Sometimes a lookout would fall sound asleep.

Food consisted of milk tablets, chocolate bars, pemmican, graham crackers and a daily ration of water, five ounces per day. Each man looked forward to his one ounce of water at noon. These supplies were running low when a sack of hard squash floated by their life boat. They ate every morsel, even to the smallest seed. In the same manner, a pint bottle of aromatic spirits of ammonia floated by, which seemed to be almost a life saver to the severely injured MacLean.

One night Flip, an EAST INDIAN seaman from Brooklyn, tried with his bare hands to catch an albatross that was hovering just a couple of feet ahead of the lifeboat. MacLean believed failure to catch the bird was lucky, because the bird probably was so strong and the sailor so weak that it could have pulled him overboard.[60]

The last afternoon they were in the lifeboat their nerves seemed more on edge than usual. The boys were swearing violently and some stood up and again started to fight, but decided to settle their disputes later on shore. Suddenly, a sea came over the boat, swamping it. The mate, commanding, succeeded in getting his crew to bail out the water and order was restored. Later, MacLean noticed that there was no more swearing "after the sea had cuffed us with a new blow."

His narrative reported that "in spite of the fact that no one heard another praying aloud, on shore (after being rescued) all confessed that they had prayed silently." The experience of Tex[61], observed to be deep in contemplation, was cited. Asked by MacLean what he was thinking, the crewman explained, "I've been a-prayin', and I knows de Lord am goin' to answer my prayer. We're goin' to land on a rock."

The night before their rescue was a terrible one with high seas dousing the survivors under an eerily clear sky and bright moon. The entire crew was huddled together in the middle of the boat under the sail trying to keep warm, except for MacLean who was forward where it was dry — but lonely. Finally, in great pain, MacLean managed to crawl back to the others where he was more content to be with them than dry.

The Rescue

MacLean's story continued:

After seemingly endless hours the morning broke gray and cold on a storm tossed sea. As always, with the coming of day, we eagerly scanned the horizon. Another hope dashed. There was nothing in sight.

All at once, Tex, who was rowing, looked forward and exclaimed 'My God, there's a ship.' Excitement must have stirred in every man, but it was surprising to me how outwardly calm the men were, considering we had spent 13 dreary days in the lifeboat and that most of us had despaired of being rescued.

Hammond was patiently putting water in Sparks' mouth with an eye dropper...The question in every mind, "Is that ship friend or foe?" went unheeded. We took chances and rowed for her. Fortunately, it was the ship of an ally, the British DURANDO coming from Bombay, India. What a welcome sight she was!

As we neared our rescuers, it seemed that the heavy seas were not willing to give us up and permit a safe transfer. Helpless, I watched in terror, fearing that the boys would be drowned or have their legs smashed against the side of the ship. At last, I saw them one by one make their way up the ladder and over the top safe on board.

I was most fearful for Fraser,[62] as after the rescue was underway, I had seen him , crazed by his pangs of thirst, drink the water that was left in the keg. It was almost a miracle he did not become violently ill.

Sparks and I were the big problem for the DURANDO's crew. Mr. Little, her first mate and a marvelous sailor, almost lost his legs trying to get me tied in the bos'n's chair, as the ship was rolling so. The line cut across my injured back, but pain did not mean a thing then, for I was happy to be rescued. Sparks, still unconscious, had to be taken up in a basket. Then our boat, the gallant little sailor, was cut adrift.[63]

The entire crew of the rescue ship, even to the lowliest coolie, wholeheartedly shared food, clothing and cigarettes with the survivors. "Since all our clothes were rotted from being constantly wet with salt water, all I had in the world was my ring and belt," MacLean recalled. He was asked what he wanted most (since he was so badly injured) and sought the impossible: fresh or even canned fruit. But the British searched their entire ship and came up with a can of apricots.

On the 14th day after being torpedoed, they arrived back in Capetown after travelling 472 miles (312 miles out in the South Atlantic Ocean and 160 miles back into the Indian Ocean). They were far off the lanes of travel as was the DURANDO, and it probably would have been months before another ship passed. When rescued, they had less than nine days of food and water left in the lifeboat. The officers of the DURANDO told the survivors that if they had appeared clean shaven (and therefore a possible ruse by a submarine lurking nearby), the ship would never have turned around to make the rescue.

During the first night ashore, Sparks, the radio operator, died from shock and exposure. MacLean recalled that only two weeks earlier when leaving Capetown, Sparks had remarked, "It is beautiful. I like it here and I want to come back some day and stay awhile." He did return, to be buried at the base of Table Mountain. Even officers and crew from the rescue ship attended his funeral. Later, the EAST INDIAN survivors heard that the DURANDO was itself sunk with the loss of all hands before it could reach England.

Search planes were sent out for three days to look for the missing rafts with their 34 men, but with no results. While recovering ashore, the survivors of the EAST INDIAN heard a news report about a German spy being arrested, supposedly a stevedore on the docks who was giving sailing information to waiting submarines. MacLean thought the reported spy had tipped off the Germans concerning the EAST INDIAN's departure.[64]

After hospitalization in South Africa, MacLean returned to America via another ship which reached Halifax, Nova Scotia. Along with some of the other survivors, he traveled by troop train from there to New York City, arriving January 2, 1943, where he received further treatment. Later he visited the Marine Office in Dearborn where we listened to his story of survival.

THE BRAZILIAN LIFEBOAT STORY

Nothing more was heard about the men on the rafts until one day in July 1943 when a letter was received in the Marine Office. It was from the father of the EAST INDIAN's Navy gun crew officer, Ensign Axtell, who had been reported missing in action and presumed lost. Mr. Axtell sent along a clipping from a Washington, D.C., newspaper about an EAST INDIAN lifeboat being washed ashore in Brazil. Soon another such inquiry was received from the sister of the purser, McHugh, with a clipping from the New York Times.

Then in August one of our men returning from Brazil brought in the original story from a Brazilian newspaper which we had translated as follows:

> From: "Diario da Noite"
> Rio de Janeiro, Tuesday, June 29, 1943. No. 3811:

DIARY OF THE SEAMAN WHO DIED ON THE LIFEBOAT OF THE 'EAST INDIAN'
Successions of Tragedies on the Open Sea
After the Torpedoing of the Fast Freighter
Death from Cold and Hunger
Terrible Agony of a Young American Seaman

MACEIO, June 28th (Asapress) — Lieutenant Nabuco Lopes, of the Medical Corps, was in Juquiz when there arrived at the beach, on the 23rd inst., a large lifeboat built entirely of wood. In this boat there were found sweaters, socks and woolen shirts, seaman's pants and oars, in addition to a small luminous buoy. Inside the boat there was an inert and rigid body of a man with blonde hair, young, emaciated and the entire body in a terrible organic condition. The corpse, wrapped in five woolen blankets, was in a bent position, with the head almost crushed, a dramatic expression still remaining on the half-destroyed face.

In the pocket of the American seaman, there was found the following diary in poor English, which was translated by Lieutenant Nabuco as follows:

"I cannot forget those terrible moments. Our steamer was proceeding at full speed, tearing through the Atlantic. We were going to load meat for our brothers in the battle. Never did the EAST INDIAN make a better voyage. There were no signs of any submarine. Keney even made some jokes about submarines and he put on a Nazi mustache and imitated the pose of the dictator.

I could not forget my little Robert in spite of the insistent recommendations of Janet. Furthermore, all of us, during the voyage, forgot the dangers of the German ambushes. We also remembered the absence of our people, the many presents we would bring back to them upon our return, the stories and incidental happenings. Yesterday was November 1st, Keney told me it was All Saints' Day and therefore we should pray for the victory of our people.

Maysie, our mascot, was jumping around happily as though, upon our return, we were sighting the Statue of Liberty. I do not know why this dog felt so happy at that time.

Night was coming. The crew had already left the mess room. I left with Keney through the passageway in order to observe the rigor of our blackout. Suddenly, treacherously, a terrible explosion occurred and the vessel tried to keep afloat. Everybody was running in spite of the continuous lifeboat drills which we had had in order to meet such a situation. I, myself, ran quickly down to my bunk in order to get the only photograph I had of my family when little Robert was born.

Terrible yells, commanding order, lost without an echo in the midst of all this confusion. I do not know where Keney went, but I heard his voice in the midst of that noise, crying out that we were going to the bottom.

At the ladder, I met Maysie, who was running without any sense of direction and happily to the engine room. I tried to pick her up but she ran away, running in various directions, barking and wagging her tail.

The lifeboats had already been lowered. Some men were already adjusting the lifeboats. Others tried to carry a wounded man, perhaps some close friend — almost brothers on that occasion. There is no doubt that many were left below, held in an agonizing prison in the holds.

When I jumped into the sea I tried to swim with all my strength in order to get away as soon as possible and not be drawn into the whirlpool of the sinking vessel. Heavy waves struck the sides of the half submerged ship and over the tarpaulins of the boats. I never thought it would be so difficult to swim under such conditions. I almost fainted. The water covered me and pulled me toward the 'EAST INDIAN'. There only remained three life boats which were getting away rapidly. After the wave of panic was under control and in the middle of this darkness I was picked up by Keney's boat. Shortly afterwards we lost sight of the other two boats. Our boat carried six men, me, Keney, two firemen, one steward and Chief Mate Garfield, a man of few words who helped us a great deal. We were six in all and all surely hoped that we would be saved. As there were only four oars we took turns in the rowing. Keney was the one at the rudder and the one who gave instructions as to the rowing in the direction in which he thought land was. We confidently lit the acetylene lamp and that live flame took away from us all our resentment against Garfield, who became an intimate friend instead of being a boss, imparting to all of us courage and faith by his encouraging words.

The first morning of tropical sun I wrote down in pencil on the tarpaulin of the boat, the day, week and month in order to keep some notion of the time. Keney suggested that we put all our money together protecting it by adhesive tape. I also used the adhesive tape in order to put together the pieces of the pictures of my family which was all torn and which made me very sad. There was an abundant supply of food and water, even if we had to spend 10 days on the water. In this hypothesis we would be able to eat like kings.

TUESDAY THE 10TH: Our hopes faded while looking for the mirage of assistance which never came. Day after day, hour after hour - no airplane and Keney attributed this unfortunate thing to the fact that we had not prayed during that tragic night. I also believed so. Three companions who could not stand the cold died but I believe they died more of hunger than of the cold. We kept their coats which diminished our suffering. However, I am spiritually depressed by these indescribable scenes. There is practically no more food left. Fortunately we caught a large turtle which was floating near us. This revived our dying hopes.

FRIDAY THE 13TH: I never liked it when Friday fell on the 13th. There is no longer any hope of being able to survive. Last night we lost Garfield, our good, faithful and courageous comrade. He took advantage of the darkness to throw himself into the water. Keney also jumped into the water hoping to save him but he was not successful. We are rationing to the utmost the rest of the turtle which even exudes a certain putrid odor. I improvised with the rims of my eye-glasses two fragile fishing hooks but I am sure I will not obtain anything with them. I only did this in order to give ingenious comfort to Keney who looked like a corpse and was sick. I myself am feeling attacks of insanity which is perhaps due to the salt water which we have added to the fresh water in order to increase the quantity. We did not row any longer. Our boat drifted, carried by the currents of the sea. Is it that the land has disappeared, submerged by the sea?

SUNDAY THE 15TH: I am desperate, Keney was delirious the entire night. He uttered unintelligible words such as "Mary," "Liberty," which he repeated continuously. He burns with fever and I gave him all the water which we still had left. At daybreak today and with the deepest sorrow and crying I left his body into the water. I would have preferred to die myself before him. Keney, besides being a friend, was the greatest hero I have ever known. It is a pity that Janet and Mary did not know this before. It is only now that I understand how fate is so whimsical. To the shores of Brazil the body of Keney was carried, wrapped in woolen garments taken from those who had been tortured by cold and hunger. He died all shrunken, his feet twisted over each other, his head sunk down between his shoulders almost between the thighs, practically in the same position in which he was born but the world of little Robert must be saved and we free men have sworn that there will not be any place for Idle castes nor will there be permitted any longer the humiliating oppression of insatiable feudal lords. Perhaps in this way our martyrdom will not be in vain."

These words ended the tragic diary of the dead American seamen, victims of Nazi aggression. This was the sad ending of a beautiful Ford ship and her crew. However, harried no doubt by wartime pressures and suspicions, Marine Office personnel rather quickly concluded that the Brazilian story was a hoax, and dismissed inquiries from next-of-kin politely with little further investigation.[65]

THE WAR CONTINUES

These war stories are related only to point out that Marine Operations had many difficult times in the past, and sometimes it was very depressing to work there with the task of talking to the next-of-kin about the loss of their loved ones. Most of the balance of the fleet survived the war but some of the ships had near misses and were damaged.

Fury of an Atlantic Winter Storm

On October 2, 1942, the Government purchased outright the Tug BARRALLTON and the small Barges LAKE ALLEN and LAKE LOUISE. These were delivered to Boland & Cornelius crews in Buffalo with orders for transfer to the East Coast via the St. Lawrence.

Finding that only Ford crews had much experience towing these barges, the Government subsequently directed the company to have its crews man the Tug BUTTERCUP and Barges LAKE CRYSTAL and LAKE HEMLOCK. With the Boland & Cornelius tow a day or two ahead, they set out November 4, 1942, from the Great Lakes Shipyards on the Detroit River for New York City via the St. Lawrence River route.

What these six vessels encountered was, except for loss of life, every bit as dramatic as being torpedoed by German submarines. The logs of the three vessels under Ford command tell the story.

In the face of what turned out to be an early and vicious winter coming on that November, the ships already had departed late. BUTTERCUP reported that heavy snow November 11 impeded vision and tow of the HEMLOCK even between Buffalo and the nearby Welland Canal entrance. The comparatively short voyage took eight hours, twice what had been needed for the CRYSTAL three days earlier.

But the real trouble didn't hit until three weeks later, December 1st, after the three ships had crossed Lake Ontario, passed up the St. Lawrence, rounded Cap-des-Rosier at the end of the Gaspe peninsula and started 200-plus miles across the Gulf of St. Lawrence for Cabot Strait into the Atlantic.

BUTTERCUP's log reads:

Dec. 1,	*10:20 AM:*	*Anchored barges giving steam to HEMLOCK*
	12:30 PM:	*Picked up barges*
Dec. 2,	*9:30 AM:*	*Anchored barges for sea*
Dec. 3,	*8:55 AM:*	*Anchored for snow*
	5:45 PM:	*Proceeded with tow*
Dec. 4,	*4:00 AM:*	*Pictan Island*
	6:00 PM:	*Tow line parted, trying to locate barges.*

Indeed, it took eight long, dark, stormy days before BUTTERCUP found HEMLOCK and CRYSTAL. In the meantime, BARRALLTON, towing LAKE ALLEN and LAKE LOUISE with inexperienced crews, had already run into the raging North Atlantic winter storm. The tow lines parted, and the ALLEN foundered and sank December 3 off the Atlantic Coast of Cape Breton Island. Since Ford personnel were no longer involved, there is no company record of the extent of casualties.[66]

The logs of the HEMLOCK and CRYSTAL relate the ordeal more dramatically than the tug's.

HEMLOCK's reads:

Dec. 4: Tug towing cable was hanging down and could not see tug...We had to drop both an chors and their full length of chain...Sea was quite rough and had to cut hawser of LAKE CRYSTAL so we would not collide with them in the heavy sea.

Dec. 5: We tried to get cable of tug in and it broke our line and slipped into the water. It must have held us all that night in the same place and we started to drift fast...LAKE CRYSTAL was not in sight. No sign of any help...

CRYSTAL's reads:

Dec. 4: 6:00 PM: Near NW Pt. Cape Breton Isl...Tug BUTTERCUP lost both HEMLOCK and CRYSTAL. LAKE HEMLOCK crew cast LAKE CRYSTAL tow line off.

Dec. 5: 8:00 AM: Daylight - driftwood going to sea against wind. LAKE HEMLOCK sighted about 6 or 7 miles NW of CRYSTAL at 10:00 AM Dec. 5th - Plane flew over 12:55 PM, came out of clouds but did not have time to signal same, do not be lieve we were seen by plane. HEMLOCK was seen again 1:00 PM Dec. 5th, about same position.

4:00 PM: Sighted vessel we took for BUTTERCUP, seemed headed for CRYSTAL about half way between CRYSTAL and HEMLOCK. Sudden snow squall and cloudy weather shut out sight of vessel or what we took for tug. Was not seen again.

Dec. 6: Saving fuel, had dynamo shut down.

4:00 PM: Sighted HEMLOCK for few minutes - was shut out of view by cloudy weather and snow. Anchor chain dragging across bow to port side at 8 foot draft mark. Causing small leak on stem.

Dec. 7: 8:00 AM: Captain, Mate and crew made all tarpaulins secure for bad weather. Anchor was not on bottom any more so decided to take it in. When it was up found all was left was the stock, feelers had been broken off.

Dec. 8: Two men placed on watch - believing or had a feeling we were near land

...5:00 AM: Watchman thought he had seen land to starboard.

...5:30 AM: Capt. called all of crew to stand by. Watchman took sounding aft, found 24 feet of water.

...5:40 AM: Capt. and Watchman lowered port anchor to bottom. Windlass and brake band had been broken. Put out about 1 and ½ shots of chain - 120 feet then gave out more chain.

..6:00 AM: Anchor did not take hold (sand bottom was found later). Felt stern strike bottom, ship swung and felt ship pounding on bottom.

..7:00 AM: Crew were all up, mostly in pilot house...Could not make out what kind of shore or whether it was land we saw or a breakwater. Looked as though we were over a shoal and drifting into deep water.

..7:30 AM (Dark): Launched lifeboat...Sudden squall came up, sea was running high, part of crew took to lifeboat which was made fast well forward and ladder had been lashed starboard side in order to get in lifeboat...When Capt. got in life boat, one of the crew cast the boat adrift. Boat was pulled or rowed ashore, crew getting selves and clothes wet when landing on beach. Crew left aboard floated a line ashore. Capt. and a few farmers launched lifeboat from beach to pick up rest of crew...All crew members safe ashore, farmers on Island (Miquelon) took crew to their homes, gave hot coffee, spirits and dry clothing.

Incredibly, in three-and-a-half days, LAKE CRYSTAL had drifted (remember it had neither engines nor propellers) some 200 miles across Cabot Strait and out into the Atlantic. Had it not run aground on tiny Miquelon, a French possession off the coast of Newfoundland, it would have been blown out into the full ocean. The crew learned they had run aground at high tide, so at low tide, they could walk "without boots" to the 261-foot-long vessel, nearly high and dry.

Barge LAKE ALLEN unloading lumber at River Rouge in the 1930's

Barge LAKE CRYSTAL loading coal at Toledo, Ohio about 1930

Barge LAKE HEMLOCK at an upper lakes port loading lumber

Barge LAKE FREELAND in ice

On the morning of December 8, the telephone rang in the Marine Office at Dearborn. It was Atte Lindstrom, the Barge Captain, calling. He had just walked several miles to a phone to report that both barges had drifted loose for several days and his had landed on a sandy beach on Miquelon, French-owned and French-speaking, 12 miles from Newfoundland and 1,000 miles from New York.

About 2 o'clock that afternoon, the CRYSTAL crewmen ashore spotted the HEMLOCK three to four miles to the northwest, also in danger of grounding. The captain ordered flares lit to warn HEMLOCK of the danger, and flares and flashlights were maintained all afternoon and night. HEMLOCK thought it was off a lighthouse, but flashed back recognition and finally managed, after hours of struggle, to secure its anchors without going aground.

The next day, the 9th, a Free French Navy tug from the colony's capital of St. Pierre, on a smaller island a few miles to the east, arrived to assist HEMLOCK, towing it back to the safe harbor. In the meantime, Tug BUTTERCUP for days had been frantically searching over a huge area of open sea and coastlines for its lost barges.

The lost Ford ships finally were reunited on the 12th, when BUTTERCUP arrived at St. Pierre. Along with two other tugs, they succeeded in re-floating :LAKE CRYSTAL at the seasonal high tide just before noon that day. Eventually CRYSTAL reached its New York destination on January 14 under tow of the BARRALLTON which, as previously noted, had lost its tows earlier in the same storm.

Completion of HEMLOCK's journey took somewhat longer. After waiting nine days for weather to improve, it departed December 23 for Sydney harbor, Nova Scotia, under the BUTTERCUP's tow. Between Sydney and Halifax on New Year's Day and again on January 3, the two vessels again experienced problems with tow lines breaking. Then the barge spent 20 days having repairs for unspecified storm damages. Finally HEMLOCK was hauled to the inland side of Nova Scotia, loaded with gypsum, and reached New York on February 8. Altogether the journey cost Ford $130,000, for which it billed the Government, offset by the fees earned by cargo hauled.

The ultimate frustration in wartime wheel-spinning came eight months later. The War Shipping Administration notified the company September 28, 1943, that it would return BARRALLTON, LAKE HEMLOCK and LAKE CRYSTAL to the Great Lakes "as they are no longer needed in the New England coal trade."

LAKE FREELAND Wins a Commendation
The six large barges which the company delivered to the Government at Chicago in August and September of 1942 were floated down the Mississippi. From New Orleans they went on to shipbuilders, as planned, to turn them back into fully engined, ocean-going vessels with midships funnels, cabins and pilot houses as they had been originally before conversion to barges by Ford. Half went to Galveston, Texas, for repowering and the others to Mobile, Alabama. The process took several months.

The (now again) steamship S/S LAKE FREELAND completed arming by the Navy on October 26, 1943. Its first purposeful wartime voyage was from Bahia, Brazil to New York with a cargo of cocoa between February 10 and March 6, 1944. It continued in Gulf of Mexico and coastal service, carrying sugar, sulfur, phosphate, chrome and general cargo in the months following. But the voyages were not uneventful.

The FREELAND's Navy gun crew log recorded the following:

On 25 June at 1200 this ship proceeding independently from Havana, Cuba, to Nuevitas, Cuba, rescued five men from a liferaft, the entire crew of plane PV-1 number 49468 which they reported had crashed in the sea 2 hours earlier. Radio Silence was broken at 1338 to notify officials concerning this rescue. — Andrew C. Robeson, Ensign DV(S) USNR

For this action, Fleet Air Wing Eleven reported: "The Navy Department Board of Decorations and Medals recommends that the Secretary of the Navy address a Letter of Appreciation to the master and crew of the S/S LAKE FREELAND for the above service."

LAKE FOLCROFT Lost to Hurricane

FREELAND's log also indicated it spent 12 days from September 12 to 20, 1944, "avoiding hurricanes." Weather was hard on the Ford ships in that period from late fall 1943 to fall 1944. In an October hurricane, S/S LAKE FOLCROFT was less fortunate than her sister ships. Her fate is spelled out in terse U. S. Navy radiograms:

```
1941 HRS 19 OCT 1944
FROM: COMGULFSE    TO: COMINCH, CNO
SUMMARY HURRICANE DAMAGE PC 824, PC 488, PC 1188, SC 1280, AM 221, AMC 54
AGROUND KEY WEST. YTM 349 AND LV 91 UNLOCATED...FS 264 DISABLED STEER-
ING GEAR. S/S EDWARD L SHEA DISABLED STEERING GEAR AND PRESENT POSITION UN-
KNOWN. S/S ORMONDALE AGROUND DRY TORTUGAS. S/S LAKE FOLCROFT REPORTED
AGROUND NEAR HAVRIA. EXTENSIVE MINOR DAMAGE TO SHORE INSTALLATIONS KEY WEST
ESPECIALLY NAVAL HOSPITAL BUT HOSPITAL CAN FUNCTION NORMALLY. NO PERSONNEL
CASUALTIES NOB KEY WEST NAS KEY WEST NAS BOCA CHICA. BOCA CHICA FIELD UNDER
WATER NO TOWER CONTROL NO VOICE. DRY TORTUGAS RADIO BEACON
INOPERATIVE

1514 HRS 20 OCT 1944
FROM: USN TUG LAPWING
COMGULFSEFRON SENDS INFO TO COM 8 COM 10TH FLT
(US FREIGHTER LAKE FOLCROFT)
US FREIGHTER LAKE FOLCROFT 3600 GROSS TONS AGROUND SINCE 0830Z 19TH 22-50-
50 N 83-46-45 W IN REPORTED 16 FEET OF WATER. ENGINE ROOM AND HOLDS RE-
PORTED COMPLETELY FLOODED. 39 SURVIVORS INCLUDING ONE WITH INJURED LEG. 3
DEAD. UNLESS OTHERWISE DIRECTED WILL TAKE ON BOARD ENTIRE CREW AND PROCEED
KEY WEST AS SOON AS POSSIBLE. MASTER REQUESTS ORDERS, WAR SHIPPING ADMINIS-
TRATION BE CONTACTED IMMEDIATELY FOR ORDERS. STATES NO POSSIBILITY REFLOAT-
ING OR DRIFTING.
```

The official report by the FOLCROFT's Navy Armed Guard stated, "At the time of the sinking, the seas were mountainous with winds reaching hurricane proportions. The vessel was driven onto a coral reef, approximately 8 miles from the coast of Cuba...There were three merchant men lost in an accident which occurred in the engine room at the time the vessel struck the reef." Crew lost on the FOLCROFT were the chief engineer, a fireman and an oiler.

Although FOLCROFT was believed lost at the time, a November 21, 1944, memo in the Navy file on the ship indicates the cargo later was salvaged and the vessel towed to Havana. But damage was so great, it was retired from service February 9, 1945, at Mobile, Alabama, when the Navy armament was removed.

Ford's remaining ocean-going Laker, the LAKE ORMOC — which had been completely reconstructed, re-engined, modernized and well-equipped for Brazilian rubber operations in 1928 — was turned over to the Government late in 1942 on a bareboat charter. But it had mechanical and crew troubles from the very beginning, becoming a "jinx" ship, shunned for good reason by others. Eventually it was banned operationally to the backwaters of the Pacific War, not unlike the fictional vessel of Mr. Roberts, the classic World War II navy story.

SAGA OF THE LAKE ORMOC

Following are excerpts from the "United States Armed Transport" (U. S. A. T.) ORMOC's Navy gun crew reports:

15 Nov 1942: Left Guantanamo, Cuba with convoy and could not maintain con voy speed and were ordered to return to base.

27 Nov 1942: Left Port Everglades; joined convoy and could not maintain convoy speed so dropped out. Our engines stopped for fifteen hours during which time we drifted.

21 June to 3 July 1943, San Pedro, Cal. to Honolulu, T. H.: The vessel lost the convoy during the second day out due to engine trouble. All pre vious attempts to remain in convoy have failed for the same reason. Also as usual the ship had to stop at least six times enroute from San Pedro because of engine trouble. The generator engine exhaust contained many large particles of glowing carbon which were visible at night for a great distance.— P. J . Stuhlreyer, Lt., USNR.

6 July to 19 August 1943, Honolulu, T. H. to Sydney, Australia: During the voyage the vessel slowed down frequently and on several occasions stopped completely due to engine trouble. The main engine exhaust smoked excessively during the latter half of the trip. Sparks and glowing particles of carbon from the generator engine exhaust were often visible at night for a great distance...The master, first and second mates are all aliens and lack the proper understanding of the Armed Guard's position aboard the ship. They also, especially the second mate, appear at times to question the Navy's authority about wartime shipping in general... — P. J. Stuhlreyer, Lt., USNR.

2 January to 10 March 1944, Sydney, Australia to Caloundra, Townsville, Milne Bay, Port Moresby, Buna, Finschhaven, Los Negros:
Departed Milne Bay 0645 30 January alone for Port Moresby, arrival being at 1030 2 February. Ship struck an uncharted coral head at 1055 1 February but insufficient damage done to prevent her proceeding to destination.
Departed Port Moresby 1830 11 February alone for Buna with water barge in tow. Tow went adrift immediately.
Departed Buna 1315 17 February in convoy with two other merchant vessels and escorted by three U. S. Navy patrol craft for Finschhaven, arrival being at 1305 18 February. Numerous explosions in water close to shore were noted at 1005 the same morning, but none was close to the ship and their source was neverdetermined... We were the first merchant ship to enter the Admiralty Group.

28 March to 4 April 1944, Hyane Bay, Los Negros Island, to Finschhaven, New Guinea: There was no action with the enemy, but two bombs were dropped by one Japanese aircraft at Hyane Bay, Los Negros Island, Admiralty Group, about 2245 12 March 1944. These landed on shore, about 1500 yards from the ship's anchorage, doing no damage to the ship.— R. C. Johnson, Lt. (jg), USNR.

6 July to 28 July 1944, Sydney, Australia to Madang, New Guinea, chartered to Australian Army, type of cargo-food and medical supplies: Sani tary conditions in the gun crew's quarters are very bad and unless immediately corrected threaten the health of the Navy personnel aboard this vessel. This is due to the fact that one of the two toi lets in the Head cannot be used and the other toilet does not func tion at all times. The Engineering Department confess their inabil ity to correct this situation...The Steward's Department has failed to furnish clean linen and towels to Navy Personnel for the past three (3) weeks.

1 August to 18 August 1944, Madang, New Guinea, to Brisbane, Australia,

type of cargo-medical and salvage: This ship has two (2) U.S.A. Army
    radio operators and they carried out all wartime radio
    instructions...No defects or deficiencies in respect to battery.
    However, living quarters of U.S.Navy Armed Guard Crew are intoler
    able because of inadequate toilets and showers and
    ventilation...Master and Chief Mate have on numerous occasions
    smoked cigarettes on bridge during blackout hours...Frequent point
    ing, training, sightsetting and loading drills held. — A. J. Cohen,
    Ensign, USNR.
5 November to 25 November 1944, Brisbane, Australia to Hollandia, Dutch New
    Guinea, type of cargo — trucks, office equipment, food, ammunition
    and tow of a refrigerator barge: Three (3) day stop in Milne Bay, New
    Guinea, for engine repairs...Sanitary conditions aboard ship still bad as it is infested
    with vermin and rats.— A. J. Cohen, Lt. (jg), USNR

These excerpts are provided both as a history of the Ford Fleet's ships and to give a flavor
of the experiences, adventures and frustrations of the young Navy officers who signed up to fight
a war, like Mr. Roberts, and found themselves assigned to a seemingly jinxed tramp steamer in the
backwaters of the South Pacific.

Lieutenant (jg) Cohen was relieved from the ORMOC by the date of the next Gun Crew
report, January 6, 1945. His successor, Lt. (jg) R. B. Heiney filed this postwar report of the ship's
ammunition supply disposal:
2 November 1945...Pursuant to US Bams Message 103 the following ammunition
    was dumped overboard on 18 October 1945 between 07°54′S-148°15′E and
    07°34′S-148°13′E in water of more than 150 fathoms and more than 10
    miles from shore: 20 mm - 21, 210 rounds, 3" 50 - 248 rounds

Two wars and nearly 50 years later, this still seems like an incredible store of ammunition
being carried by one little tramp steamer which never needed — fortunately — to fire a shot in
anger or defense.

In total it can be said proudly that our Ford ships and dozens of our marine personnel
served their country well. Many, as we have seen, made the supreme sacrifice. Toward the end of
the war, the next-of-kin of each Ford officer and crewman lost to enemy action received the
Mariner's Medal as posthumous recognition of their service.

M/S LAKE ORMOC

After the war: DISPOSAL OF THE OCEAN FLEET

The war ended on September 2, 1945, with the Japanese surrender to General MacArthur in Tokyo Bay. The War Shipping Administration had no further use for the surviving ships; neither did the company. During the war, charters were made with other Great Lakes operators to carry Ford's raw materials. After the war a decision was made to continue using our big ore boats while eliminating the tug and barge business.

Times were changing. The cost to stockpile auto parts to be shipped to the East Coast in the canal vessels was too high; so this operation was also discontinued. The tire plant had been shut down and the rubber plantation in Brazil was sold, thereby eliminating the need for the LAKE ORMOC.

In addition, the Government had converted the six large barges back into steamers and had erected conventional superstructures for ocean service on the three canal vessels which were not sunk. Cost of putting them back the way they were in company service before the war would have been prohibitive. None of these ships fitted the company's needs in 1946. However, we did continue to move new cars in intracoastal waterways, lakes and rivers by barges and car carriers under charter.

The Tug DEARBORN was sold to Captain Morgan Howell of Detroit in 1946. We were then using Great Lakes Towing Company's tugs to move vessels around in the turning basin. Another reason for disposing of the DEARBORN was that the captain was caught sleeping on the tug one day and was fired on the spot. The selling price for the tug was $80,000 and it was renamed INTERSTATE.

The balance of the fleet that went to war was disposed of as follows, either by Ford if it still owned the vessels, or by the Government if it had bought rather than chartered them during the war:

Small barges LAKE FARGE and LAKE FRUMET — sold to Coast and Inland Navigation Corporation, New York for $50,000 each. Both were scrapped in 1953.

Tugs HUMRICK and BUTTERCUP and small barge LAKE LOUISE — title was taken in 1942 by the U. S. Government in exchange for $380,000 (the sunken LAKE ALLEN was also included in the price). LOUISE was bought from the Government in 1944 by Seaways Transportation Company of New York City and renamed GORDON C. COOKE. She sank in a storm April 22, 1947, off Ocean City, New Jersey.67

Tug BARRALLTON — sold to Republic of Columbia, South America, for $127,000 in 1944. This was quite a premium over the $25,000 each her three sister tugs had sold for in 1933-34.

Tug BARLOW and small barges LAKE CRYSTAL, LAKE HEMLOCK and LAKE KYTTLE — sold to Sound Chartering Corporation, New York City, for $200,000 in 1945. CRYSTAL sank February 14, 1946, off Watch Hill, Rhode Island, while in tow from New York to Boston. HEMLOCK sank in a storm in Long Island Sound, December 13, 1957. KYTTLE was re-sold to Sheridan Barge Corporation of Philadelphia in 1950, renamed JAMES SHERIDAN and sank January 20, 1960, in a storm in Long Island Sound off Saybrook, Connecticut.

Steamer LAKE FREELAND — sold to Inter-American Shipping Service, New York City, for $132,500 in 1946. Renamed NAVEMAR, she was sold to the Argentine government in 1947. When scrapped in April 1973 at Campana, Argentina, she was the last of Ford's Lakers.

Steamer LAKE INAHA — sold to Bright Star Steamship Company, Houston, Texas, for $135,000 in 1946. Renamed CAPTAIN JOHN and later SANTA MARTHA, she foundered November 22, 1954, off the coast of Brazil.

Steamer LAKE PLEASANT — sold to Compania Punta Alta, Panama, for $99,750 in 1946. Renamed STAMO and later ADRIATICA, and scrapped about 1957.

Steamers LAKE SAPOR, LAKE FRUGALITY and LAKE FOLCROFT — sold in 1946 to Francis
I. S.Chu, Shanghai, China, for $145,687, $144,300 and $15,000, respectively. The last
was so badly damaged in the October 19, 1944, hurricane off Cuba that it was only good
for scrap. SAPOR ran ashore and broke up on Mine Shima Reef in the Pacific, February
14, 1947, while enroute from New Orleans to Hong Kong with a cargo of barreled gaso
line and quonset huts. FRUGALITY was renamed EASTERN VENTURE and later EAST-
ERN LUCKY, and sank in a storm off Swatow, China, December 12, 1959, enroute from
Hong Kong to Yokohama, Japan, with a cargo of scrap iron.

M/S NORFOLK — sold to Erie St. Lawrence Corporation, New York City, for $255,000 in 1946.
Stranded on East Coast in 1948 and abandoned to underwriters. Bought by N. M. Paterson
& Sons of Fort William, Ontario, in 1950. Rebuilt and renamed HUMERDOC. Scrapped
in 1967.

M/S LAKE ORMOC and S/S CHESTER — sold in 1947 to Nelson Line Inc., New York City, for
$245,000 and $120,000, respectively. ORMOC was sold Norwegian in 1948, renamed
SIGNEFJORD. Renamed GUNNY, sold Italian, sank after stranding near Cape Rizzuto,
Ionian Sea, December 22, 1962. CHESTER was renamed LOURIVAL LISBOA in 1947
by Brazilian owners, and GUARARAPES in 1949. Scrapped about 1955.

S/S EDGEWATER — sold to McColl Frontenac Oil Co., Montreal, Quebec, for $120,000 in 1947.
Renamed ORION in 1949 by her new owners, Cleveland Tankers, Inc., this ship remained
on the Great Lakes as an oil tanker for many years. She was sold for scrap in 1964, con
verted to a sand barge in 1965 and sank in Lake Erie in 1968.

The settlement procedures with the Government regarding wartime charter agreements,
and the insurance claims involving these ships, continued for several years after the war. The
decisions to accept or reject settlement offers were made solely by Captain O. A. Johnson as
recommended by N. J. Ahrens who was Marine superintendent.

Ex-barge LAKE FREELAND after World War II as powered Steamer NAVEMAR

THE NEW FORD MOTOR COMPANY

In the midst of World War II, the company faced a terrible crisis. Henry Ford I reached his 80th year in 1943. Two months earlier, his sadly powerless son Edsel had died suddenly at the age of 49. The Ford family rebelled at the tyranny of Harry Bennett, on whom Mr. Ford, who was more and more becoming senile, depended for carrying out his orders.

Mr. Henry Ford II, Edsel's eldest son, was released from his service in the Navy and came home to take over the company at the age of 26. There was a deep concern in Washington that Ford might not be able to meet its war production goals. His first step was to hire Mr. John Bugas[68] who had been special-agent-in-charge of the Detroit office of the Federal Bureau of Investigation. His second was to fire Harry Bennett.

After the war when peacetime production could be resumed, the company and Henry Ford II found themselves losing millions of dollars each year under the old management system mentioned earlier. Something had to be done. "Young Henry" brought in Mr. Ernest Breech, a General Motors financial expert who in turn brought in many other new faces from our arch-rival across town. Those brought in by Mr. Breech and Mr. Ford also included the so-called Whiz Kids from the Army Air Corps, most of whom became top executives of the company, and college graduates whom Mr. Henry Ford I would never hire.

Captain Johnson's Last Days

The Harry Bennett "group" was slowly removed from the company payroll over a period of many months. This purge eventually included Captain O. A. Johnson. After he left the company, Captain Johnson bought the Steamer W. D. REES in 1946 and obtained a contract from Ford to haul coal from Toledo to the Rouge Plant. This ship continued in operation through 1948. Following Captain Johnson's death on January 2, 1948, his widow tried to manage the vessel. However, she was unsuccessful and the vessel was sold in 1950.

One of Captain Johnson's benevolent activities was a joint venture with Grant Piggott and Joseph Braun, when they bought the J. T. WING, the last schooner left on the Great Lakes, used by then to haul pulp wood. With money out of their own pockets these three men sponsored this sailing vessel as a Sea Scout ship. The venture unfortunately was discontinued because of difficulty in controlling costs and getting competent people to operate the ship. In 1948, the WING was moved to Belle Isle in the Detroit River where it became the nucleus of the Dossin Great Lakes Museum. Due to an invasion of termites, the ship had to be destroyed by burning in 1956. A new and beautiful museum building was then erected at the same location where the WING once lay.

Ford Starts its Comeback

The company had made a very considerable contribution to the war effort with production of 8,600 B-24 four-engined bombers at Willow Run, 57,000 aircraft engines and 278,000 jeeps. The first postwar 1946-model Ford V-8 automobile came off the line June 2, 1945, and the last bomber on June 28. The new car was presented to the new President of the United States, Harry S. Truman, by Henry Ford II, soon (September) to become the new President of Ford Motor Company.

The automobile industry was rapidly trying to convert back to peacetime production and meet the huge pent-up demand for new cars. This was caused by the fact that none had been produced since early 1942, the veterans coming home had no cars, and veterans and civilians alike had a lot of dollars saved up from wartime. Spending had been curtailed by serving overseas for those in the Armed Forces and rationing at home. War work also had afforded new wage-earning opportunities for many people not employed previously in industry, such as women and blacks.

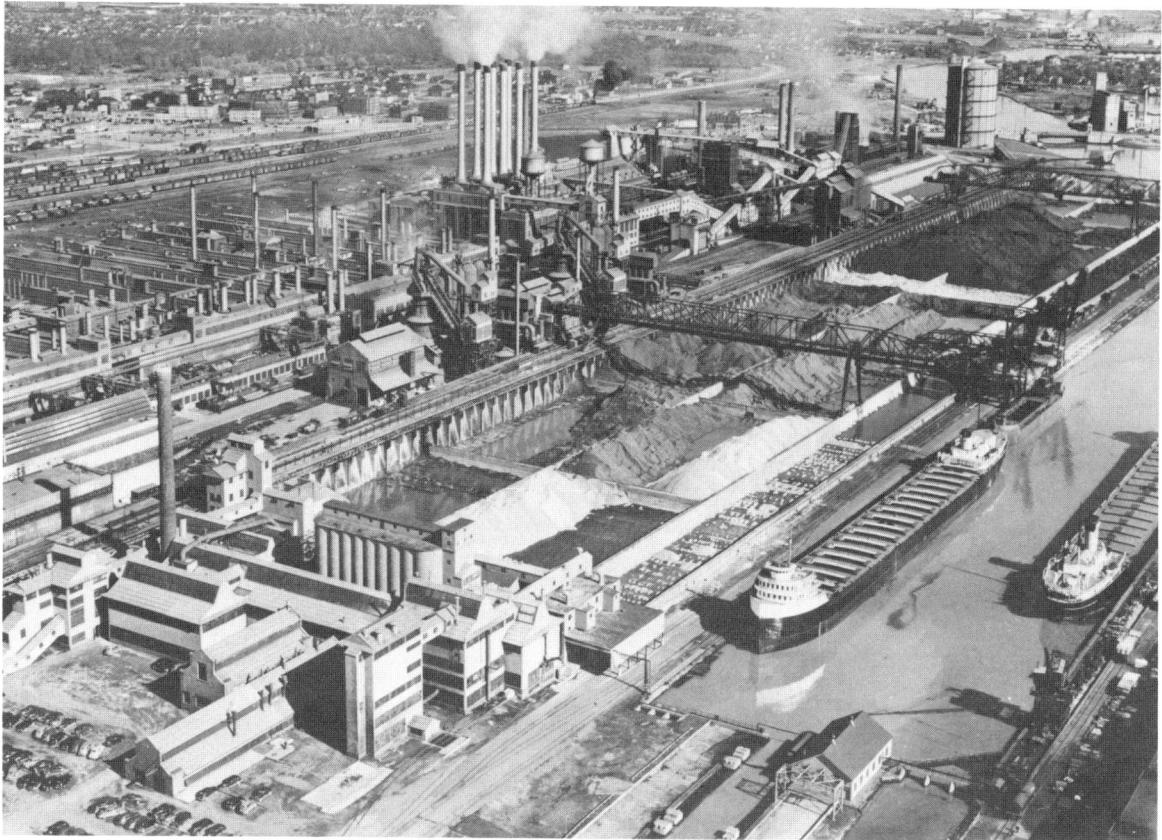
Ford Rouge plant and boat slip about 1950

Loading coal at Toledo, Ohio at the Chessie System dock # 4 about 1960

Capt. Meyers and Benson Ford on his namesake at the Soo Locks about 1955

The first postwar cars were just slightly restyled 1942 models, except for some new name-plates like Kaiser and Fraser, built at the former Ford Willow Run bomber plant. Then all-new cars began to be introduced, mostly in 1948 for the 1949 model year. The new Fords, Mercurys and Lincolns had new bodies and new chassis designs, reflecting the influence of the new company executives.

Mr. Henry Ford I died in his home, Fairlane, on April 7, 1947, at the age of 83. Much has been made of the fact that, because flooding of the Rouge River caused a power outage, this man who so changed the world died as he was born, by light of candles and kerosene lanterns.

The company's U. S. car, truck and tractor production reached 1,426,691 in 1949, up 73 per cent from 1939, and the highest since 1930. Foreign production had reached a record 173,790 the year before, and climbed another 14,000 for 1949. But Ford Motor Company still was trailing Chrysler Corporation for second place in car sales.

Postwar Marine Office Changes

Following the war, the Marine Operations of the company bounced around quite a bit. In 1945, the Traffic Department, along with Marine Traffic, had its offices moved from Schaefer Road to the B Building at the Rouge which was located in the assembly plant (and one-time Eagle Boat plant) across the road from the head of the Boat Slip. Captain Johnson had a small square window cut in the wall so he could see the ships at the dock from his second floor office.

It was during our time in the B Building that the Old Guard, including Captain Johnson, were replaced and a new traffic manager was named. Marine Traffic later was transferred to the Transportation Department and we moved to offices in the Rouge Transportation Garage in the World War II Aluminum Foundry building. We operated the ships from that office with Mr. Ahrens as Marine superintendent under Dave Doig, the Transportation manager. Mr. Fuhrman had been placed on Medical Leave and Mr. Ahrens, Alex Ingram (our port engineer) and I made up the entire office force.

Mr. Ahrens was one of the old timers. He had been with the company since 1918 and in Marine Operations since 1926. Just as I experienced later on, he always recalled the times when he was called out in the middle of the night by some shipping incident. One night in 1949, for instance, he got a call at 2 a.m., telling him the BENSON had gone aground in the St. Marys River. He had to fly up there after daylight and supervise its freeing. It took three tugs and two Coast Guard cutters to pull it back into the channel.

It was at this time that I began to handle the important responsibility of dispatching, although we were down to only two ships, the M/S HENRY FORD II and the M/S BENSON FORD.

Mr. Ahrens retired at the end of the 1954 shipping season and Jordan A. Schanbeck was then named Marine manager. Although he had worked for Mr. Doig in the Transportation Department, he had no experience in the Marine Department. He was raised in Grosse Pointe and was one of several young men who were acquainted with the Ford family, and whom we felt were being groomed for higher positions in the company.[69]

In 1957, Marine Operations and Power Operations were transferred to the Steel Division of the company. Our offices were then relocated to the Rouge Office Building on Miller Road which was the general operating office for the Rouge Plant complex. Unfortunately, Mr. Schanbeck fell off a cruiser while fishing in Lake St. Clair and drowned in July 1958. Ironically, he apparently had never learned to swim. I was appointed Marine manager on August 1, 1958.

SCHEDULING AND DISPATCHING SHIPS

To give you an idea of how the Ford Fleet was tied to car and truck sales, let me describe the role of Dispatcher, the first responsibility assigned to me in the immediate postwar period.

Planning

Many plans had to be laid before a dispatcher could schedule the first ship to load a cargo of iron ore or coal. The first plans were made in the company's Central Office (as it was called before being renamed World Headquarters in the Sixties) many months earlier when it was determined how many vehicles Ford planned to build during the coming Model Year.

That type of analysis was a new "science" which the postwar influx of new management brought, much of it from General Motors. They estimated the strength of the national economy and, from that, the likely total industry sales level. Then they calculated Ford's probable market share for each type of vehicle, based on both Ford's and the competition's selling points.

From the vehicle production schedules, it was then determined how much and what type of steel would be required. An allocation was given to our Steel Division to produce its share for our Stamping and Casting plants. The balance of our steel was purchased from outside steel companies to fulfill the production requirements. (Ford was unique in the automobile industry in having its own steel plant and, of course, the mines and ships to supply it.) Steel Division's Production Control Department then determined the raw material requirements of iron ore, limestone and coal that would be required to make the steel. Iron ore and limestone are charged directly into the blast furnaces. Coal is first made into coke in the coke ovens; the coke then is added to the blast furnaces in the iron-making process.

After the Marine Department was given the "annual buy" of raw materials, the dispatcher coordinated a schedule with dock operations to make certain materials would be on hand at all times to support production, while at the same time insuring that the storage bins would not be loaded beyond their capacity. The dispatcher then divided this tonnage over the period of the sailing season and determined how much was to be delivered each month. Available vessel capacity was determined and a monthly delivery schedule prepared along with an annual projection. At this point it had be determined whether Marine Operations had enough, or too much, vessel capacity to deliver the material. If too much, then the start of the sailing season could be delayed and if not enough, then additional vessel capacity had to be procured through contracts with other Lake shippers.

These projections all took place during the winter months while the ships were laid up and their crews far away on winter layoff. (A few men were always kept on to do maintenance work on the machinery and crew quarters to make them ready for spring fit-out.) It was the middle of January and February when the Marine Operations manager and his dispatcher were hard at work trying to determine a fit-out and sailing date for each of the ships in the Fleet. When these dates were established, the dispatcher might find time for a week's vacation before issuing his first sailing order to the master of the first ship to depart for the season.

Scheduling

In the back of his mind, the dispatcher had to remember not to ever schedule such a departure on a Friday. This was one superstition never ignored in the Ford Fleet; a captain would gladly depart the dock on the first trip at 12:01 a.m. on Saturday — but never two minutes earlier on a Friday.

The dispatcher by now had been provided information on the various grades of iron ore purchased and the ports and loading docks where the ore would be loaded. Years ago, when only red ore was available, it was not uncommon for us to have ten or fifteen different grades of iron ore to deliver. They came from many different ports, such as Escanaba and Marquette, Michigan; Ashland, Superior and Allouez, Wisconsin; Duluth, Minnesota; and Port Arthur and Michipicoten, Ontario. Later, only the lower-grade taconite ore was produced, and its pellets were loaded at just a few large automated docks near Minnesota's Mesabi Range. This made the dispatcher's job much easier.

After determining how much of each grade was required each month the dispatcher scheduled the ships to deliver the cargoes. He issued written orders to each ship's captain in duplicate. The master signed and returned one copy to the dispatcher to acknowledge receipt. The dispatcher told the captain what dock to proceed to and what type of cargo to load. The ship had to follow these orders exactly, because if it should go to the wrong dock, there would be no cargo waiting to load.

Before the Marine Office dispatcher issued sailing orders, he arranged with the ore company's dispatcher to make certain that the cargo would be available at the mines or loading dock storage areas. Before the ship arrived, he would have checked to insure that a clear dock would be available for the ship to load, and the same for the unloading port. Finally, he had to make certain that storage space would be available for the cargo when it arrived at the Rouge Plant. Once he lined up this first cargo he had to start working on the second, third and sometimes the fourth cargo in advance for each ship in the Fleet. Sometimes it took several days to prepare a cargo for loading. And once a ship has put into a dock, the dock operators expect it to load promptly so the dock can be cleared for the next ship.

After the dispatcher had made all of these detailed plans there was one big thing that he could not control — the weather. Weather delays are a dispatcher's nightmare. Once a ship was delayed the whole schedule changed. Sometimes it worked out, sometimes it didn't. Years ago when we had so many small ships (the tugs and barges and the Lakers) that could not navigate the Lakes in bad weather, they would bunch up, creating bottlenecks at both ends waiting to load or unload. The larger ships of today can continue to sail in bad weather and, since there are fewer of them, congestion is reduced considerably.

Checking

As the ship moved up the waterways the dispatcher was constantly checking to make sure that the cargo would be ready to load on arrival. The ore company dispatcher was also checking daily to make certain that the ship was on time. It is amazing how perfectly this cooperation worked. Very few delays were caused by the dispatchers. When either the ship was delayed or the cargo was late in arriving at the dock for loading, the phones started ringing regardless of the time of day.

When the captain was a few hours away from his loading port, he would report into the dock by radio-telephone to give them his arrival time and ask if his cargo was ready. If it was not, it did little good for him to complain to the dock because they were serviced by the railroads and they could hardly load the cargo if it had not arrived. So the captain's first move always was to call the marine dispatcher, even if it was three o'clock in the morning, to find out what was going on. The dispatcher then called the ore dispatcher and he in turn called the people responsible for getting the cargo down to the dock — the mine, the railroad or the switching operation within the dock yard itself.

Once the cargo was located and the arrival time established, all concerned were notified and the dispatchers could go back to their beds. These problems have been greatly reduced in recent years with longer-term storage of pellets at the loading dock, allowing the inventory to be taken from stockpiles at the dock rather than being dumped from railroad cars on demand.

When the ship was downbound from the Lake Superior mines, the arrival time became very important to many people. The wives and friends of the crew members kept calling, wanting to know when to pick up their men. Many times they also wanted to know when the ship was going to leave and where it was going so that they could make other plans. Various other people needed to know the expected arrival time: those delivering groceries, clean laundry, shore side supplies and fuel oil; service men for radars, radio-telephones, gyro compasses and other equipment aboard ship; those responsible for emptying sanitary holding tanks; U. S. Coast Guard or American Bureau of Shipping officials coming to check the ship; union representative or attorneys wanting to contact personnel aboard the vessel; new crew members coming aboard; hospital personnel wanting to check a crew member for treatment; passengers planning on boarding the ship; and those providing transportation for the disembarking passengers.

From the above it is quite clear that when a ship was delayed in the fog with all of these people standing by waiting for it to arrive, the Marine Office dispatcher could easily be criticized for not doing his job even though he had been up most of the night trying!

Limestone and Coal Cargoes
Limestone is much easier to handle than iron ore or pellets, inasmuch as it generally came from only one port, the largest limestone quarry in the world, located at Rogers City, Michigan. It was easy to work with the people at Michigan Limestone & Chemical Company, a division of U. S. Steel, as their schedules were flexible. Cargoes always loaded at one dock and discharged at the same location very seldom caused any problems.

Coal, on the other hand, was an extremely difficult commodity to load into ships. First, most coal was dumped directly from railroad cars into the ships. Larger ships loaded 200 to 300 cars of coal at a time and the trains had to be held in railroad storage yards prior to the ship's arrival. The coal might have come from several different mines located on several different railroads and bought from several different companies.

A coal cargo consisted of one, two and even three different grades of coal that had to be kept separate. This meant that the ship's first mate had to give the dock foreman advance notice on how he wanted to load the cargo, namely, how many tons in each of the ship's compartments. Then the yard foreman made up his train accordingly before pushing them up onto the coal car dumper at the loading dock. If the yard foreman directed too many cars to the ship, the cars had to be returned to the yard and, if too few, the mate could not load the ship properly. To keep the ship in trim, several loading runs had to be made through the ship from the after to the forward compartments.

The coal moved up to the docks on consignment numbers or names and was controlled by the Ore and Coal Exchange in Cleveland. This exchange was supported by the railroads as a independent agency to control movement of ore and coal and insure prompt return of empty railroad cars. No coal could be shipped without issuance of the proper permit by the Exchange. Before any shipment was made, the marine dispatcher had to send a request to the Exchange identifying shipper, mines, shipping point, rail routing, dock, and name of vessel to be loaded. The permit number was placed on the Bill of Lading, indicating that the shipment was authorized, and the cargo then could be assembled by using these permit numbers.

During the winter months, when the coal could freeze and cause serious dumping problems and delays to rail equipment, special Post-Season and Pre-Season permits were issued to provide much stricter control. The Exchange could cancel a permit at any time if their orders were not being complied with, and thereby halt movement of the coal until the situation was cleared up.

The marine manager in a small operation like we had at Ford also depended on the dispatcher to handle other duties. The dispatcher was responsible for activities such as ordering crew replacements from the union hall and making certain that they got their physical examinations at the Plant Medical Center; keeping departmental records and those required by government agencies; keeping abreast of rail rates, and routing the coal movement via the lowest cost alternative, including any volume rates available. He also had to provide the captains, chiefs and stewards with the necessary supplies to operate their vessels.

We provided a private telephone line in the dispatcher's home and a radio-telephone on his desk that allowed him to talk directly to those ships within a 60-mile range of the Rouge Plant. He was required to be available, or make someone else available, to take the ships' reports beginning at 8:00 o'clock every morning during the sailing season. It was our policy to have the ships report in every day so that we would know where they were and if everything was okay. The ships were also required to report in if they were delayed for more than four hours, and at certain other times if they anchored. They were always required to report immediately any mechanical failures or serious injuries to a crew member.

CHANGING TIMES

Prior to 1945, the ships' main purpose was to haul cargo. Other than calculation by the engineers of the gallons of fuel per mile that their engines consumed and the hours required for each trip, there seemed to be very little cost analysis. The bills would come in and be approved for payment. Actual profits or losses were unknown.

Following the war, when most work was done on a cost-plus or time-and-material basis, things began to change and we were required to become more accountable to management. As I have related, new people came into the company — from General Motors, right out of the service or as graduates of business schools — who were given key positions in the Controllers Office. Soon they began to check into our operations; this did not set too well with the old timers who had not really been accountable to anyone.

Initiation of Marine Annual Reports

Because of this new trend, I prepared my first annual report for Marine Operations at the end of the 1947 season, the year I started to dispatch some of our ships. My very first report indicated that our cost to operate the M/S HENRY FORD II and M/S BENSON FORD was $60 per hour and they hauled a total of 1,286,372 net tons of iron ore, limestone and coal that year. Chartered vessels delivered a total of 2,474,145 net tons, which included foundry sand.

At that time, the established ore rate from Duluth was $1.00 per gross ton whereas our cost to haul was 67 cents per ton. I calculated our total profit for the year at $210,000. As far as I know, this was the first time that anyone ever attempted to calculate profits for the ships. Lowest rates were always negotiated, but once they were established, nothing further was done to see if the ships were profitable or not. No questions were asked: just get the ships to deliver the raw materials.[70]

In that report, I attempted to cover the many aspects of Marine Operations, such as weather conditions, accidents, costs of operation, tonnages carried, unusual happenings, etc. During the 1947-48 winter operation I found that coal delivered by Nicholson Transit vessels saved the company $985,223 over what it would have cost to bring this coal into the plant via all-rail delivery. My report also indicated that the two Ford vessels saved the company another $358,870 by delivering raw materials to the Rouge Plant more cheaply than it would have cost by hiring outside vessels. Thus a basis was established to evaluate the profitability of Marine Operations which could be used to determine future plans.

I had great difficulty getting anyone to read these reports for a long time and was even told to discontinue preparing them because they were "unofficial" (i.e., hadn't been ordered from above). However, I continued preparing them on my own time and found them very valuable in later years when they provided backup information that no one else had.

My first report on food costs indicated that we had reduced our crew and passenger meal costs to 71 cents per meal from 85 cents in previous years. Proving a point did wonders. Competition between the stewards was great when we could show them where improvements could be made!

My 1950 report indicated that Ford vessels delivered only 12 per cent of the cargoes received at the Rouge Plant and only 21 per cent of the total tonnage. (This may have influenced the plans, announced in January 1951, to build the S/S WILLIAM CLAY FORD.) The HENRY and BENSON broke all existing records for late loadings at the port of Marquette in 1950. Records dating back to 1890 showed the previous latest loading was December 12, 1925. Both ships departed Marquette on December 14th.

Changes in Raw Materials

The year 1950 also marked our first loads of Brazilian iron ore, which was trans-shipped at Montreal and delivered inefficiently to Rouge in small Canadian canal vessels. It took three of these vessels to deliver 5,488 gross tons of ore. Shortages of high-grade red ore were being felt, and the steel producers were starting to look for better sources of high-grade ore. In 1951, we started to receive Liberian ore in addition to the Brazilian ore. Eventually these ores were replaced by taconite from Minnesota, which came in the form of processed gray pellets.

When foundry sand was received by boat in those immediate postwar years, it was unloaded into as many as 100 railroad hopper cars located on two railroad tracks laid along the East Boat Dock. The unloading machines would load the cars which were then hauled by locomotives to the sand storage area located outside the plant alongside the Willow Run (now I-94) Expressway. From there it was trucked back to the Foundry as needed. Because vessels frequently were not available in those years, it was necessary to rail a considerable amount of sand, at higher costs, into the Rouge Plant .

By 1952, our raw material requirements had risen to a total of over five million tons of coal, iron ore, limestone, dolomite, sand, pig iron, scrap and borings. This required 653 total cargoes delivered by 15 different steamship companies, and made it extremely difficult to schedule the arrivals of each one to avoid delays. The need for the S/S WILLIAM CLAY FORD was becoming more obvious — and urgent.

As described at greater length later, the CLAY arrived on the scene in August 1953, and made 22 trips before the end of that season, November 25.

Trials and Tribulations of the Fleet

The Ford Fleet was always recognized as having a very good safety record. However, accidents will happen due to the many, many hazardous conditions encountered. Every year back in the Fifties seemed to bring on new challenges in this regard. Sometimes they were quite independent of the routine shipping accidents, breakdowns, bad weather, etc., we faced.

For example, when the banks of the Rouge River cave in, problems increase immensely. That happened twice in 1956. The Peerless Cement Dock, on the Rouge between Ford and the Detroit River, was overloaded and caved in, blocking our plant traffic. A little later the same year, the Cronin Coal Dock slid into the Rouge River, again blocking all traffic. In addition to those problems, that year there was a tug strike, a steel strike and officers on other Lake fleets were unionizing in preparation for a strike.

During 1957, the water levels on the Great Lakes reached their lowest point in modern history. To illustrate how this affected our operations, to keep from running aground, the average cargo on the CLAY dropped to less then 16,000 gross tons, whereas she was built to carry 19,000. Then for a while everything seemed to be going well until July 5, 1958, when (as related earlier) my boss, Jordan Schanbeck, tragically drowned in Lake St. Clair.

After considerable consultation, I was named the new manager of Marine Operations at the age of 41. It certainly was a new era inasmuch as I was the only one available who had very much experience in that function. There was no one else with experience even to help or assist me in the new job. Fortunately, there was a young man in the Steel Division, Richard DeWalt, who was available. He joined the Marine Department as dispatcher and was a tremendous help to me during the next several years.

During my first few months in this new and tremendous responsibility, we had "only" a few things happen that caused us some "little" problems. The BENSON struck the Algoma Steel Corporation dock at the Soo, the HENRY collided with the USS FARMINGTON in the St. Clair River and the CLAY lost a blade from her propeller in Lake Superior when I had talked Captain Pearce out of retirement for one trip to replace Captain Olsen who wanted to be home while his wife was in the hospital.

Our misfortunes continued into 1959, when we had three bad accidents caused by dredging operations for the opening of the St. Lawrence Seaway (described in greater detail later in this narrative). I thought that my job surely would be on the line. But, by sticking together with the captains and providing satisfactory explanations to our management, we all survived that very bad year.

Things were generally much better in 1960. Water levels were going up and we were able to make many improvements to the vessels. The wooden doors on the HENRY and BENSON were replaced, as was the electrical wiring on the HENRY. We built new crew quarters on the HENRY and modernized her galley. We also started a program to remove the mud from the water ballast tanks on all the ships because it was accumulating so fast that it was affecting their carrying capacity. But the year could not pass without a barge sinking in the Rouge River. Its owners failed to notify anyone until after the HENRY struck it dead on and crushed it into little pieces. The HENRY had to go to the shipyard for repairs and the river was blocked while the barge was being removed piece by piece. I guess one could say that there was never a dull moment in the Marine Department.

In 1961 we had many more major projects that required attention. We built new crew quarters on the BENSON and started a re-winding program. We painted her cargo hold and installed stern anchors on both the HENRY and BENSON. The CLAY needed a new row of blades on her Low Pressure turbine and we installed a new heating boiler on the BENSON. We also installed new rubber life rafts on all ships.

I will never forget the radio-telephone call that season from the master of the BENSON. He advised me that they had just looped the stern anchor-chain around the propeller and the crewmen were trying to get it off! He had been at anchor in the St. Clair River during fog and was backing up to raise the anchor when it became entangled. I called Stanley Dupont at McQueen Marine in Amherstburg, Ontario, asking for help. He advised that our ship's crew could not get the chain off by themselves and that he would start out immediately with his crew to help the disabled boat. I also left immediately, driving the 60 miles to St. Clair, where I hired a tug to take me out to the ship. After the McQueen people arrived, it took them 34 hours to remove several loops of chain from the "wheel" and lift the anchor from the bottom. While they were analyzing the situation, I was standing in the pilot house with the captain when the ship suddenly started to drift slowly downstream with the current. The captain, who shall remain nameless, looked at me and said "What'll we do now"? All I could say was, "Let her go until she stops." She did - about 15 feet from a boat house on the shore. "What a relief!"

In 1962, we added the S/S ERNEST R. BREECH and the S/S ROBERT S. McNAMARA to the Fleet. Now we started to look again like one of the major fleets on the Lakes. And we were able to carry 84 per cent of our tonnage, with profits increased considerably.

I remember well an early morning one September, when the captain of the HENRY called me at home from Port Arthur, Ontario. Loaded, they were just leaving the dock there when they encountered a heavy fog bank which obscured their view. While turning, the ship struck the pier, punched a hole in her bow and started taking on water. When the captain called, they were in the process of plugging the hole with an old mattress. He reported: "We struck the dock and have a hole in the bow and are taking on water. But don't worry, we won't sink, we have a line on the dock." Don't worry? How could I not worry! This was only a small part of what the manager of a fleet of ships goes through each day, even before reporting for work at 8 a.m.

Postwar Coal Operations

The Nicholson Transit Company hauled our winter coal until 1949 when the T. H. Browning Lines submitted a competitive bid. These two companies continued the winter coal run from then until 1963.

During the time that Nicholson Transit was pioneering extended season operations, their ships required the assistance of ice breaking tugs which were hired from McQueen Marine. When the ships would get stuck in the ice, the tugs would be called out to free them and escort them to open water or to their destination. During the Fifties, the U. S. Coast Guard, whose responsibility it was to assist waterborn commerce and to maintain and keep the navigation channels open to shipping, began to furnish ice breaker service to the ships in this trade. The winter run was called "Operation Coal Shovel."

Despite all of the hazards of winter operation, no ship Ford operated or chartered has ever been lost or even seriously damaged by the ice. (Note that cargo was loaded above the hatch openings and the hatches were not closed. It was never the practice to close the hatches for this short run to Toledo where, even if a ship did sink, it would not go below the main deck line.) The ships do receive bow damage that can easily be repaired. Considerable strengthening has been built into the hulls of the ships to make them stronger when they come into contact with the ice. Additional compensation was usually awarded by the company to the operator carrying coal for Ford when damage occurred or the hulls had to be strengthened.

During the post-season operation, it was customary for the insurance underwriters to require sailing clearances. These had to be obtained from the U. S. Salvage Association or the Salvage Association of London before the vessel left any port. (U. S. Salvage represented the American Underwriters and Salvage Association, the Lloyds Underwriters.) This was done for the protection of the underwriters and provided for the safety of the ships and crews.

As an indication of how efficient the winter operation was, the vessel freight rate in 1935 was 28 cents per net ton and in 1954, 38 cents per net ton, a 30 per cent decline in constant dollars.

From 1935 to 1948 coal was moved by the Steamers JAMES WATT, E. C. POPE, FELLOWCRAFT, FLEETWOOD, STEEL KING, PERSEUS and SULTANA. These were older ships, built between 1887 and 1905.

During the winter operation from December 2, 1947, to March 1948, the Steamers JAMES WATT, E. C. POPE and PERSEUS delivered 631,577 net tons of coal to the Rouge Plant at a rate of 40 cents per ton. Nicholson and Browning carried the winter coal until the winter of 1962-63 when both companies, due to the age of their vessels, discontinued the operation of their fleets. It then was necessary for Ford Motor Company and this writer to come up with a "Better Idea" which will be described later.

Passengers and Guests

Most Lake fleets permit passengers to take trips aboard their vessels during the summer months. Indeed, most of the larger ships have passenger quarters built in. Some fleets use these facilities to entertain business associates as well as company executives.

At Ford Motor Company this privilege was usually restricted to company officers who used these trips to relax and gain a better knowledge of our Marine Operations. Because the Internal Revenue Service considered this a gratuity, the officials were billed personally for their passage to comply with the tax requirements. The trips would last from three to five days and reservations would have to be made many months in advance to assure passage.

Each officer on a Ford ship was permitted to take his family on a trip once each year. This was one way to help the family accept the fact that the man of the house was going to be away from home most of the time during the sailing season.

Many requests were received from the general public wanting to know how they could take a trip on one of our Great Lakes freighters. These outside requests could never be accommodated because of the limited number of spaces available and the need to take care of our own people. A ship like the S/S WILLIAM CLAY FORD would only make about 15 trips during the passenger season (June-July-August) and several of them would have to be reserved for the officer personnel and authorized business trips.

Consequently it was not possible for the general public to take trips on any of the Ford ships on the Lakes, even if they had been willing to pay. After all, we were not in the passenger business after the war, except for building and selling passenger cars.

PERSONNEL MATTERS & UNION RELATIONS

Up until 1941, all Ford employees were non-union. However, when the United Auto Workers (UAW) organized the plant workers, Captain Johnson decided that it would be better for the Ford seamen to belong to a maritime union rather than one controlled by the auto workers. He contacted Joe Curran, president of the National Maritime Union (NMU) in New York and arranged to negotiate a contract with them.

At that time there were other seamen's unions on the Lakes, but they were affiliated with the American Federation of Labor (AFL), and the UAW being a Congress of Industrial Organizations (CIO) affiliate, insisted that if it couldn't have the Ford sailors, they had to stay with the CIO.

The NMU was the largest union operating on both the East and West Coasts. The company has never been struck by the NMU and considerable gains have been made by the union on behalf of its members. At this writing (1981), the Ford Fleet was the only bulk fleet operating on the Great Lakes with an NMU contract; however, that union had contracts with other tanker fleets, car ferries and the Corps of Engineers ships.

The Officers
In 1947, the Foreman's Union in the Rouge plant called a strike of its members, including some of the officers on our ships, who refused to sail. In the plant, production continued without the foremen. The men who were higher management and other salaried personnel, such as myself, were assigned various jobs to keep operations going. With the help of the hourly people, some operations ran much better without the foremen on the job than they did with them. In my case, I was assigned with Jordan Schanbeck to run the Ford railroad within the plant on the afternoon shift. We would turn out more switch orders than had ever been turned out on this shift in the past, and the switch crews had plenty of rest time between switches. After about two months, the foremen returned to work without a union and the officers again returned to work on the ships.

Following the Foremen's Strike, the company offered to each of us who worked during the strike the privilege of purchasing a new car at company cost. This was a real benefit, as new cars were hard to find because of pent-up demand from the war years when none had been produced, and dealers sold them for premium prices. Our cars were built and delivered immediately following the placement of our orders. Most of us paid for these 1947 models with overtime money that we had earned during the strike, but we all felt that the company treated us very well.

From that time on, Ford marine officers were non-union and except for Hanna our boats were the only wholly non-union-officered on the Lakes. Ford Motor Company took the position that these officers were part of the management of the company and treated them as such. The company felt that the men did not need a union to represent them or to bargain for them. This could be done by personal contact the same as with any other salaried employee. The officers were included in the Ford Stock Savings Investment Plans, Medical Plans, Contributory Retirement Plans, etc. They were also granted the same salary benefits paid by other Lake fleets and the same vacation programs that were prevalent. Because of their seven-day, 24-hour operations, seamen are granted considerably more vacation time than shore-side workers.

During the past 50 years, seamen in general have been raised from a very poorly paid group of men to what is now considered a very respectable wage. In all, the Ford officers in the later postwar years were getting the best of two plans — automotive and maritime — and this was both good and bad.

For the men who wanted to work in a non-union fleet Ford was, with one exception, the only one left for them to join. There are many who do not like to be dominated by union leadership and the requirement to pay high initiation fees and dues. On the other hand, a Ford officer found it hard to leave the Fleet because he was considered a scab and not welcomed into the union unless it was short of qualified personnel. Then he would be accepted.

During the Seventies, the various unions representing the deck and engine room officers in other Lake fleets tried to unionize the Ford officers by personal contacts and threats published in various publications. However, up to the time of my retirement in 1975, no election had ever been requested or held.

Some of our officers had held cards in the MEBA (Marine Engineers Benevolent Association) and the MM&P (Masters, Mates and Pilots) when they worked in other fleets and their organizers used this as their basis for organizing.[71] Most of these men, however, joined the Ford Fleet because they wanted a greater opportunity for advancement and the additional benefits that Ford could offer as a captive fleet, because our sailing seasons were longer and provided more work than any other fleet on the Lakes.

All of the new men in our Fleet were selected by me from a long list of available people who submitted applications. Many excellent employees were hired and became very loyal to the company. They knew that the conditions at Ford provided much more than they had been receiving from other employers. Most of the pro-union men in our Fleet were the old Ford men who couldn't cope with changing times. If they did not raise their licenses, they could not be promoted. New men were taking the higher-paying jobs because of their qualifications. Employees who had been disciplined for various reasons such as drinking, absenteeism, insubordination, etc., also looked to the union for protection. They, however, were outnumbered by the loyal employees who tried to make the Ford Fleet the best on the Lakes. They took great pride in the fact that they were succeeding.

Wages and benefits for our seamen have been increased considerably and now, working with the Union, these men can earn a very comfortable living with good working conditions which was not possible a few years ago. Over the years, the seamen have gained greater insurance and pension plans and considerably more vacation time in addition to higher wages. They are probably the only ones who must work seven days a week while they are aboard the ship. Most of them work split watches of four hours each which makes it very difficult for them to get home even when the ship is in port. However, now, with the granting of summer vacations, it is much easier for them to be away from home for long periods of time.

Crew Size Changes

Working with the National Maritime Union, it has been necessary to negotiate many changes in the size and job assignments of the unlicensed crews. As new equipment became available it required reconsideration of crew sizes and we negotiated these changes with the Union without too much difficulty.

Up until the mid-1960s, we carried three electricians and three assistant engineers on the two diesel ships. We also carried only one wiper in the engine room. It was felt that if we eliminated the three electricians and added another second assistant engineer and two wipers it would make a better operation, inasmuch as it was impossible for the Union to supply qualified electricians at that time anyway. This was done and was a big improvement.

When the steam boilers were automated about 1970, we were able to eliminate the three firemen aboard each steam ship. In 1974 we were able to reduce the wipers on these ships from three to two when we agreed to work them seven days a week instead of five. In 1974 we also eliminated the three deckwatchers after agreeing with the Union to make one of them a deck maintenance man. The steward classification was eliminated and the Union agreement replaced the cook with a steward/cook at higher pay. When the M/S HENRY FORD II was converted to a self-unloader, two conveyormen and two gatemen were added to operate and maintain the conveyor system.

Now, we jump back a few years to explain the need for all of the new men in the Fleet which had only two vessels from 1943 to 1953, and encountered very little change during that time. A new ship was to be added to the Fleet.

THE NEW FORD FLEET

Following World War II, there was very little shipbuilding, and the need for larger and faster ships to replace the boats that were then over 50 years old was apparent. I was still working for Mr. Ahrens and remember well the morning of January 24, 1951. To the surprise of everyone in the Marine Department, an announcement was made in the morning paper by Del S. Harder, the company's manufacturing vice president, that Ford had contracted with Great Lakes Engineering Works for a 647-foot bulk freighter similar to the Steamers RESERVE and MAUTHE which were under construction for Oglebay Norton and Pickands Mather & Co.

The S/S WILLIAM CLAY FORD
The keel for the new Ford ship was laid on April 19, 1952, and she was launched on May 5th, 1953. The ship was christened by Mrs. William Clay Ford, who named it in honor of her husband, the third grandson of the late Henry Ford I and the son of Edsel Ford.

The new ship had a 70-foot beam and a depth of 36 feet from the spar deck to the hull bottom. Her 7000-hp steam turbine for main propulsion was more than twice as powerful as the BENSON and HENRY, and she could carry 19,000 gross tons at mid-summer draft. She would carry a crew of 35 men and the estimated cost to build her was $5,381,470. This new ship had the latest navigational aids installed, including radio direction finder, radar, fathometer, gyro-compass, gyro pilot and ship-to-shore radio-telephones.[72]

Indeed, the CLAY, as we called her, was completely modern in every way, including electric stoves, stainless steel galley and not more then two men in a room. This was quite uncommon at that time; on older vessels, space was at a premium. The CLAY was one of the first ships built with interior passageways which eliminated the entrance to the crew quarters from the outside deck. Tunnels ran from the forward to the after end on both sides of the ship. This eliminated the need for the crew to walk on deck in bad weather. On the older ships it was necessary to wear a safety belt fastened to a "life line" to keep from being washed overboard during heavy seas.

The CLAY featured the first steam turbine in the Ford Fleet and it was necessary to select and train a new engine room crew and officers who were documented by the Coast Guard with high pressure steam licenses. This vessel was completely different than the diesel ships and the old type up-and-down reciprocating steam engines operated on lower steam pressures. With its 7000-hp and massive 17-foot 6-inch propeller, the boat required high pressure steam to turn the high and low pressure turbines that drove a double reduction gear attached to the tail shaft and propeller.

This modern ship also had an electro-hydraulic steering gear, larger electric winches and anchor windlasses. All this made the selection of the crew to sail her extremely important. Captain Pearce was appointed the first master of the CLAY, so it was necessary to appoint a new master for the BENSON, inasmuch as Captain Bernard Olsen now became master of the HENRY replacing Captain Pearce. At a meeting on March 29, 1951, long before the CLAY was even well under construction, it was decided that Carl W. Meyers would become the BENSON's new skipper. Since he had never piloted a ship before, his training period would begin immediately under theguidance of Captain Pearce. George Peterson was selected as the new Chief Engineer for the CLAY. He had been with the company before World War II and had left when the Fleet was largely disbanded during and after the war.

Times changed all of the old training methods and in the later days of the Ford Fleet it became customary to have a continual training program going on at all times on each ship. Most pilots (mates) had their Masters License which qualified them to become a master when neededand they were given the opportunity to handle a ship during docking and undocking and in the rivers, so that they had the experience to take over at any time.

Trial Run of the WILLIAM CLAY FORD

At 7:00 a.m. on August 1, 1953, the S/S WILLIAM CLAY FORD, all decorated with flags and loaded with good things to eat and drink, departed from the shipyard for her "sea trials." Many important guests were aboard and the serious business of testing all of the equipment and machinery aboard the ship began. This writer was aboard. Despite the fact that I had served in the Marine Office since 1941, it was my first ride on one of the Ford ships. I was particularly proud because it was not customary to let any of the office help go aboard the ships. Even Mr. Ahrens did not make the trip, which indicates in a small way how times were changing.

We departed the shipyard on the Detroit River and headed upstream. Captain Pearce had to make a very important decision immediately. The ship had to make a 180-degree turn to proceed downstream to Lake Erie and there were some doubts that a ship so long could make this turn. Everything being new, this was a challenge to his own skill as a master and to the equipment. When the ship cleared the dock and "hard right rudder" with full power was applied, the ship made the turn with ease, to the relief of the crew and every one aboard, and proceeded toward Lake Erie where the Trial Run tests were to be held.

The Trial Run took 15 hours. The ship passed all requirements satisfactorily. She was "officially" delivered to the Ford Motor Company at 1:15 p.m. on August 5, 1953, and departed the shipyard barely two hours later, upwards bound for Superior, Wisconsin, to load iron ore.

The next challenge, on the downward leg, was to get the ship through the Rouge River inasmuch as a ship of that size had never been up to the Rouge Plant. The river, with its six bridges and 21-foot-depth at low water datum, presented many problems for the master which he had not faced before. But because of the greater maneuverability of these newer ships, which included more horsepower and larger rudders, the passage up the Rouge was uneventful — and has never caused any real problems since.

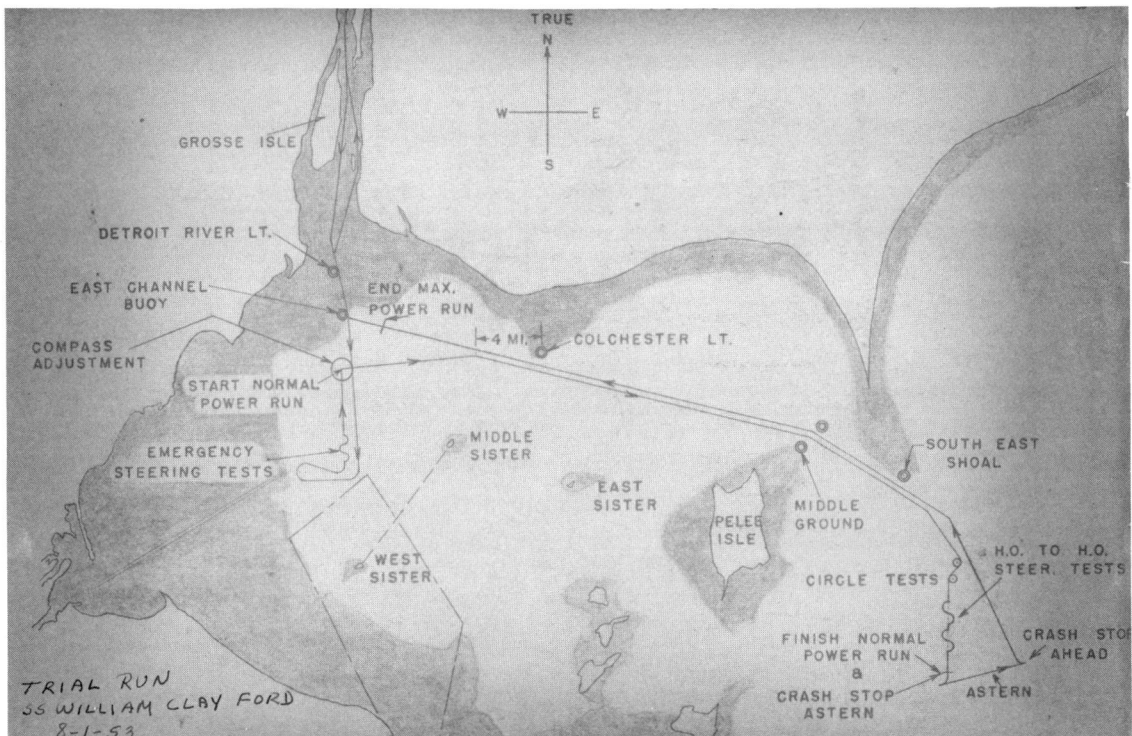

Trial run of the "CLAY" on August 1, 1953

Keel-laying for Steamer WILLIAM CLAY FORD

Launch of the S/S WILLIAM CLAY FORD early in 1953

Pilot house of the S/S WILLIAM CLAY FORD

Inbound on the Rouge River with iron ore pellets

Engine room of the "CLAY" showing main turbine

Underdeck passageway on
S/S WILLIAM CLAY FORD

FORD MOTOR COMPANY, 1950-1979

To put in perspective the changes to our Fleet beginning in 1953, it is necessary here to record briefly the history of the auto industry and Ford Motor Company for the growth years of the Fifties and Sixties and the challenges of the Seventies.

Ford in the Fabulous Fifties

The decade of the Fabulous Fifties, as they were called, started out with another war, the Korean "police action," but the company wasn't as much affected as in World War II. The first important event was that we regained second place in sales from Chrysler in 1950, and for a few years even felt we could regain first place from General Motors. It was a period of excitement, of looking back in 1953 on the occasion of the company's 50th birthday, of many new manufacturing and assembly plants, and introduction of many new cars and trucks.

The year 1953 was marked by the dedication of the Ford Research and Engineering Center in Dearborn on land where there were soybean farms in the 1930s. The 40 Millionth Ford Motor Company vehicle, a Mercury convertible, was produced on September 9, 1953. In 1954, the Ford Thunderbird was introduced.

Industry car, truck and bus sales surpassed eight million in the United States in 1950 and nine million in 1955. The buyer's market had returned, and competition was fierce. Major new investments were expended for new engines and automatic transmissions, which had been introduced just before the war on a few higher priced cars and now were offered by all makes.

Perhaps the most significant event for Ford in the Fifties was when public sale of company stock began on January 17, 1956. It was not long before Ford became one of the "blue chips." The company decided to take on General Motors and organized five car divisions — Special Products (for the new Continental Mark II introduced in 1955), Lincoln, Mercury, Edsel and Ford. The idea was to face off against the Cadillac, Buick, Oldsmobile, Pontiac and Chevrolet dealer organizations, but it didn't work. The Edsel was introduced in 1957 with much fanfare, but landed in the middle of a recession. Also, its appearance was ridiculed, a sad thing for the Ford family with their father's name on the car.

The new Ford administration building, a 12-story tower at the corner of Michigan and Southfield in Dearborn, was dedicated September 26, 1956. It was first called the Central Office Building (COB) and later World Headquarters (WHQ). It replaced the old Administration Building on Schaefer Road, where I had first gone to work for the Marine Office in 1941, which now became the home of Lincoln-Mercury Division when the Lincoln Division was disbanded. The Special Products and Edsel Divisions fell by the wayside as industry and company sales declined in a deep recession.

Our company wasn't the only one to suffer through expansion and contraction in the Fifties. Kaiser, Fraser, Nash, Hudson and Packard nameplates disappeared due to mergers and closures, and more were to come. Some of the big supplier companies, such as those building bodies, also closed as their production was "integrated" into Chrysler and Ford. In our case, it wasn't all bad because that helped increase the demand for raw materials shipments in our ships.

Another influence that began to be felt in the late Fifties was the importation of small cars from Europe. The leader was Volkswagen from Germany, with Renault from France also a factor, as well as Ford and GM cars built in England and Germany.

The decade closed with several milestones. In 1958, the company announced it was entering the heavy and extra-heavy truck field. The 50 Millionth vehicle, a 1959 Ford Galaxie, was produced April 29, 1959, in the old Eagle Boat "B Building" at the Rouge, the Dearborn Assembly Plant, across from the head of the Boat Slip. By this time, the Ford car had grown in size, equipment and finish so it was comparable if not superior to the pre-war traditional "medium-priced" cars.

Also in 1959, Ford Motor Credit Company was formed, the "compact" Falcon car was introduced and the Edsel was discontinued. For the industry, U. S. vehicle production totaled 6.7 million, above average for the decade, whereas that level had been the absolute peak for the final year of the Forties. The Ford share of car sales had improved to 28 per cent, a big gain from the 21-22 per cent levels of 1939 and 1949. Ford's combined car and truck sales in the U. S. exceeded two million. Import share of sales was just nine per cent of U. S. vehicles.

The Zooming Sixties

The traditional concepts of "low-priced," "medium," and "luxury" cars were about to change in the Sixties as the industry got into what was called "product proliferation." It started with the "compacts" introduced by American Motors (successor to Nash and Hudson) and the "Big Three" on the eve of the new decade.

Then in 1960 came the "luxury compacts," led by the Mercury Comet. Next were compact trucks, including the first Ford Econoline van. In the fall of 1961, for the 1962 model year, Ford introduced its "intermediate" Ford Fairlane and Mercury Meteor models. There was also a "sporty" version of the Ford Falcon. All this meant there was no longer just one Ford passenger car, as had been the situation through 1956. Now there were five different sizes and shapes — the Thunderbird, Galaxie, Fairlane, Falcon and Econoline Bus.

It seemed like there were as many top management changes, except for Mr. Henry Ford II, as there were new products at the company in the Sixties. Mr. Ernest R. Breech, who came from General Motors to help rebuild the company in 1946, retired in 1960 as chairman of the board. "Young Henry" became chairman. For a brief period until he was appointed Secretary of Defense in the new Kennedy Administration, Mr. Robert S. McNamara was Ford's president. He had been one of the "Whiz Kids" from the Air Force who joined the company right after the war. He was succeeded as president early in 1961 by Mr. John Dykstra, a manufacturing executive who had been brought over from General Motors by Mr. Breech.

It was also about this time that Marine Operations and Steel Division came organizationally under the company's Manufacturing Group, which had been headed by Mr. Dykstra, so we felt close to him.

In 1963, Mr. Arjay R. Miller, another of the Air Force "Whiz Kids, " replaced Mr. Dykstra as president. He was appointed vice chairman in 1968 when Mr. Ford brought over Mr. Semon E. Knudsen, a top General Motors executive and son of a Ford executive back in the Twenties, as president. Mr. Knudsen didn't last more than a year or so, and the decade closed with Mr. Lee A. Iacocca, who had joined the company as a "college graduate" engineering trainee at the Rouge Steel Plant in 1946, becoming president.

In 1961, the company bought the old line appliance company, Philco, and merged it with the Aeronutronic Division that Ford had started in the Fifties to participate in the Space Industry. The next milestone was production of the 60 Millionth vehicle in 1963.

By far the most important product introduction of the decade was that of the Mustang on April 17, 1964. That was followed by the Bronco four-wheel-drive recreational vehicle in 1965, the Mercury Cougar (then a luxury version of the Mustang) in 1966, and the compact Ford Maverick (a replacement for the Falcon) in 1969.

As the decade closed, foreign imports, still led by the VW "Beetle, " were increasing their share of the American market, and Ford was once again expanding overseas by creating Ford of Europe. However, unlike the 1920s, it did not call for launching an ocean fleet by the company again.

The significant trend in the automobile industry for our Marine Operations was increasing public demand for large V-8 engines. By the end of the Sixties, Ford was offering a 460-cubic-inch (CID) V-8 in many of its passenger cars, more than twice as big as the original 221-CID- V-8 introduced in 1932. In effect, twice as much cast iron per car was required, and all the coal, limestone and taconite ore to make it.

In addition, the recreational vehicle market dominated by big-engined trucks with camper tops was also booming. New engine and casting plants were built to meet the demand. Even without "RV" tops, light trucks were becoming popular as "macho" substitutes for passenger cars, and trucks were gaining in their proportion of total vehicle sales.

Although the nation was much upset about the Vietnam War, Ford again was not involved, not even as much as it had been for Korea. Like most of the rest of the country, it was "business as usual."

The Sixties can't be closed without mentioning that this was when the Government began regulating our business in a big way. First there were scattered state regulations concerning vehicle safety and pollution-control equipment. Then in 1966-67, the Federal Government took over the lead from California, and so-called "stationary source" pollutants — the smoke from manufacturing plant and ship stacks and the effluents from the sewers — began to come under stringent control nationwide just as vehicles had. Where once factory smoke was a sign of good times and prosperity, it soon became a sign of bad (corporate) citizenship.

The U. S. automotive industry finished out the decade with 1969 vehicle sales of 11.5 million cars and trucks, again above the average of 9.2 million for the decade as a whole and continuing the significant upward trend in volume. Ford's share of the market declined slightly to 26 per cent but volume went up 50 per cent to 3.0 million. Foreign vehicles sales in the U. S. were still in the 9-10 per cent area.

The Shaky Seventies
The 1970s started out as a continuation of the boom times of the Sixties but, as hinted, there were threats on the horizon of growing import sales, Government regulations and international involvements.

It all came to a head in the fall of 1973 with the so-called "Yom Kippur" Arab-Israel War. As a result of the Israelis beating the Arabs who were trying to exterminate them, the Arab oil sheiks called for an oil embargo. This had huge and lasting results on the automobile industry and, ultimately, Marine Operations. All of a sudden, the public feared they wouldn't be able to get enough fuel for their big-engined cars and recreational trucks (not to mention their pleasure boats). Gasoline and all other kind of fuel prices doubled almost overnight. Worldwide inflation and recession followed.

The first consequence in the U. S. automobile market was a totally unanticipated surge in demand for economical small cars. Although our company had introduced the sub-compact Ford Pinto in 1970 and had other reasonably economical models like the Maverick and Mustang and the imported European Capri in its "stable," there was no way to meet the demand when the manufacturing system was dedicated to large car and engine production which could not be turned around "over night."

Ironically, the Volkswagen Beetle, which could have filled this demand, was hit with German inflation which made its price not so attractive and also difficulty in meeting U. S. engine pollution regulations. Into this breech stepped the Japanese auto companies with a large variety and volume of inexpensive, economical and, for the first time, attractive cars.

Ford's product introductions in the Seventies included the "downsized" Mustang II in 1973; the mid-sized Ford Granada and Mercury Monarch in 1974; the European-built front-wheel-drive Ford Fiesta in 1976 (imported to the U. S., 1977-80); the new compact models Ford Fairmont and Mercury Zephyr in 1977; the smaller, more economical "big" Ford Crown Victoria and Mercury Grand Marquis as well as the new Mustang in 1978, and the lighter-weight, more fuel-efficient Lincoln Town Car in 1979.

As a result of the fuel crisis in 1973 and another similar panic in 1979, the Government imposed fuel economy standards, mainly effecting the domestic industry.

As far as Marine Operations was concerned, the reversal in demand for big engines and big vehicles meant far fewer raw materials needed to be shipped. Because of the huge costs involved in retooling to downsize cars and develop new, more economical engines and transmissions, the company looked even to Marine Operations for significant efficiency contributions.

The combination of inflation and low-cost foreign competition also meant the company had to take a whole new look at costs of doing business. One result was increased sourcing of components and even engineering outside the U. S. Another realization was that Japanese competitors in particular were producing relatively high quality products due in large part to better ways of manufacturing, including worker involvement.

From an organizational point of view, early in the decade the company was reorganized into three groups — North American Automotive Operations, (NAAO), International Automotive Operations (IAO) and Diversified Products Operations (DPO). The last, of which Steel Division and Marine Operations became a part, included such other automotive supply operations as Plastics, Paint and Vinyl, Electrical and Electronics, Climate Control, and Casting; and non-automotive operations like Aerospace and Ford Tractor.

Mr. Henry Ford II became quite interested in real estate developments for the company and, in particular, the Renaissance Center on the Detroit River in downtown Detroit. It was the great honor and pleasure of Marine Operations to have several of our ore boats salute the "topping off" ceremony of the first Renaissance tower by sailing up the river, whistles blowing, on the evening of July 29, 1974.

Ford reached its 100 Millionth U. S. vehicle production milestone in 1977 with a Ford Fairmont Futura at the Mahwah, New Jersey, assembly plant near New York City. Ironically, this was one of the plants soon to be closed as domestic (and Ford) sales began to shrink and quality demands from the public rose.

In 1978, Mr. Iacocca was replaced as president of the company by Mr. Philip Caldwell. Also, Mr. Benson Ford died; he had been inactive in company management for many years. The 150 Millionth company vehicle produced world-wide, a 1979 Mustang, was driven from the Dearborn Assembly Plant.

The decade closed with industry sales at 14.1 million cars and trucks in 1979. This continued an upward trend in volume overall, but Ford saw its share decline to 24 per cent while the import share had about doubled to 18 per cent. The company's absolute sales volume was slightly higher than ten years before in terms of units (at 3.4 million), but the tonnage of iron and steel going into passenger cars was drastically less and getting worse. The factor which "protected" Marine Operations was the fact that the truck proportion of Ford vehicle sales had increased from 15 per cent in 1959 to 35 per cent in 1979, and trucks generally are heavier with more steel content.

Ford Rotunda and Rouge plant about 1955

EXPANSION OF THE FLEET

The Ford Fleet remained at three ships from 1953 until 1962, when the rumor began to go around that the Pioneer Steamship Company of Cleveland was going out of business. One of its vessels, the Steamer CHARLES L. HUTCHINSON, was a modern ship, built in 1953 by DeFoe Shipbuilding Company, Bay City, Michigan.

John Helenhouse, then Primary Operations manager for Ford Steel Division, and I went to Cleveland to see Gene Hutchinson, who was then the principal owner of Pioneer, regarding the purchase of the ship. Although we had considered several other vessels for purchase, the HUTCHINSON was the one I recommended that would best suit our trade. The ship was laid up for the winter in Buffalo harbor. After a survey was made by the writer, it was recommended to our superiors that the vessel be purchased. A project for $4.6 million, including refitting, was approved by the Ford Board of Directors and the ship was purchased for $3,475,000. A project for $80,000 was approved for refurbishing the vessel.

There are many legal documents that must be obtained whenever ships change ownership. For instance, before a name can be used it must receive clearance. The ship must be documented with Customs. It must get a Load Line Certificate from the American Bureau of Shipping and the U. S. Coast Guard must issue a Certificate of Inspection before the vessel can sail. The Bill of Sale, coverage of the ship with both P & I (Protection and Indemnity) insurance as well as Hull and Machinery insurance, must be secured. The responsibility for ownership change of the HUTCHINSON was turned over to the Detroit law firm of Foster, Meadows & Ballard which was recognized as one of the most competent firms in the country handling admiralty cases. They took care of the paper work covering the transfer and all other legal matters pertaining to the change.

The S/S ERNEST R. BREECH

Ford took over the HUTCHINSON on a "bare boat charter" basis at 3:00 p.m. March 9, 1962. Captain Sven Fagerstrom, formerly master of the HENRY, was appointed the new master and Leland Feese was named chief engineer. A crew was selected and sent to the ship at Buffalo. The ship was then fitted out, including renovation of the quarters, painting of the hull and cabins, etc.

When the fitout work was completed and the ship was ready to sail, however, Buffalo Harbor and the entire eastern end of Lake Erie was still completely frozen over. Because there was no way that the ship could get through the ice fields on its own, it was necessary for us to arrange for the Coast Guard Ice Breaker MACKINAW to come to Buffalo. It was to escort the ship through the heavy ice out into open water so that she could be dry-docked at the American Shipbuilding Company, Toledo, Ohio, for the customary underwater survey of the hull.

The work at Buffalo was completed March 30, 1962, and the ship departed for Toledo at 1:00 p.m., escorted by the Cutter MACKINAW. It was the first time that a ship had ever departed from Buffalo escorted by the MACKINAW. The HUTCHINSON was placed in the Toledo dry-dock April 1.

On April 10, the HUTCHINSON departed for the new Cobo Hall dock in downtown Detroit where arrangements had been made for her christening. The ship tied up at 6:00 p.m., the largest vessel ever to berth there. The re-naming ceremonies were scheduled for 10:00 a.m. the next morning, including an open house for the general public and a reception for company executives and their guests. The ship was re-christened the S/S ERNEST R. BREECH by Mrs. Breech whose husband was the former board chairman. Fully dressed in her new name and colors, the ship sailed at 5:00 p.m that same very full day.

A total of 33 days elapsed from the time the ship was taken over in Buffalo until the day she departed on her first voyage for Ford. Meeting this schedule was one of my greatest challenges as manager of Marine Operations. We had no margin for error. In Buffalo, we had to overcome many difficult situations to pass Coast Guard inspections. This included getting the anchor windlasses to lift the bow anchors, changing the name on all of the equipment and putting new and strange people aboard to operate the engine room equipment — the boilers, turbines, pumps, etc. For the first few days it was below freezing and we had to put the crew up in hotel rooms and food had to be prepared specially for them. Because of the cold weather it also was difficult to paint the outside steel cabins, causing many delays.

The BREECH was 642 feet long, with a beam of 67 feet and a moulded depth of 35 feet. She had a 4000-hp steam turbine and a cargo capacity of 18,700 gross tons at mid-summer draft. In terms of power and size, she was between Ford's original 1924 ore carriers and the CLAY. The ship had accommodations for eight passengers with a forward galley and lounge. She was much slower than the CLAY, making only 16.5 mph light and 15.5 loaded. However, she was quite economical to operate which made her very competitive with the other ships in the Ford Fleet. She had been the flagship of the Pioneer Fleet in the past and was maintained in excellent condition.

Following the first year's operation, it was found that, due to conditions unknown at the time of purchase, her "bull gear" (reduction gear) was showing considerable wear and required replacement to pass Coast Guard final inspection. A new gear was ordered and installed at DeFoe Shipyard in Bay City at a cost of $80,000. Mr. Hutchinson reimbursed the company for this expense because he sold the vessel to Ford with the understanding that it would pass all Coast Guard requirements.

The S/S ROBERT S. McNAMARA

Later in 1962, it became evident that it was going to be next to impossible to obtain vessel capacity for our winter coal requirements from Toledo. As mentioned earlier, Nicholson Transit Company had gone out of the steamboat business and Browning Lines advised us that they would not be able to operate any of their ships in the winter trade. This meant that either the HENRY or the BENSON would have to haul our coal requirements during the winter of 1962-63. This movement was necessary because of a lack of coal storage space at the Rouge Plant, coupled with increased production of iron and steel because of the expanding automotive market. It would have been very costly to have this coal delivered via rail, inasmuch as no facilities were available to dump the coal from the railroad cars and the rail freight rates would be considerably higher.

During our previous discussions with Mr. Hutchinson, we had considered the purchase of one of his older vessels, the S/S W. H. McGEAN, which had been built in 1909. We heard that this ship was going to be scrapped by Pioneer, so an inquiry was made to see if this vessel was available. It was, and a project request was made for $80,000 to purchase the ship, plus $15,000 for refurbishing.

This vessel was laid up at Toledo. After the ship was bought, a crew was put aboard starting October 9, 1962. She was fitted out and dry-docked for inspection at American Ship in Toledo. On November 8, 1962, the ship was re-named at the Rouge boat dock in honor of Mr. Robert S. McNamara, a past president of the company who at that time was United States Secretary of Defense. The sponsor of the ship was Mrs. Charles Patterson, wife of the then Ford executive vice president. Gustav Goransson was appointed master and Al Bottrell was named chief engineer.

At the time, this purchase was quite a gamble because the ship was 53 years old and her condition was unknown to us. We did know, however, that she had a good engine and Pioneer had kept this ship in a seaworthy condition. When dry-docked, her hull was found to be in excellent

Christening ceremony at the River Rouge plant in 1962

Capt. Goransson, Charles Patterson
and Mrs. Patterson holding portrait of
Robert S. McNamara

109

condition. Overall, she certainly had a very limited life expectancy, but would fill the gap for at least one winter. At 500 feet long with an 1800-hp triple-expansion, low-pressure, steam reciprocating engine, the McNAMARA was smaller and far less powerful than Ford's other bulk carriers.

Thinking back, I can remember when this project was presented to Mr. Patterson (then our vice president) for approval. I was asked by my boss, Bill Conn, the general manager of Steel Division, to go along to explain why we wanted to buy this old ship. When Mr. Patterson saw me with Mr. Conn, he turned to him and said in his thick Scottish accent, "I suppose you want to buy another boat?" Mr. Conn sheepishly replied, "Yes, that's why we're here." Mr. Patterson asked, "How much?" and when Mr. Conn answered, "$80,000," Mr. Patterson said, "Go ahead and buy the damn thing," without any further questions being asked. That was the beginning of a very profitable ten years for Ford Marine Operations.

After the first winter in the coal trade the ice had damaged the bow of the McNAMARA so severely that extensive repairs were necessary. We recommended that a high strength steel bow be installed, and during the summer of 1963 the ship was dry-docked at Fraser Shipyard in Superior, Wisconsin, where a new bow of T-1, Type-A steel was installed. These plates were all welded together to eliminate the need for rivets, and additional stringers and frames were used to back up the new plating. The ship returned to the winter coal trade and never again was damaged by the ice. This was the first application of type T-1-A steel for exterior hull plating. Now it is used extensively to strengthen ships.

This old ship had another first when, in the summer of 1966, the telescoping hatch covers were eliminated to be replaced with six-foot high sides, and every other arch was removed, thus making wider openings for the unloading buckets at the Rouge to operate when off-loading cargo. The work was done at G & W Welding Company in Cleveland. This was the only ship of this size on the Great Lakes, and possibly in the world, that was left completely open. Considerable difficulty was encountered to get approval from the Coast Guard and the American Bureau of Shipping to do the work. However, all of their requirements were met and restricted approval was granted. The ship was limited to the Toledo-to-Detroit coal run which was acceptable to the company, inasmuch as there was more coal available to haul than the ship could carry in any one year.

During the nine years that the McNAMARA operated, she delivered 14,319,515 net tons of coal. She made a total of 1,437 trips and returned to the company considerably more in coal cost-savings than was spent on her refurbishing and repairs. Considering the size and age of the vessel, this was a remarkable feat.

By July of 1972, due to her age (64 years) and physical condition, the McNAMARA was withdrawn from service. The excessive cost involved to maintain her in a seaworthy condition would have been prohibitive. The principal defects were the damage done by the unloading buckets to her side tank and tank top plating and internal structures which had been worn to the point where they needed complete replacement. This would have cost several hundred thousand dollars. Even given these repairs, her expected life would not have been very long because of other increasingly strict Coast Guard requirements because of some notable ore ship sinkings between 1958 and 1972.

Her struggle for survival continued after she was sold for $25,000 to Dale Osborn of the Detroit Bulk Dock Company, who intended to sink her hull for a dock face at his facility in the Rouge River. When he could not get approval from the Corps of Engineers to do this, he sold the ship for scrap. On April 7, 1974, the Tugs TABOGA and BARBARA ANN towed the McNAMARA to Lauzon, Quebec, where a deep-sea tug was to tow her to Santander, Spain, for scrapping. On December 4, 1974, the McNAMARA and S/S BUCKEYE MONITOR left Quebec in double tow.

However, before the trip ended, the BUCKEYE MONITOR broke loose from the tow and sank, but the McNAMARA, still fighting to the end and despite her open cargo holds, completed her final voyage across the Atlantic where she ended her great career. Her triple expansion engine and two Scotch boilers were still in good operating condition up to the very end.

She had been the first Great Lakes vessel to comply with the Michigan Pollution Control Act of 1971 and was issued Emblem No. 101 by the State of Michigan, the first number issued.

New Marine Office Building

In 1965, a new Marine Office Building was constructed at the head of the Boat Slip. This provided nearer and better access to the ships. For several years some management people had felt that we should be closer but nothing was ever done about it. Our vice president at this time, Dennis Bracken, promoted the idea that we find a location near the Boat Slip. He was a strong supporter of the Fleet and took a trip annually on one of the ships.

It was first decided to locate the building near Gate #1A on Dix Road near the Dix bridge. However, through much persuasion, we were able to change the location to the north end of the Boat Slip. Several bids were received and many changes were made before the project was approved. With the insistence of our executive vice president, Mr. Charles Patterson, the entire area around the Marine Office was landscaped with many trees and green lawns. Ample paved parking was provided for the office personnel and the ship's officers.

A recent (1981) visit to this area has shown me that many changes have taken place since my retirement. Now the trees are gone and the view is blocked by two huge storage tanks which are a part of a new pollution control system for the Rouge Plant.

The S/S JOHN DYKSTRA

The Ford Fleet continued to grow in 1966 when the S/S JOHN DYKSTRA was added. The acquisition came about in the following fashion.

Wilson Marine Transit Company of Cleveland had the S/S JOSEPH S. WOOD (ex RICH-ARD M. MARSHALL) under charter from the Northwestern Mutual Life Insurance Company, the owners. Wilson was paying the insurance company a charter fee of $500,000 a year, an unprofitable arrangement for Wilson. In order to pay the charter fees, Wilson had to keep this vessel in operation and lay up some of the other older vessels in its fleet. Because of competition from opening of the St. Lawrence Seaway, they did not have enough business to keep them all in operation. The WOOD had been built by the DeFoe Shipbuilding Company at about the same time, 1952-3, that the BREECH had been under construction there.

On a chance meeting I had one day with Ernest Andberg, then vessel manager of Wilson and a good friend of mine, he mentioned the possibility that the WOOD might be for sale. A meeting was held with Wilson in Cleveland on December 17, 1965, and an agreement was made whereby they would recommend to Northwestern Mutual that the ship be sold to Ford for $4.3 million. (The ship had cost $6 million when she was purchased by Northwestern from Wilson in 1957.)

On February 14, 1966, the Ford project request was approved for $4.6 million and a purchase agreement was signed. Marine Operations had great difficulty in getting approval to purchase this ship because Steel Division had accumulated many other important projects with greater priority for investment.

The vessel was laid up in Ashtabula, Ohio, and this writer, Richard DeWalt (who succeeded me nearly ten years later as Marine Operations manager), James McIntosh (a former Coast Guard official and consultant to us) and Carl Swanson, the second assistant engineer on her when she was built, went to survey the ship and evaluate its condition before the agreement would be signed. It was decided to tow the vessel from Ashtabula to Toledo to put her on drydock for survey before a final recommendation was made.

Arrangements were worked out with Great Lakes Towing Company to pull the vessel to Toledo for $7,412. We put a shipkeeper aboard on February 11, even before the title changed hands, because we were quite certain we would buy the ship. Wilson had to make arrangements to have the storage cargo of iron ore unloaded by March 25. We started to put the crew aboard on March 28, and the ship departed Ashtabula in tow of a Great Lakes tug on March 31. She was dry-docked at Toledo April 1. The underwater hull survey was made and accepted by Ford. After a decision was made to purchase the vessel, she underwent her five-year survey, had her name changed to S/S JOHN DYKSTRA and the new Ford "script-in-oval" sign (based on the old Model A radiator badge) placed on her stack.

I remember this time very well, because the Marine Office a year or so later had quite a go-round then with the Corporate Identity Office people from the "Glass House" (World Head-quarters Building) over paint schemes for our ships. The Identity people, who were changing the appearance of Ford products and facilities all over the world, including dealerships, wanted us to paint our hulls blue, the newly adopted main Ford color. From the beginnings of the Fleet, the Ford ships were painted black (hull), tan (stack) and white (cabins and pilot house). The Marine Office felt that painting the hulls blue would be unsafe, because blue would blend in with the blue water of the lakes (actually, as reflected from the sky) and, in effect, be like camouflage and make them hard to see. Our arguments prevailed and the hulls remained black. The new blue went on everything above the white cabin level — funnels, masts, covers, air vent "horns, " etc.

We also were able to get immediate delivery on a bow thruster for the "new" DYKSTRA, which was installed before the other work was completed in the yard. The ship departed Toledo in tow of two Great Lakes tugs April 23. She arrived safely at the Rouge Plant where the fit-out crew was put aboard. Here she was initially painted in the prevailing Ford ship colors and the crew and passenger quarters were refurbished. The ship's name had to be imprinted on all life saving equipment, and many other items had to be renewed to bring the ship up to Ford standards. Captain Gustav Goransson was named master and Carl Swanson was appointed Chief Engineer.

The re-naming ceremonies were held at the Rouge Plant on May 11, 1966, with Mrs. John Dykstra re-christening the ship and naming it in honor of her husband, a past president of Ford Motor Company. The vessel joined the Ford Fleet immediately and was a very great asset to the company. Under the skillful command of Captain Goransson and with her powerful engine she became recognized as one of the best ice-breaking ships on the Great Lakes.

The DYKSTRA was 644 feet long, with a beam of 67 feet and a moulded depth of 35 feet. She had a 5000-hp high pressure steam turbine and a cargo capacity of 18,600 gross tons. She could maintain a speed of 18 mph light and 16 mph loaded.

At opening of the 1975 navigation season, the Ford Fleet was capable of hauling all of the company's requirements of iron ore, coal and limestone. When excess vessel capacity was available, the ships were chartered out to carry cargoes for other companies requiring assistance. This provided a very profitable operation for the company.

S/S ROBERT S. McNAMARA upbound with coal in the Detroit River in 1967

S/S WILLIAM CLAY FORD loading iron ore at Northern Pacific Railway ore dock
in Superior, Wisconsin about 1961

FIVE-YEAR INSPECTIONS &
FLEET MODERNIZATION

It was, and still is, a Coast Guard requirement that every Great Lakes vessel be placed on drydock every 60 months for inspection of the underwater portions of her hull, seacocks, rudder, propeller, etc. With five Ford ships operating, this was an average of one a year. (In the larger fleets it would be a continual process to inspect their ships to keep them seaworthy.) This inspection required the master, mates and chief engineer to maintain a running record of all accidents and shutdowns or malfunctions of equipment that could be checked only when the ship was dead and out of water. With this information, the Marine Office would prepare a "project proposal" for Steel Division management after an estimated cost was made. A Purchase Order would be placed with the lowest-bidder shipyard for the work and a date for outage would be set.

The ship would then be placed on a drydock which provided inspectors access to the bottom of the ship's hull and, in the case of the older ships with riveted plates, the number of worn or leaky rivets would be marked with chalk. Several thousand might be found on an older ship. Back in 1975 the cost to replace rivets was $5.50 each. Indented and worn plates also would be marked for replacement. The propeller blades, tail shaft and rudder would be checked for damage, and replacement or repairs made when necessary. Spare propeller or individual propeller blades were always kept on hand because they might be needed at any time in case of a grounding or striking bottom. The pintle bushings on the rudder would usually be replaced while in drydock because it only could be done then.

Other major repair jobs were usually planned to be done while the ship was in drydock. These included cargo hold reconstruction and major engine room replacements such as boiler, generator or turbine equipment. It was important for everyone to keep accurate records of work needed between dry-dockings because, once the ship was back in the water, there would not be another opportunity for five years.

Winter-month dry-dockings were very cold and working conditions extremely difficult. The ship would freeze in the ice before it was placed on drydock and tugs were required to break the ice and maneuver the ship around into the dock.

We took advantage of these inspections, as well as developing technology and available resources, to modernize our ships continually in the postwar years, as detailed below.

Navigation and Communications Equipment

Prior to World War II, very little navigational equipment was available for the masters to navigate their vessels. They depended on their skills as seamen and the skills of their officers. They had the regular liquid compass, the steam or electric fog whistle, a direction finder, depth recorder and a chart room full of Lake charts (which were not always up-to-date).

During foggy weather they would go to anchor wherever they could find shelter and wait for the fog to clear. In storms they would seek shelter behind islands, in shallow water where their anchors would reach bottom. This is where they depended on their depth sounder. A deck lookout was always posted on the bow in all kinds of weather to listen for whistle signals from other ships and to locate buoys, range lights and other approaching ships.

The old-time masters thus had to be very capable. Even so, many collisions and accidents occurred which would not be condoned today with all of the modern navigational equipment available.

From their beginnings the HENRY and BENSON carried wireless radio operators for con-

Close-up of Ford's most modern stack design

New marine office building, 1955

S/S WILLLIAM CLAY FORD (1) after lengthening to 767'

S/S BENSON FORD (3) passing downbound in the St. Mary's River in 1985

S/S WILLIAM CLAY FORD (2) upbound in the St. Mary's River in 1987

M/S JOHN DYKSTRA (2) at River Rouge in 1982. Never operated under this name

tact with the Marine Office through the communication system at the Ford airport in Dearborn. The J. W. Westcott Company had lookout offices at Port Huron, Michigan, and Amherstburg, Ontario, Canada, in addition to their office in Detroit, and they recorded all ships passing at those points. It was one of the ways we would find a ship's location and calculate the expected arrival time at the Rouge. This unique practice continued until the mid-Sixties. We would also get our ships' passings each day at the Soo via Western Union.

During World War II, many new developments provided entirely new navigational equipment for ships and airplanes. The most important ones were navigational radar and the gyro compass. Most people may not know that a liquid compass does not always point to true north, but to magnetic north, which changes several degrees in various locations on the earth. The gyro compass eliminates the need for continuous calculations for course directions that are indicated on the Great Lakes charts as "compass variations" over the courses the ships follow.

Ford ships were provided with new equipment to improve safety and efficiency as technical developments in communications and navigation equipment became available. At the end of the 1948 season, wireless operators were replaced on the HENRY and BENSON with new ship-to-shore radio telephones. Radar was installed at the same time, and these two new pieces of equipment helped ensure the safety of the vessels. They now would be able to navigate with a greater degree of accuracy, be able to seek out better anchorages and their officers would know exactly where they were at all times regardless of weather.

The CLAY had all of this new equipment installed when she first sailed in August of 1953. The HENRY and BENSON received their new gyro compasses also in 1953. This made navigation much easier and more accurate for their masters.

By 1958, VHF radio telephones had been developed and were installed alongside the old AM sets which provided greater coverage but were affected by adverse weather conditions that made them useless at times when they were needed most. The new FM sets increased the number of channels that were available for the masters to use and were not affected by weather conditions. While their range was less than 100 miles, they were very helpful for ship-to-ship or close-range ship-to-shore communications.

In 1966 a ship-to-shore radio-telephone was installed in the Marine Office. This provided close-range communications directly with the ships. The radio had a range of about 60 miles and could easily cover the area from Port Huron to Toledo. This radio kept the Marine Office in constant touch with all ships in the area and was a valuable asset in ordering deliveries of fuel, groceries and other supplies.

Unloading Equipment

In the earlier years, ships were unloaded of their bulk cargoes at the Rouge Plant with two machines called Huletts. These were replaced by large clambucket-type machines that unfortunately tended to damage cargo holds. First, one of the new bucket unloaders was built to augment the two Huletts. Then the Steamer CARL D. BRADLEY struck one of the Hulett machines when departing after unloading a cargo of limestone, tipped it over and it became a big pile of junk. It was replaced with a bucket-type machine. The last Hulett was torn down and replaced with a third new machine like the others. These buckets could lift 20 tons of material at a time. The three machines on the Ford dock were very difficult to operate and experienced operators were hard to find. Consequently, the cargo holds on all our bulk vessels received a considerable amount of damage that had to be repaired continuously.

By 1952, the original 28-year-old set of tank tops and side tanks on the HENRY and

BENSON were worn out from the bashings of the dockside unloaders. The side tanks and tank tops are the inner parts of the ship that hold the cargo and form a space for the ship to carry its water ballast when light. The carrying of ballast water when travelling light has always been necessary to make the ship more stable in rough weather and to keep the propeller under water. During the winter of 1952-53, channel-type tank tops and side tanks replaced plate steel. These were much stronger and would last considerably longer.

Other Modernizations

The passenger quarters on Ford ships were refurbished several times after the war to make them more suitable for the company guests carried during the summer months. Additional living quarters were added to the HENRY and BENSON to provide better living conditions for the crew. In 1959, we installed 25-man rubber liferafts to replace the old wooden rafts that were carried up to that time. These rafts would provide greater safety for the crew in case of a sinking.

During the winter of 1958-59, stern anchors were installed on the HENRY and BENSON to give them an advantage when it was necessary to anchor downstream in the rivers. We received a shock when someone miscalculated, and only about one-half of the 90 fathoms of anchor chain would go into the chain box installed on the BENSON. The box had to be cut in half and enlarged to accommodate all of the chain.

At the close of the 1962 season, the HENRY had the first-ever diesel-engine "bow thruster" installed on a bulk ship. All previous installations were in self-unloaders and were electric drives. Bow thrusters were also installed on the CLAY and BENSON in 1963, and on the BREECH in 1964. These bow thrusters eliminated the need for one or two tugs at the Rouge to turn the ships around in the turning basin as well as for tug assistance at the coal and ore docks. They also made it much easier for the officers when making non-Ford docks and approaching the Soo locks.

Environmental Requirements

The State of Michigan passed the Michigan Watercraft Pollution Control Act of 1970 which became law effective January 1, 1971. This law prohibited the discharge of sewage into the waters of the Great Lakes.

Little was known about how to comply with this law and, as a consequence, there were no plans or technology under development. On the first of March 1971, the office of Henry Ford II advised Marine Operations that the company was going to comply with this law and issued orders to have the ships completely pollution-free before they sailed early in April. A crash program was initiated and the six ships were completed in six weeks. The Ford Fleet was the first fleet on the Lakes to meet the requirements of the Act and, as stated before, the McNAMARA was issued the first certificate.

At that time the only system available for use was installation of holding tanks. Monomatic toilets which drained into the holding tanks were installed by the crew on each ship with the help of Nicholson Terminal and Dock Company workers. The chemicals used were similar to those for airplanes. The holding tanks were pumped out at the Rouge Plant by an independent outside company and then emptied into an approved sanitary sewer system outlet.

The First Self-Unloader in our Fleet

As the requirements for raw materials to meet expanding car and truck production continued to increase, it was evident that some relief had to be given to our dock unloading facilities. Several studies were made over a considerable length of time to determine what the best solution would be. We reviewed the alternatives of building a new self-unloader, buying a used vessel, building a tug and self-unloading barge and the possible conversion of one of our present ships in-

M/S HENRY FORD II in original colors, downbound abreast Grosse Ile, Michigan in 1954

M\S BENSON FORD (1) in post-1970 colors

M/S HENRY FORD II as a self-unloader

M/S HENRY FORD II as a Rouge Steel self-unloader

S/S ERNEST R. BREECH in post-1970 colors, downbound in the St. Mary's River July 17, 1975

S/S ERNEST R. BREECH upbound at the Soo Locks in original colors

S/S ERNEST R. BREECH downbound in the St. Mary's River July 1984 in Rouge Steel colors

S/S JOHN DYKSTRA (1) in original colors

S/S JOHN DYKSTRA (1) in post-1970 colors

-to a self-unloader. It was decided to convert the HENRY because her tank tops, side tops and ship service generator system all had to be renewed anyway. Two Worthington ship service generators in the BENSON had already been replaced and her cargo hold was in much better condition than that of the HENRY.

After the project was approved and bids were received, two contracts were let: one to Stephens-Adamson Inc., Belleville, Ontario, for the total conveyor system, and one to American Ship Building Company, Lorain, Ohio, for the installation of this system and other related work and equipment. The conveyor system was built in the United States by Borg-Warner, the parent company of Stephens-Adamson, later a subsidiary of Allis-Chalmers.

The ship arrived at the American Ship Building dock on November 1, 1973, and work was completed on August 6, 1974, nearly three months behind the scheduled delivery date of May 15 and well through the sailing season. This installation was unique because it was the first ship, either American or Canadian, which had both a loop belt and reclaiming machine installed in the cargo hold.

Inasmuch as the principal cargo was to be coal, the reclaiming machine was installed to eliminate the need to put crew members into the cargo hold to push the coal onto the belt. Wet, fine coal has the tendency to stick and will not flow by itself, thus requiring men to go into the hold with shovels and force the coal to move through the hopper openings. This was a dangerous job and it was our intent to eliminate such hazardous work for the crew. It was the first installation where the main cargo-hold-belt went up and over the loop-belt arrangement. To permit the machine to travel the full length of the cargo hold to move all of the cargo onto the main cargo-hold-belt, it was necessary to install a movable bulkhead.

Along with this installation, two new AC diesel generator sets were installed for the unloading system and two new DC generator sets were installed for ship's service. Wings with all navigational controls were constructed on both sides of the pilot house to provide the master with an unobstructed view aft when docking.

Tax Incentives

The Merchant Marine Act of 1970 provided that vessel operators could set aside their fleet earnings tax-free, as long as the funds were used for new construction, re-construction of existing vessels or acquisition of new vessels. Such an account was established at Ford in 1970 and the re-construction of the HENRY was completed with funds set aside under this act.

Many new American ships were built under this act since it was the only way that major construction or re-construction could be justified dollar-wise. Revenues generated by the old ships could not support the high cost of new construction. This program made possible the replacement of many older vessels with new and larger ships that were more efficient to operate, thus reducing the cost-per-ton-mile to deliver their cargoes. The Federal Government easily recovered its investment through taxes applied after these investments had been depreciated. Income tax then had to be paid on the profits earned.

Lengthening of the WILLIAM CLAY FORD

The final phase of modernizing the Ford Fleet began at the end of the 1978 sailing season with the CLAY at the Fraser Shipyards in Superior, Wisconsin. There, in a procedure not unlike that which took place with six of the old Laker barges in the late 1920s, the CLAY had a 120-foot section added to her length. In drydock, she was cut in half while the new section was constructed. Then "like a jigsaw puzzle" the three pieces were joined up on the water in the spring of 1979 and welded together.

M/S BENSON FORD (1) in original colors

S/S BENSON FORD (2) downbound in the St. Mary's River during 1983

Fraser used a crew of 120 to accomplish the task — boilermakers, carpenters, welders, machinists, electricians and crane operators. While the ship was in drydock, a new stern thruster also was installed to improve the vessel's maneuverability in docking.

The reworking was completed in May, 1979, and by June, the ship was back at work carrying taconite pellets from Duluth, Minnesota, and Superior, Wisconsin, to the Rouge Plant. In the 1978 season, in her then-647-foot length, she had carried a total of 1,096,371 tons of raw materials. With the addition of the 120-foot midsection, the CLAY was now 767 feet long and had a crew of 28. Her 7000-hp steam turbine engine was capable of producing speeds up to 16 miles an hour at her full load of 23,900 gross tons at mid-summer draft. She was much the largest, fastest and most maneuverable ship of the Ford Fleet.

However, changing technology on the docks soon was to make even this remodeled ship obsolete.

Lengthening of the "CLAY" 120 feet at Superior, Wisconsin 1979

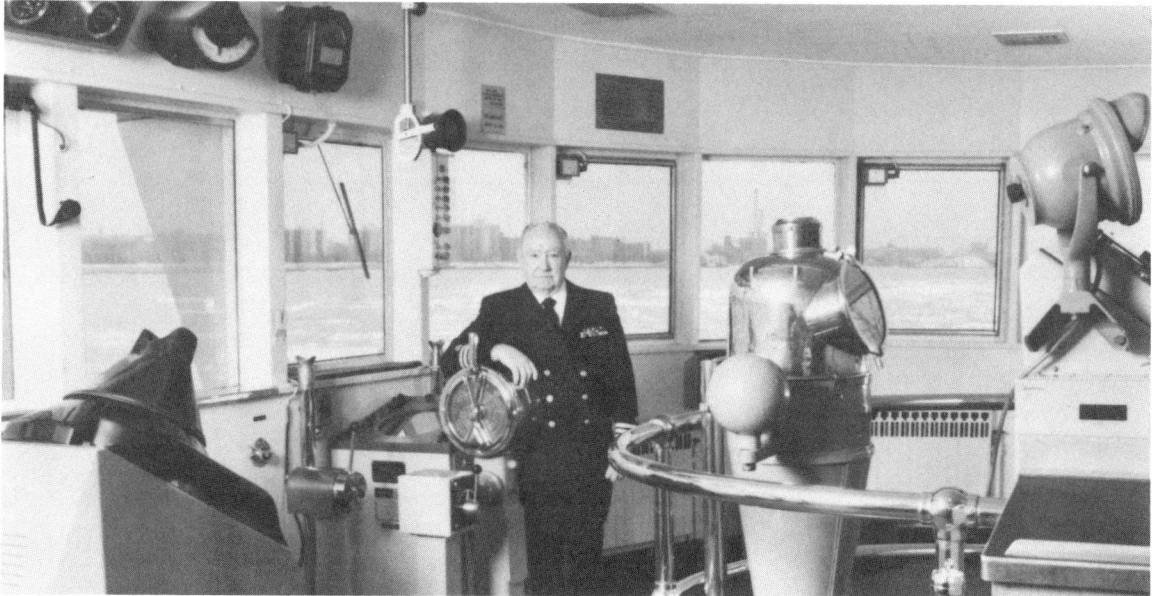

Capt. Donald Erickson, the "CLAY's" last master before it was retired

127

Capt. John J. Pearce

Capt. Bernard Olsen as a young officer

Captains: Erickson, Brent, Goransson, Fagerstrom, Meyers,
Pearce, Inch and Olsen at Spring meeting, 1978

Capt. Carl H. Meyers at chadburn
of M/S BENSON FORD

SHIP ACCIDENTS

Accidents are always a great worry to a marine manager. This includes ship accidents as well as personal injury accidents on board. Many times as Dispatcher and later as Manager, I was called and advised that a ship had gone aground, struck bottom or dock or had collided with another vessel. I was the first one to be called and it was my job to get the necessary assistance and to make arrangements for help and/or repairs.

When a ship was loaded with cargo it was considerably more difficult to make a judgement on what to do. The master's judgement was not always the best at the time. However, not being on the scene and being unable to accept a captain's telephoned version of exactly what happened made it extremely important to be right. The ship might be at sea or had to travel over deep water to reach a safe port. Captains always had a tendency to minimize the amount of damage and a survey would nearly always reveal considerably more damage than the shipboard personnel would indicate. It did not take me very long to expect the worse and hope for the best.

I would then have to pass information about the accident on to my superiors. They always expected exact details which were not always available to me. Many times, when extensive damage was involved, it was difficult to explain to them exactly what happened until a complete investigation and survey was made.

Shipping Channel Problems
Modernization of the Great Lakes shipping channels was taking place during the Fifties and particularly in 1959, work was rushing for the opening of the St. Lawrence Seaway to provide easy access to and from the Atlantic Ocean for larger vessels. (You'll recall the specially designed World War I "Lakers" which formed the nucleus of our ocean-going fleet, and the many locks even those small ships had to pass through between the Great Lakes and the Atlantic.) Dredging to provide for deeper-draft ocean vessels caused considerable difficulty for the Great Lakes captains who still had to make their trips despite the closure of large sections of the channels for these purposes. As a result, three major groundings to our ships took place during the 1959 season when we encountered unaccustomed hazards. The river channels were sometimes cut in half and navigation made even more difficult with equipment obstructions and, at times, bad weather.

The BENSON went aground at Brunner-Mond in the Amherstburg Channel of the Detroit River on June 12. It took 5 ½ days to get her off. We had to remove part of her coal cargo and she needed the assistance of six tugs, all pulling at one time, to free her. Damage included 41 shell plates on the bottom of the ship and she was out of service for 30 days for repairs.

I remember this incident very well because it took place when, for the first time and as the relatively new (10 months) Marine Manager, I had been permitted to take my mother and father with me on a Great Lakes trip. We were on the HENRY at Marquette in Michigan's Upper Peninsula when my boss called and ordered me home by air immediately. I was awakened at four in the morning just as the ship was ready to depart. I found Marquette a very lonely place at that hour and could not imagine how I would be greeted when I arrived back in the office if the BENSON were still aground. Well she was, and many hours were spent on the telephone, lining up tugs and other pieces of salvage equipment to try to get her off.

On August 16, the BENSON went aground for the second time, this time in the St. Marys River, and she required dry-docking again with the replacement of 11 more plates. Then on September 25, the HENRY went aground at Johnson's Point in the St. Marys River and required dry-docking and replacement of 18 plates.

This — my first full shipping season as manager — was the most difficult year we ever had and the only year while I was manager that our insurance claims exceeded our premiums.

Accident Investigations

The insurance underwriters were always notified immediately of accidents. They would assign the U. S. Salvage Association and the Salvage Association of London to have their inspectors take over the salvage and repairs. Their report would also include an account of exactly what happened after interviewing the crew and other people involved. The Coast Guard and the American Bureau of Shipping would also have to be notified, to get their inspectors on the scene to make certain the ship was seaworthy before it could be moved. The Coast Guard had responsibility for the safety of the crew and the Bureau, for the seaworthiness of the ship. The Coast Guard always inspected the ship, but generally accepted the Bureau's recommendations.

All of these people would board the ship as soon as possible wherever she was docked to make their inspections and report. Bureau inspectors would advise what repairs were necessary before they would issue a new Load Line Certificate. They would lift the old certificate as soon as they boarded the ship. Likewise the Coast Guard lifted its Certificate of Inspection and would not issue a new one until all repairs were made to its satisfaction. The Coast Guard also would interview crew members involved in the accident and determine if there was negligence on anyone's part. In the event of a preliminary finding of negligence it could revoke an officer's license or a seaman's document until the necessary hearings were held and the individuals cleared.

The Dangerous Lakes

Despite all the advances in communications and navigation technology and the rigid Coast Guard and American Bureau of Shipping inspections, the Great Lakes remain extremely dangerous waters for even the most conscientious of operators. Three ore-boat sinkings in modern times are etched into the memories of all Great Lakes mariners.

In November 1958, the 640-foot-long limestone carrier CARL D. BRADLEY was steaming in ballast through Lake Michigan from Buffington, Indiana, back to her home port of Rogers City, Michigan. The ship had been built in 1927 and was owned by Bradley Transportation Line, a subsidiary of United States Steel.

The ship was almost to the top of Lake Michigan on Tuesday, November 18, with no premonition of any unusual danger from high southwestern winds and waves in a raging early winter storm. Suddenly at 5:31 p.m., those in the pilot house on the bow observed the BRADLEY stern cracking away. She went down with only two survivors, one the mate, out of 35 aboard. In good weather the place where she sank, 47 miles northwest of Charlevoix, Michigan, would have been in easy sight of several Lake Michigan islands.

Eight years later to the month, the 60-year-old, 603-foot ore-carrier DANIEL J. MORRELL, owned by Bethlehem Steel's Cambria Steamship Company, was upbound in ballast through Lake Huron, just below the tip of Michigan's Thumb. A miserable blizzard had begun blowing across Michigan and the Lakes on Monday morning, November 28, when the MORRELL and sister ship EDWARD Y. TOWNSEND departed their safe havens in the Detroit River. They were headed to pick up a taconite pellet load at the western end of Lake Superior and deliver it back to their Bethlehem docks at Buffalo.

The MORRELL had handily withstood in Lake Superior the same storm that had done in the BRADLEY in Lake Michigan. This time the wind was tearing down from the northeast out of Canada. The captains of the two sister ships were communicating via radio-telephone, with the MORRELL some distance ahead of TOWNSEND, in heavy snow squalls where they would have been out of sight of one another even if close at hand. Other captains in the vicinity, including our James A. Van Buskirk in the M/S BENSON FORD downbound for the Rouge with a load of taconite, were listening in. Shortly after midnight, Tuesday, November 29, 1966, the MORRELL's captain, Arthur I. Crawley, reported he was having trouble maintaining headway. The wind was blowing his ship sideways toward Harbor Beach some 25 miles distant. She was not seen or heard from again.

The first certainty of the MORRELL's fate came at one o'clock Wednesday afternoon, more than 36 hours later, when the Coast Guard recovered a body in a MORRELL lifejacket off Harbor Beach. Late that afternoon, the sole survivor of the 30 men aboard was plucked from a liferaft in which his companions were three frozen corpses.[73]

Ford's closest touch with one of these tragedies came in the fateful November of 1975, nine years after the MORRELL went down and just a few months after I retired. Our Captain Donald Erickson was upbound on the S/S WILLIAM CLAY FORD on the 10th, not far west of the Soo locks, when a terrible Lake Superior winter storm persuaded him to seek shelter in Whitefish Bay. Downbound across Superior from the taconite mines trudged two loaded ore boats: U. S. Steel's ARTHUR M. ANDERSON and the EDMUND FITZGERALD. Owned by Northwestern Mutual Life Insurance Company and chartered by mining company Oglebay Norton's Columbia Steamship Company, the 711-foot-long FITZGERALD had been built in 1958 and was equipped with all the most modern equipment.

Around 3 p.m. Captain Erickson overheard the FITZGERALD's captain tell the ANDERSON that he was taking on water. At 7:10, the ANDERSON radioed a distress inquiry: It had lost sight of the FITZGERALD west of Whitefish Point — had any other ship sighted her? Shortly the Coast Guard broadcast an appeal for other ships to assist in a search.

Alone among ships sheltered from the storm, Captain Erickson and the CLAY set out into that grim dark night to join ANDERSON in the search. But not a sign was found of the FITZGERALD. She was gone mysteriously and without a single survivor, yet another reminder of the Lakes' dangers and cruelty.

For their courage in seeking to help their fellow mariners, Captain Erickson of the CLAY and the ANDERSON's master, Bernie Cooper, received Coast Guard medals. Their ships and crews were awarded individual letters of commendation. It was one of the proudest moments of the Ford Fleet.

Accident Complications

Regardless of their severity, accidents were always a nightmare for fleet management, if for no other reason than all the complications.

After the extent of damage was determined and the necessary repair work planned, then a repair facility had to be selected. The ship might have to go to a shipyard and possibly put on drydock for the repair work to be done. If it was an insurance claim, the underwriters would negotiate the cost of repairs; but if it was to be a company expense, then Marine Operations and/or the Ford Purchasing Department would become involved in negotiations.

At the same time it was necessary for the Marine manager to prepare a project proposal to obtain approval for repair funds. This typically required a lot more explanation before the Divisional Controller would issue authorization even though the ship and the supply pipeline were tied up. Once all this ground work was completed the necessary repairs could be made and the ship certified to sail again.

If a ship was going to be out of service for any length of time, there were many other decisions to be made. Generally most of the crew would be laid off and transportation home from the site of the accident provided for them. A decision would have to be made as to keeping the galley open for the men remaining on board. A source of supplies and laundry at the site had to be obtained. A security watch had to be set up and gate passes issued to the crew.

Needless to say, a major accident also caused many problems for the dispatcher who had to revise schedules to cover delivery obligations. He would have cargoes waiting at a dock for loading that had to be re-scheduled or diverted.

When the repair bills came in, they had to be checked for accuracy and paid. The project could then be closed and the inevitable, unpredictable next accident awaited. The hazards encountered with the weather and the narrow channels the ships navigated always presented conditions sometimes beyond the skills and qualifications of the officers and men who sailed these large ships. These Great Lakes ships were the safest in the world, but accidents have happened from the beginning of navigation on the rivers and lakes and there will be more in the future.

Ship accidents also included those which occurred aboard, in the engine room, on deck or in quarters. Failures of the steering gear, the boilers or generators and many other components of the ship caused accidents. These could include fire or explosions in the engine room or other parts of the ship. Environmental accidents involved discharge of oil or oily substances into the water, discharge of unlawful sanitary wastes into the water and air pollution by emitting smoke from the boilers, generators or bow or stern thruster engines.

Personal injury accidents were always of intense concern, whether minor, serious or life-threatening. Ford had a hospital in the Rouge Plant near the Boat Dock that provided immediate attention to any injury occurring on the premises but treatment became far more complicated when a crewman was injured at sea. If the injury was minor, treatment could wait until the ship reached its destination. If immediate attention was needed, the ship would head for the nearest port or request that the Coast Guard send out a helicopter to take the injured person to the nearest hospital.

When such incidents took place, the Marine manager frequently would be left in the dark as to what happened until there was a chance to interview the crew and obtain accurate reports from the hospital. This was hard to do over the phone. Fortunately, serious personal injury accidents aboard Ford ships have been rare.

While I was manager we had two seamen die aboard ship from natural causes. I will never forget those nights when I had to go to their homes to advise their families that the husband in one case and the father in another had died on the ship. In both cases, the deaths happened shortly after midnight and it was about three in the morning when I picked up a nurse at our plant hospital to go along with me to handle any problems. Knocking on a front door with a message like that was one of my most difficult tasks.

Insurance Coverage
With Great Lakes ships making so many docks and travelling through the narrow channels in the rivers and lakes, the possibility of an accident was quite evident. The captains had to pass other ships in these narrow channels, and there were many intersections where the upbound and downbound ships had to cross shipping lanes. Because of the great risks involved in operating a fleet of ships and the extremely high costs to repair damages due to accidents, it was necessary to carry Protection & Indemnity and Hull & Machinery insurance coverage.

This was obtained from insurance underwriters and brokers who generally worked through Lloyds of London for the coverage. Large policies might be divided among many companies so

that no one company would be hit with a large loss. Premiums were usually based on the safety record of all of the insured customers. Therefore a fleet with a good or perfect record might receive an increase in rates in a particular year because other fleets may have had a bad record. On the other hand, this would help a fleet with a bad record in one year, because with overall coverage, their insurance rates might not go up as much if the rest of the fleets had a good year.
Safety Awards

The Ford Fleet had one of the best safety records on the Lakes and we received several awards from the National Safety Council and the Ford Motor Company. It was customary that when we reached one million man-hours without a lost-time personal injury, we would give each member of the crew a personal safety award. The crews always seemed to appreciate this gesture very much and worked hard to accumulate another one million man-hours without a lost-time personal injury.

During my many years in Marine Operations we always had a good ship-operating safety record. As mentioned, only in 1959 did our claims exceed our insurance premiums and the accidents that we incurred that year were due to the dredging in the rivers for the deepening of the St. Lawrence Seaway.

Especially after all the difficulties we had had on my first few months on the job, one of my greatest pleasures was when Mr. Benson Ford presented Marine Services with a safety award in 1960 at the National Safety Council Convention in Chicago.

Winter Maintenance and Inspections
When the ships docked for the last time in the fall of the year everyone was anxious to go home. However, the ship had to be "laid up" first and this was a big job. All of the working gear had to be stored and other items prepared for future Coast Guard inspections. The boilers were shut down slowly and all other engine room equipment serviced as prescribed to prevent damage during layup. The galley was cleaned and all food items disposed of.

Layup normally took from three to ten days, depending on how hard the crew worked. If they wanted to go home badly enough they worked much harder. Others stretched out the work as much as they could to stay on the job. Once this work was completed the crew was laid off for the winter and each member given his final paycheck. Shortly thereafter, each received earned vacation pay, bonus money and any other benefits due.

Following layup certain crew members were kept on the payroll to continue whatever miscellaneous work was still to be done on the ship. On deck, the rooms had to be cleaned and painted; much of the navigation equipment had to be repaired by outside service technicians, and an inspection of the cargo hold was usually made to find leaks needing repair. In the engine room, specified duties were assigned under the chief: engineers would be assigned to work on the boilers, the main engine and generators, and the motors and pumps. It seemed like there was always more work than could be completed before the Christmas holidays so it generally was necessary to return afterwards. Then, if there was any time left, the layover crew could take some winter vacation, too. All during this time the Coast Guard and the American Bureau of Shipping would be reviewing the ship's records, inspecting and letting the company know what changes or maintenance would be required to meet safety standards. All this work had to be completed before the ship could sail in the spring.

When the spring sailing date for each ship was set, the galley crew was the first to be called back. They had to order the food supplies, make up the rooms and be ready to prepare the meals when the rest of the crew arrived. Next the engine room crew came aboard to start up the boilers and other equipment. The ship was usually on shore power during the winter to provide lighting and electric heat for the layup crew. About a week or ten days later the deck crew would come aboard to fit out the deck equipment.

Altogether a ship would be ready for Coast Guard inspection in about three weeks. When the American Bureau of Shipping completed its inspection, it issued the master a "Load Line Certificate," indicating how deep the ship could be loaded during the sailing season, divided into Winter, Intermediate, Summer and Mid-Summer periods. This certificate really indicated how much freeboard could be left exposed for safe operation of the ship during the various sailing periods.

The Coast Guard then would issue a Certificate of Inspection which had to be posted in a conspicuous place aboard the ship. If a ship failed to meet U.S.C.G. requirements for personnel safety anytime during the season, the certificate could be "pulled" and the vessel could not sail again until all requirements were met.

Clare Snider (left) presenting safety award, 1959

Clare Snider accepting National Safety award from Benson Ford, 1960

MARINE MANAGEMENT

Captain John J. Pearce was a most remarkable man, and one who could be considered an old timer even from the turn of the century when water transportation was on a decline and land transportation was beginning to take over with the advent of the automobile.

He started out as a newspaper reporter, but switched to a sailing career in 1910 after first writing about it and later getting summer jobs on the Lakes while attending Oberlin College. After 13 years with the United States Steel Corporation, where he worked his way up to first mate, he was invited to join Ford Motor Company in 1924 as first mate on the BENSON. In 1925 he was made master of the BENSON and in 1926 was transferred to the HENRY after Captain Johnson was promoted to marine superintendent. He retired in 1956.

Under Captain Pearce's guidance many capable officers were to follow, including Captains Andy Pederson, John B. Martin, Bernard Olsen, Carl Meyers and Sven Fagerstrom. Many, if not most, of our officers were of Scandinavian descent or were from the Upper Great Lakes area where many Scandinavians settled.

For example, Captain Fagerstrom, a native of Sweden, joined the Ford Fleet as a wheelsman on the HENRY in 1927. He then became mate and master of the Barge LAKE KYTTLE, and moved to the Tugs HUMRICK and BUTTERCUP between 1928 and 1932. From 1933 to 1945, he served as master of several different Ford tugs. After the war, he became second mate on the HENRY, eventually advancing to master in 1956. He then became first captain of the BREECH in 1962.

Captain Olsen was born in Norway and joined Ford as second mate on the BENSON in its first year of service, 1924. He became first mate of the HENRY in 1926, and from 1937 to 1941 was master of the EDGEWATER. During the war, he became Ford's port captain. He was named first mate of the BENSON in 1944, advancing to master in 1949. In 1953 he transferred to the HENRY as master, and in 1956, to the CLAY. He retired in 1965.

Captain Meyers also joined the Ford Fleet in 1924, as a deckhand on the HENRY. He rose to first mate of that ship and was named captain of the BENSON in 1953, a position he held for ten years until retiring. In his 39 years of sailing with Ford, he made more than 2,100 trips.

One of Captain Pearce's very favorite proteges, Donald Erickson, began as a young deckhand on the HENRY. A four-year Navy veteran, Erickson rose rapidly, being named master of the HENRY at the age of 34 in 1962 after serving only 14 years in the Ford Fleet. He was the last master of the CLAY, serving in that position from 1963 to 1984. Capt. Erickson retired from the company in 1986.

Recapping the top Ford Marine management positions, we find that not too many changes have taken place during the past 50 years, which indicates the stability of the operation and the devotion that these men had to their jobs.

Here is a listing of the heads of the Marine Office and the masters of the postwar Ford Fleet of Great Lakes bulk carriers:

Manager or Superintendent

Captain Oscar A. Johnson — 1925-1938	Norman J. Ahrens — 1938-1955
F. Jordan Schanbeck — 1955-1958	Clare J. Snider — 1958-1975
Richard DeWalt — 1975-1979	John G. Nye — 1979-1985
James R. Commerford — 1985-1988	

Master — M/S HENRY FORD II
Oscar A. Johnson
John J. Pearce
Bernard Olsen
Sidney Inch
Sven Fagerstrom
Donald Erickson
James R. Brent
Michael A. Gerasimos
James Van Buskirk
Theodore Cogswell

Master — M/S BENSON FORD
Stakes (first name unknown)
Daniels (first name unknown)
John J. Pearce
Andy Pederson
John B. Martin
Bernard Olsen
Carl H. Meyers
Gustav Goransson

Master — S/S WILLIAM CLAY FORD
John J. Pearce
Bernard Olsen
Donald Erickson
James Van Buskirk

Master — S/S ERNEST R. BREECH
Sven Fagerstrom
Gustav Goransson
James R. Brent

Master — S/S JOHN J. DYKSTRA
Gustav Goransson
Mark Ganey
James Van Buskirk
Michael A. Gerasimos

Master — S/S ROBERT S. McNAMARA
Gustav Goransson
James R. Brent
James Van Buskirk
Joseph Cusack

Relief Masters
Charles R. Van Buskirk   Theodore Cogswell

REFLECTIONS

For 17 years as Ford's Marine Operations Manager, and before that for several years as Dispatcher, my duties and responsibilities varied greatly from day to day. This brought many happy memories and some unpleasant ones.

I know that I was little different from anyone else placed in a similar position and another fleet. Marine people who have reached the top come from the same mold, if they can hold onto their jobs for a long period of time. They are alike because they are dedicated. They trust each other and most will never go back on their word. Contracts are made over the phone and may carry over from one year to another and nothing in writing is exchanged. One cargo of ore involves as much as five or six days of work for a ship and $100,000 or more in freight charges. The managers and dispatchers work together, and they play together, year in and year out. This aspect, along with the men who worked for me, brought me some of the most unusual and interesting memories that a man could ever have.

In these closing pages I find that another generation has taken over management of the Ford Fleet. The entire office force which assisted me through the 17 years I served as manager has either retired or moved to higher positions.

Len Schimm (dispatcher) now plays golf with me on Tuesdays. Dick DeWalt, who replaced me as manager, has been promoted to manager of Power Operations. Bill Ludt has gone South. We were replaced by John G. Nye, manager; Jim Commerford, port engineer, and Joe Hommick, dispatcher.

The officers who joined Ford with the addition of the S/S WILLIAM CLAY FORD in 1953, the S/S ERNEST R. BREECH and the S/S ROBERT S. McNAMARA in 1962, and the S/S JOHN DYKSTRA in 1966 are now (1981) all reaching retirement age and will be replaced by another group of young men, and maybe women, who will devote their lives to their ships.

Looking Ahead

Rapid changes in both the ships and the men who sail them makes one realize that the maritime industry here on the Great Lakes is far ahead of most any other industry. Old ships that were small and uneconomic to operate, due mostly to high labor and maintenance costs, have long since gone to the scrap pile. Several of them have been replaced by a single thousand-foot self-unloader which carries five or six times as much cargo, with the same or fewer crew members, as one of the older ships. The self-unloader requires no shoreside equipment to unload her cargo.

Two types of unloading equipment were used for many years, namely, bucket machines and Huletts. With inexperienced operators, both types were doing an unusual amount of damage to the cargo holds of ships. The repair or replacement of cargo holds was very costly and was always under the watchful eye of the Coast Guard inspectors who were prone to "pull a certificate" (i.e., refuse permission for a ship to sail) if they found leaks in the cargo hold area.

The unloading equipment at the various coal and ore docks has been getting old and costly to operate. Breakdowns cause ship delays. These docks were continually plagued with labor troubles which, along with equipment failures, resulted in long delays for the ships. These would then disrupt schedules, causing delays to ships and other dock operations back up the supply pipeline. Many dock facilities have closed permanently or else they shut down on weekends and nights. This also delayed ship schedules to the point where something had to be done to keep the large ships in operation. The answer increasingly has been self-unloaders.

Self-unloaders like our modernized M/S HENRY FORD II required only a dock unloading foreman to put the cargo on a storage pile. He directed the boom operator where to drop the cargo.

On some docks the cargo was moved away on conveyors. This did require additional operating personnel; however, it required far less help than the old unloading rigs.

Many ships in the thousand-foot class, all self-unloaders, now are plying the Lakes. The larger ships have both bow and stern thrusters to assist moving them in close quarters where they can discharge their cargoes with very little shoreside help.

The crews also have changed. Men who took up sailing when they were very young, many of them following in the footsteps of their fathers or relatives, were devoted sailors. This job was their life and they were very proud of it.Their wives and families understood this and, in most cases, accepted the fact that the ship came first. The men knew that when the ship left the dock, they had better be on it or they were out of a job. Even when there were emergencies or illness in the home, the sailor still left the problem with his wife and family and made certain he did not miss his next watch. Once fit-out started in the spring he was required to be aboard the ship seven days a week until lay-up in late fall. On ships that did not maintain a steady run, such as to the Rouge Plant, many of the men did not see their families for weeks at a time. As anyone can imagine, this did cause many serious problems. It also built strong men and women who, each in their own ways, coped with the situations.

It is different now. Both officers and unlicensed men earn and are granted summer vacations which were unheard of 30 years ago. Medical programs have provided sick time and benefits. When a seaman gets sick, it is good reason for him to leave the ship, even if he is not seriously ill. Personal time is granted for weddings, graduations, etc. This is an effort to keep the capable and reliable men aboard these large ships. No longer do sailors put their jobs first. Most of them are so competent they can readily find work ashore which provides weekends off and regular daily working hours. By providing these advantages along with higher pay scales, Great Lakes operators have been able to get qualified people and operate their ships more efficiently and safely.

Women also are getting into the maritime work force. The Maritime Officer training schools are encouraging women to enroll and some women have sailed on the Ford ships as engineers and cadets. This provides them with sailing experience while going to school. For many years women have worked on passenger ships. Canadian vessels have employed women for many years in their galleys. Some American ships also had women working in their galleys but that was quite rare. It is only recently that women have been licensed to serve as ship officers.

These new people will be faced with new problems that must be solved each day. I remember that when I was having one of my worst days and was complaining to my boss, he reminded me, "If there were no problems to solve, you wouldn't be needed."

Clare J. Snider
Dearborn, Michigan
1975-1981

138

Clare J. Snider
1916 - 1981

139

FINAL YEARS OF THE FORD FLEET
by Michael W.R. Davis

A previous section of this book described the tremendous cost pressures Ford and others in the domestic automobile business faced by 1980 from the combination of inflation, low-cost import competition, Government-mandated costs, and customer demands for both new products and substantial quality improvements.

In the wake of the automotive industry recession which began in 1979 as a result of the second fuel availability crisis, the management of Ford's Diversified Products Operations (DPO), which included Marine Operations, adopted an operations analysis technique recommended by the Boston Consulting Group. Fundamentally this analysis forced management to look at the various distinct businesses under DPO in terms of their potential earning capacity and demands for investment. Decisions were "forced" as to whether (1) to continue investing in a business, (2) to maintain the business with minimum new investment, or (3) to disinvest the business by selling it or closing it out.

In the decade of the Eighties, this led to some of the following actions among DPO's divisions:

• Casting Division closed its Sheffield Aluminum Foundry in Alabama, and the relatively new Michigan (iron) Casting Plant property at Flat Rock, Michigan, was sold to the Mazda Motor Company of Japan (in which Ford had a 25 per cent interest) for a new automobile assembly plant.

• Ford Tractor Operations first merged with farm-equipment-maker New Holland, and then later was 80-per-cent bought out by Fiat of Italy. The company's Aeronutronic space and defense business was sold. The paint and vinyl plants were sold.

• On the other hand, DPO's electronic, climate control and plastics development and manufacturing operations were considerably enlarged and strengthened. All were key to advancing automotive technology and sales appeal.

• Steel Division, of which Marine Operations was a part, seemed to stay in the middle ground and actually enjoyed substantial reinvestment for a time. Steel's challenge was to improve its position by incorporating such large-investment but energy-saving manufacturing technology as continuous casting and new products such as coated steel. The Division was renamed Rouge Steel Company in 1981.

In the meantime, the domestic automobile industry continued to suffer from reduced sales and market share. Car and truck sizes also continued to shrink, and smaller cars for a time took a larger share of the industry. The impetus for lighter weight to improve fuel economy resulted in the increased use of aluminum and plastic. This meant sharply reduced demand for iron and steel.

Ore shipping on the Great Lakes in 1979 was a fairly typical "good year" in terms of tons shipped — 79 million — and rates. However fuel prices for ships mushroomed just as for automobiles, increasing shipping costs and squeezing carrier profits.

Then followed this discouraging trend in the Eighties:

Year	Million Tons of Ore Shipped	Year	Million Tons of Ore Shipped
1980	72	1985	52
1981	75	1986	45
1982	38	1987	55
1983	52	1988	61
1984	57	1989	59

As a consequence, Ford found itself by the early 1980s with excess shipping capacity.

In addition, as Clare Snider predicted in his closing words in the preceding chapter, self-unloading became more of a controlling factor for the Ford Fleet. Dockage became either difficult to schedule or too costly if ships were not self-unloaders. There were sequential consequences of this.

First, at the end of the 1981 shipping season, the M/S BENSON FORD was "benched" for the first time in nearly 60 years and put up for sale. In its final year, it carried 440,000 tons of iron ore, coal and limestone. After laying idle throughout the 1982 season, the following year it was renamed JOHN DYKSTRA and the DYKSTRA was renamed S/S BENSON FORD in a name swap.

The old BENSON/new DYKSTRA subsequently was towed from the Rouge on June 23, 1983, with the intention of it being used as a barge by Gerald Sullivan. However, this service never was undertaken. The pilot house of the original BENSON was removed at Cleveland in 1986 for use as a summer cottage on South Bass Island, Lake Erie, where it remains. The hull was sold for scrap.

In the 1983 shipping season the old DYKSTRA (new BENSON) hauled 815,000 tons of iron ore and 77,000 tons of coal, substantially more than the ship whose name she took in its last year of service. The self-unloading M/S HENRY FORD II carried 150,000 tons of iron ore, 1,400,000 tons of coal and 254,000 tons of limestone. The CLAY hauled an even one million tons of ore and 24,000 tons of coal. For the BREECH, 1983 saw the beginning of a new role in which the ship began to be removed from its traditional role of shipping Ford raw materials. Instead, it was chartered out, mainly to carry grain from the upper Midwest to Buffalo. Its cargo that year therefore consisted of 400,000 tons of ore, 122,000 tons of coal, 20,000 tons of limestone and 600,000 bushels of wheat.

The next step in the sad decline of the Ford Fleet took place at the end of the 1984 shipping season when the S/S WILLIAM CLAY FORD was retired to be sold for scrap, even though only five years before it had been lengthened to carry more ore. In her place, the company purchased two self-unloaders from Cleveland Cliffs Steamship Company of Cleveland, Ohio.

The first was the 826-foot-long S/S WALTER A. STERLING. It had been built as the tanker SAMOSET for Socony-Mobil Oil Company in 1942 at Sparrows Point, Maryland, by Bethlehem Steel. Subsequently it became the U.S.Navy Tanker USS CHIWAWA, and was bought by Cleveland Cliffs in 1960. It was converted to a bulk carrier in 1961 with a new 510-foot midsection, lengthened again by 96 feet in 1976 and converted to a self-unloader in 1978. It also had the necessary bow thruster added in 1966 and stern thruster in 1982, and was rated at a capacity of 29,000 tons.

The other was the 767-foot-long S/S EDWARD B. GREENE, built in 1952 by American Shipbuilding Company, Toledo, Ohio, for Cleveland Cliffs. It was lengthened by 120 feet at Fraser in 1976, three years before the CLAY, and converted to a self-unloader in 1980. It also had been equipped with bow thruster in 1965 and stern thruster in 1982, and was rated at 25,250 tons capacity. Both ships, like the CLAY, had 7000-hp steam turbines.

The STERLING was renamed S/S WILLIAM CLAY FORD when it entered Ford service at the beginning of the 1985 shipping season, and the GREENE became the third BENSON FORD.

The old DYKSTRA (second BENSON) was sold for scrap in 1987. Ford's shipping plan for 1985 used the three self-unloaders — the two new ships and the venerable M/S HENRY FORD II — to haul company raw materials. The BREECH was chartered out to haul pellets to non-Ford Canadian steel plants at Hamilton, Ontario, and grain to Buffalo.

In the meantime, John Nye, who had succeeded Dick DeWalt as Marine Operations Manager in 1979, retired in 1985. James R. Commerford, formerly Dispatcher, was promoted to replace him but left the company in 1988 as operations were winding down.

Before long, there was not enough Ford traffic to utilize the HENRY and it was chartered out to International Salt, now AKZO, to haul salt for the short remainder of its useful shipping life. Unfortunately the salt corroded the cargo hold as might be expected. In 1988, Ford sold the BREECH and it was renamed KINSMAN INDEPENDENT. It remains in service on the Great Lakes as a bulk grain carrier.

The end came on March 13, 1989, when Ford announced that Rouge Steel Company was selling Marine Operations, including the three remaining vessels, to Lakes Shipping Company, a newly formed affiliate of Interlake Steamship Company of Cleveland. Included in the agreement was a long-term shipping contract for the Lakes Shipping Company to haul raw materials to the Ford Rouge Plant for the Rouge Steel Company.

Ford's announcement stated:
The sale of the Rouge Steel ore carriers and negotiation of a long-term transportation agreement are responses to evolving business conditions. In the past two years, changing marine transportation requirements resulted in the sale of the S/S ERNEST R. BREECH and the permanent layup of the M/S HENRY FORD II. If one of Rouge Steel's two remaining active vessels were to be put out of service for any reason, the interruption in the flow of raw materials could cause serious consequences for its steel operations. After very detailed studies were conducted, the management of Rouge Steel concluded that a long-term transportation agreement was the solution that best served the interest of its core steel-making business.

Thus the second WILLIAM CLAY FORD departed Ford service after only four years and was renamed the S/S LEE A. TREGURTHA. The third BENSON likewise was renamed S/S KAYE E. BARKER. Both remain in operation, presumably serving the Rouge Plant.

The M/S HENRY FORD II, rotted by salt corrosion, was towed to Toledo's "Frog Pond" on June 23, 1989, where she still awaits the scrapper's cutting torches. (In August 1992, rusting away and hatches boarded up, she was tied to a weed-strewn Maumee River dock near the giant coal loaders from which she had carried millions of tons during her 65 years on the Great Lakes.) On December 15, 1989, Ford completed the long-threatened disinvestment of Rouge Steel by selling 80 per cent of the subsidiary to a new consortium headed by Worthington Steel of Columbus, Ohio.

The final event in the more-than-70-year grand history of the Ford Fleet, whether dated from Henry Ford's acquisition of the yacht SIALIA in 1916 or launch of the first Eagle Boat in 1918, was placement of the pilot house from the original S/S WILLIAM CLAY FORD at the Dossin Great Lakes Museum on Detroit's Belle Isle. That event took place April 3, 1991. The structure was formally opened to the public as part of the museum on March 18, 1992.

Pilot house of original BENSON FORD at rest as a private residence on South Bass Is., Ohio

Final resting place of "Clay's" pilot house - Dossin Great Lakes Museum, Belle Isle, Michigan

APPENDIX I
THE SHIPWATCHER'S GUIDE
(by Clare J. Snider)

For all of those who have never had an opportunity to become involved in the actual operation of a fleet of ships, I would like to pass on some bits of information that may be informative about these ships .

Most of what I will describe relates to the big ore carriers you see on the Great Lakes; but much of the general information may also be informative about ocean-going vessels as well.

Thousands of interested people, with little or no knowledge of the operation or function of a ship, will sit on a river bank or some other good vantage point and watch in awe as a freighter quietly passes them by. Thousands stand on the viewing platforms at the Soo Locks and have little or no idea of where the ships are going, what they are carrying or how fast they will go. The following paragraphs will answer some of their questions.

What is a Ship ?
First, a ship is a huge piece of machinery that may be from one day to some 75 years old. It may be a couple of hundred feet to over 1,000 feet long. It may carry from a few hundred tons to 50 or 60 thousand tons; even more on the high seas. Most mariners make the distinction of classifying a boat as a vessel that could be carried on a ship, but many people will call all vessels "boat." However, you would never call an outboard fishing boat a ship. The beautiful piece of machinery we call a ship is also a hotel, a restaurant and a power house as well as a transporter of two, three and even four railroad train-loads of cargo each trip.

The crew of a ship is composed of the officers, or licensed personnel, and the men, or unlicensed personnel. On the Great Lakes it has been traditional for the officers to be promoted up from the ranks, although in recent years licensed officers have been coming to the ships directly from schools such as the Merchant Marine Academy at Kings Point, New York.

The Pilot House and Deck
The ship is always under the command of a captain or master. The pilot house is manned by a mate (also called pilot), a wheelsman (also called helmsman) and sometimes a watchman. In the rivers, while passing through locks and making or departing docks, the master pilots the vessel. He is also responsible for the actions of the mates when they are piloting the ship. Thus, a captain or a mate is like the driver of a big truck, except that he has a wheelsman to steer and an engineer to push the throttle. On some of the newer ships, the pilot can even perform both of these functions.

The Deck Department usually consists of the master, a first, a second and a third mate, three wheelsmen, three watchmen, a deck maintenance man and three deckhands. Some ships carry from one to three deckwatchmen who assist with the deck work.

Engine Room
The engine room is under the direction of the chief engineer. Ships are powered by steam or diesel engines and the ship engineers must have the appropriate operating licenses. The engine room crew (formerly called the "Black Gang" from the days when they had to shovel coal to fire the boilers) may consist of the chief, a first assistant, one or two second assistants, a third assistant, three oilers and from one to three wipers.

When the captain or mate in the pilot house signals the engine room to instruct the engineer on watch to move the ship either forward or astern, he does this via the engine room telegraph or "chadburn" as it is usually called. The officer in the pilot house also instructs the engineer how fast to turn the engine. The engineer acknowledges that he has received the proper signal with the indicator on the chadburn. An engineer must be standing by at the engine room console at all times to be able to make these adjustments to the propulsion of the ship.

Loading and Unloading

When a ship arrives dockside to load cargo, extreme caution must be taken to maintain balance. The first mate, usually in charge of the loading, must work closely with the engineers who pump out the ballast tanks as the cargo is loaded evenly throughout the holds. If this is not done, the ship could sustain heavy damage or even sink while the cargo is being loaded.

The mate must have a loading plan for dock personnel on how he wants the cargo dumped. Typically for an ore boat, it starts at the after end with a minimum amount loaded through the hatches into each compartment, moving forward. Then another run will be made along the ship and finally a third to top off, which will put the ship in even keel and trim.

All during this loading operation, the engineers pump water ballast from the tanks under the cargo hold being loaded. This ballast is required when the ship is sailing in a light condition to make it more stable and to keep the propeller under water. Sometimes some of the ballast is pumped out when running in the open lake to gain speed and to make the ship operate more efficiently. Sometimes when operating in ice the ballast is pumped out of the forward tanks to let the bow ride upon the ice, thereby breaking it with the weight of the ship. But before docking, the ballast must be returned to the ship's tanks, lowering the vessel to permit entering under the ore dock over-hang. On the newer docks where cargo is loaded by conveyor belts the same amount of ballast is not required.

When the ship is being unloaded the same precautions for stability are necessary. Cargo must be removed evenly through the ship and some ballast must be pumped in as the cargo is removed. The unloading of the ship can be supervised by any of the mates.

When the ship is finished loading or unloading it is the mate's responsibility to make certain all crew members ashore are called back on time. A sailing board is usually posted with the departure time so that crew members leaving the ship will know what time to return.

Steward's Department

The Steward's Department is headed by either a steward or a steward/cook and is responsible for both meals and housekeeping of crew and passenger quarters on board. The Steward's Department is operated differently in nearly every fleet. However, it generally consists of the steward/cook, sometimes a second cook or night cook, a waiter (or messman) and one or two porters.

In the Ford Fleet it was the practice for many years to carry a steward who was considered one of the officers on the ship. His principle duties were to accommodate the passengers as well as supervise the galley crew. Because of the conflict of interest between the two jobs and general position restructuring for greater efficiency, this position has been eliminated in favor of the combined position of steward/cook.

The Steward's Department is very confining because it is just like running a hotel. These few men must serve three meals a day, seven days per week, do all the housekeeping and maintain everything on schedule. The meals are served at a table or tables as the men come off watch. Sometimes they must eat in a hurry. The galley crew must maintain all of the individual cabins on the ship, plus the recreation rooms, hallways, etc., as well as the galley itself.

The steward orders all of the necessary food items and supplies to provide first class meals for a trip that may last from one day to two weeks (longer on ocean cruises). He is usually supplied with ample refrigerator and freezer capacity that reduces his storage problems. However, considerable planning must be done to operate a well organized galley.

The cook never receives much praise from the crew, regardless of how well he does his job. For many years at Ford, we tried to control our meal costs but we found that it was far better to provide good, nutritious meals than to try and scrimp. It never took very long to hear from the captain, the crew or a Union representative when the food was poorly prepared or in short supply. So, a happy crew was a crew that was well fed. It was always necessary to have a happy crew to have a ship that was well maintained and operated efficiently.

While the deck crew maintains the exterior of the ship and navigating equipment and the engine room crew keeps the power plant operating perfectly, the galley crew, in addition to serving the meals, keeps busy checking its huge inventory of linens and bedding, changing the bunks and preparing to send the soiled linen ashore for cleaning. Each crewman is supplied with clean bed linen twice a week and such other items as hand and bath towels, wash cloths, etc. At Ford, a room porter made the beds and cleaned the rooms. However in some fleets the crews, with some compensation, are required to maintain and clean their own rooms.

The inventory that the Steward's Department keeps might surprise a landlubber, but it covers many of the same items that one would have in a home. Included are sheets, pillow cases, blankets, bedspreads, bath and hand towels, wash cloths, rugs, cooks' pants, shirts in different sizes, aprons, dish clothes, dish towels, and rags. It also must include drapes, window curtains, throw rugs and runners. Bags full of laundry go off each trip and bundles of clean laundry come aboard each time that the groceries are delivered, at the completion of each trip five days or more in length.

The Watches

The crewmen on a ship basically work three different shift arrangements — watch-standers, day workers and the captain and chief engineer who are on call at all times and work whatever hours or watches necessary. The watch-standers work two four-hour watches each day, 4 to 8, 8 to 12 and 12 to 4, both a.m. and p.m. The day workers are on from 8 a.m. to 4:30 p.m. with a half-hour for lunch. The captain and chief always are on duty when the ship is making or leaving a dock, while in the rivers, while going through the locks and when fog, wind or bad weather make navigation difficult.

Traditionally the first, or chief, mate, is in charge of the 4-to-8 watch, because that used to be the time when navigational "fixes" on the rising and setting sun were taken. The second mate takes the 12-to-4 watch, and the third, the 8-to-12. The same pattern is followed in the engine room.

The Deck Crew reports to the mate in charge of their watch and maintains the ship outside of the engine room and the galley. They are responsible for loading and unloading the cargoes and also assist navigating the vessel. They order the necessary deck supplies, prepare the payrolls, handle the Coast Guard deck inspection and maintain all the navigation equipment such as radio-telephones, radars, compasses and depth sounder. The mates must keep the master notified about the weather and all changes that are specified in each "Notice to Mariners" they receive. They must continually check and repair all lines and cables, ladders, running lights, etc., to make certain these are safe to use and are working properly at all times. Once the ship leaves the dock after spring fit-out, much of this equipment never stops running until the ship is laid up in the fall.

Down in the engine room, the engineers must keep all of their equipment running during heavy peak loads and for long periods of time. Whether the ship has huge diesel engines with their many parts or a steam turbine with high pressure boilers, there are hundreds of pumps and motors, electric generators, emergency generators, bow and stern thrusters, winches, steering gears, refrigerators and freezers and an integrated sanitary system to be serviced.

In the event of a failure or stoppage of any moving part in the engine room, the engineers must be ready to switch to an auxiliary system or be able to repair on short notice. Modern ships are equipped with emergency generators that start up immediately in the event of a power failure on the main generator and they provide power to certain necessary equipment such as the steering gear, lights and other emergency equipment. The radio-telephones have battery standby power for emergency use.

Many improvements have been made in connection with the operation of steam generating boilers on the steam ships, whereby the boilers have been automated and the need for the use of "firemen" to attend them has been eliminated. Much of this new equipment requires considerable talent to operate and maintain. The engineers on a large ship must be highly skilled and qualified.

The ship requires huge amounts of fuel oil and lubricants that must be ordered in ample supply. Thousands of spare parts must be kept on hand and available. The engineers must be able to make some repair parts in their tool room (machine shop) when parts are not available.

During the winter layup period, the engine room personnel are kept aboard to repair and overhaul their equipment. Unfortunately, most of these men would like to take the winter off inasmuch as the sailing seasons are so long. However, they do not like to depend on outsiders to work on their equipment so they prefer to do the work themselves. Outside crews and various shipyards also are called in to do major repair work and hull repairs.

Many years of experience are necessary to design, build and navigate the beautiful ships which move through the Lake system. Safety is a must, so they are designed and built with backup systems that can be used if any components fail. With the exception of the main propulsion system, auxiliary equipment for practically any function can be activated immediately, including steering gear, generators, most pumps and electrical transmission lines. All newer ships have an emergency generator that starts up automatically when the main power source fails. The ship must have a qualified crew who know how to use this equipment efficiently.

When a failure occurs, what a captain needs is the time to get the ship in position, so use of his rudder and navigation equipment are most important. What the engineers want is time to find and correct the problem. This is extremely important when a failure occurs in the rivers or channels or when making a dock or entering or leaving locks. These failures do occur and are of great concern.

The need to keep the ship clean and healthy is most important. To keep the crew free from disease when they are living in such close quarters is a continuing problem. At home we may take our essential utilities such as water, sewer, heat and power systems for granted, and most of us therefore are unfamiliar with how they work. But on shipboard the men must operate their own sanitary system because they no longer are allowed to empty the wastes into the waters of our Great Lakes. They purify their own potable water and generate their own electricity.

In addition to all of this, the ship must make a profit for her owners, or otherwise another means of hauling the cargo would be found.

From Deckhand to Captain

Everyone looks up to the "old man," the "skipper" or the "master" of a ship. He is called Captain. Regardless of his ability, he is the boss or master of his ship. How does he get a job like that? Well generally, he starts as a deckhand or cabin boy when he is very young.

Before a young man aspiring to a sea-faring (or in this case, lake-going) career can get a job on any ship, he first must get his seaman's papers which are issued by the U. S. Coast Guard. The U.S.C.G. Officer-in-Charge of Marine Inspection will not issue a seaman's document until a man has the promise of a job. Therefore a young man must get a shipping company to say that it has a job opening and that they will hire him if he can get his seaman's papers. When he gets this commitment, the Coast Guard will issue temporary papers so that he can take a job. The validated document will be forthcoming in about three months. In the meantime, he is limited to a job opening only with the company that made him the job offer. (It is a policy of the Coast Guard not to issue papers to anyone who has a criminal record or has been charged for the use of narcotics of any kind. The Coast Guard will check his criminal record before a document is issued.)

After obtaining his seaman's papers he must then go to the union hiring hall and register for a job. He must pay a registration fee and put his name on a waiting list. If he is available in the hall when his name reaches the top of the list for the job for which he has registered, he will be sent out to the prospective employer to be hired as a ordinary seaman, or deckhand, aboard a ship. As soon as he starts to work, he must then pay union dues and work under their contract conditions.

Prior to being hired, however, he must pass the employer's physical examination. Many young men today are turned down because of their health. Anyone who has used controlled drugs of any kind will not be issued a seaman's document and, if this information had been withheld from the Coast Guard, the physical examination will likely discover its effect on the health of the applicant and he will be turned down. He must be neither too small for the job nor too large because a shipboard job requires a considerable amount of climbing.

Once hired, the young man is sent to the ship and is welcomed aboard by the mate on watch, escorted to his room and shown his bunk. Each employment position on a ship has a specific bunk assignment. He will be given job and safety instructions aboard ship. A "rite of passage" or acceptance will be his first thrill-ride on the "bosun chair" over the side to the dock when he has received sufficient instructions. Then after he "lets go" the lines he will be instructed to "run" for the ladder that is placed over the side of the ship, climb to the rail, over the fence and onto the deck. Once he has done this he will know whether he will make a sailor or not!

As a deckhand, he learns the trade by performing the menial duties aboard ship — cleaning, painting, chipping off old paint from the hull, etc. His principle duties, however, are to handle the mooring lines on the dock. At all times when a ship is not at sea it must be tied to a dock or pier. When passing through locks, as at the Soo, lines must be placed on the pier. While a ship is being loaded and unloaded it is generally necessary to shift the ship and the deckhands must be on the dock to move the lines from one bollard to another. This may occur at any hour of the day or night.

A deckhand must take aboard the groceries and laundry and haul off all the trash that has been collected. He usually lives and sleeps in the most crowded rooms because he is the "low man on the totem pole." He works from 8 a.m. to 4:30 p.m. every day of the week, plus overtime when it is necessary to work at night. A deckhand usually will be expected to work 60 or 70 hours per week if a ship is in the stone or coal trade.

As the Great Lakes seaman moves up through the higher job classifications on board, he will perform duties that require increasingly more skill and knowledge. When he is able to perform those duties requiring greater seamanship, he can even climb the ladder to a licensed (officer) position if he so desires.

If a man can pass this first trial, likes this type of work and shows an interest in advancement, he can obtain his AB (able bodied) seaman document from the U. S. Coast Guard, after serving a certain amount of time aboard ship and writing a Coast Guard examination. Once he obtains his AB ticket he can be promoted to a watchman and then to a wheelsman as he becomes more skilled. These are the steps to becoming a deck officer.

The highest unlicensed deck job is that of helmsman or wheelsman. A wheelsman spends his time in the pilot house with the captain and mates and steers the ship at their command. He must follow explicit instructions from the pilot, particularly in the rivers and in making docks. One mistake or misunderstood order can be disastrous. Not very many seamen have the "knack" or ability to steer a ship, but those who can, have the opportunity for further advancement.

At this stage, he can study for his First Class Pilot's license for the Great Lakes which is required of all mates. An engineer can use his license both on the ocean and the Lakes, but an ocean pilot's license does not apply on the Great Lakes, nor does a Great Lakes license apply to the oceans.

When a seaman feels that he can qualify himself for an officer position, he must first have the confidence of the officers under whom he has served. If they will recommend him, he can study on his own or, during the winter months, can attend one of several schools which are operated especially to prepare candidates for the Coast Guard pilot's examination. Most Ford men went to the Lake Carrier's Association school in Cleveland.

When the AB is ready, he requests permission to write the examination from the U.S.C.G. Officer-in-Charge of Marine Inspection. This will take a week or more to complete. The exam is given in several different stages. He must complete and pass one step at a time. If he passes, he will be issued his First Class Pilot's license for the Great Lakes. This will permit him to sail as a first, second or third mate. His license will restrict him to those waters of the Great Lakes covered by his license, such as Duluth to Buffalo. (The St. Lawrence Seaway requires an additional license for which a mate must qualify before piloting a ship in those waters.) In order to qualify, he will have to make several trips through those waters as an observer. After he has obtained his pilot's or mate's license, he must then look for an opening in some fleet that needs a third mate, or sail as an AB until a job opens up in a fleet for him. Then, if his work is satisfactory, he waits to be promoted to second and then to first mate as openings occur.

Before being promoted to first mate, an officer usually is required to have his Master's license so that he can take over for the captain if an emergency arises. The Master's license is considerably more difficult to obtain. Many candidates fail the exam and never get a Master's license. Those who do win the license must again wait for a captain's slot to open and, again, for many this never comes about. You can see from the foregoing description that it is a very long and difficult road from a boy on the banks of the river to master of a ship. That is possibly the reason a captain is called "the old man."

The promotion process for engineers is similar to that for mates. However, as noted, their licenses are good for both the oceans and lakes but are divided between steam and diesel. Some engineers have both. It is necessary to have actual sailing experience on both before they can write for these licenses.

With the building of the newer, larger and far more efficient Great Lakes ships, it is evident that the number of personnel required to operate a Great Lakes freighter has been diminished considerably during the past few years. It is, therefore, even more difficult to hold a position and even more difficult to be promoted.

APPENDIX II: WORLD WAR II REPORTS
(by Michael W. R. Davis)

Appendix II has five sections: the first is an introductory commentary about German submarine warfare operations; the second contains the correspondence which led to this book being brought to publication; the third is about the first Ford ship (the LAKE OSWEYA) lost to enemy action, the fourth is a copy of the official report of the ONONDAGA sinking, and the fifth has all the documents about the EAST INDIAN because there is a mystery about whether the lifeboat or liferaft washed ashore in Brazil months later was a hoax or not.

The copies of actual documents relating to Ford ships lost during World War II are reproduced as faithfully as possible, including typographical errors, misspellings and known factual errors (such as the classification in some documents of the EAST INDIAN as a steamship ["S/S"] rather than as a motorship ["M/S"]).

Careful reading of the war documents reveals much about the times — what kind of records were kept and how information was transmitted; the youth, marital status and homes of the Ford ship crewmen; the rumors of spies even in official reports; errors in reporting or recording details, and anxieties about what happened to loved ones. Together, the documents present a small but detailed slice of American history which should be better known: that of merchant ships at sea in wartime.

A. German Submarine Operations

Two of the five sinkings of Ford ships by German submarines during World War II are notable because of the apparent gallantry of the U-boat captains. At the first of these, the GREEN ISLAND loss on May 6, 1942, the U-boat surfaced, ordered the crew under gunpoint into lifeboats and safety, and then torpedoed the Ford ship. The sinking took place at high noon about 50 miles south of Grand Cayman Island between Cuba and Jamaica. At the second, on November 3, 1942, off the Atlantic coast of South Africa, the U-boat surfaced after torpedoing the EAST INDIAN about 5 p.m. and, after asking questions of the survivors, offered them supplies and compass bearings to safety (which were defiantly refused by the American seamen). It could be argued, of course, that the "gallantry" was merely a ruse to obtain information subsequently used to sink other ships.

Postwar information on the voyages and fates of these two Nazi submarines and their captains is instructive as to war and to the pallid Allied defenses of the time.

The GREEN ISLAND and the U-125

This GREEN ISLAND was sunk by the U-125, commanded by Ulrich Folkers, an apparently compassionate U-boat officer awarded the distinguished Knight's Cross by the German Navy in March 1943. The U-125 was on its second war patrol off the American coast and had scored its first "kill" of the voyage, the 5100-ton LAMMONT DUPONT, on April 23 while still far out in the Atlantic east of Bermuda. The submarine then courageously (or outrageously, depending on your interpretation) slipped through the Windward Channel past the major U. S. Naval Base at Guantanamo Bay, Cuba, and into fertile hunting grounds between Jamaica and Cuba. There, at 1723 hours on May 3, it sank the 2000-ton SAN RAFAEL less than 100 miles north of Montego Bay. The U-125 continued almost straight west and the next day at 2021 hours, claimed its third victim, the 5700-ton TUSCALOOSA CITY at position 18°25'N-81°31'W.

Two days later, on May 6, Ford's GREEN ISLAND was the fourth ship to be sunk, the first of a two-in-one-day record. The U-125 reported sinking GREEN ISLAND at 1215 hours, position 18°25'N-81°30'W, almost the exact location where the TUSCALOOSA CITY had gone down barely 38 hours earlier. Then, eight hours later on May 6 at position 19°14'N-82°34'W, or slightly northwest, the U-125 sank the 6400-ton EMPIRE BUFFALO.

The submarine evidently stayed in that position, or returned to it. Three days later at position 19°24'N-82°30'W, she sank the 12000-ton tanker CALGAROLITE at 1814 hours. Five days later, May 14 and still in the same vicinity, U-125 claimed its seventh sinking of the patrol, the 2500-ton COMAYAGUA, at 1812 hours and position 19°00'N-81°37'W. Moving more to the northwest toward the Yucatan Peninsula of Mexico but still south of Cuba, on May 18 she completed her patrol by again nailing two ships in one day. The victims were the 8900-ton MERCURY SUN at 0500 hours and position 20°01'N-84°26'W and the 2600-ton WILLIAM J. SALMAN at 2100 hours and position 20°08'N-83°46'W. That ended a hugely successful patrol in which nine ships totaling 47,000 tons were sent to the bottom by the U-125.[74]

One can't help wondering where our intelligence and our defences were, since the sinkings followed a discernible pattern, the submarine was operating within reasonable range of U. S. air stations and all of the sinkings were relatively close to one another. But, as explained in the section of the book on the early months of America's entrance into the war, all was chaos.

A year later, the U-125 met its fate in a massive battle between U-boats and British convoy escorts south of Greenland the night of May 5-6, 1943. Caught on the surface in a dense fog bank, the U-125 was rammed "abaft the conning tower" by the HMS ORIBI and then depth-charged by the HMS SNOWFLAKE and HMS VIDETTE. Folkers managed to get off a radio distress signal before his boat went down with all hands. The battle claimed 13 merchant ships and six attacking submarines in all.[75]

Curiously, no official records on the GREEN ISLAND could be located in either the National Archives or the Ford Archives. The account is wholly from secondary sources, including whatever notations Clare Snider may have made at the time or later recalled.

The EAST INDIAN and the U-181
The German submarine which sank the queen of Ford's ocean-going fleet, the EAST INDIAN, was the U-181. Her captain at that time was Wolfgang Luth. Before sailing the U-181 to the South African coast, Luth had commanded the U-43, attacking convoys in the North Atlantic, and together with his Indian Ocean successes, ended up being Germany's second biggest submarine ace. He won an Iron Cross in 1940 and was credited with sinking 225,700 tons and 43 ships by war's end. (The EAST INDIAN was the second Ford ship to have the particular misfortune of crossing the path of a U-boat ace. The LAKE OSWEYA was sunk by the U-96 under Heinrich Lehmann-Willenbrock, Germany's eight-ranking submarine ace of World War II, credited with 166,600 tons and 22 ships).[76]

An examination of the U-181's record after it sank the EAST INDIAN makes it clear that the information Korvettenkapitan (Commander) Luth obtained from the EAST INDIAN's third mate helped doom many other freighters within the next month. So the submarine's offer of aid to the seaman in the lifeboats and on the rafts may not have been all gallantry. However, there is at least one other account of Luth allowing a crew to get off a ship into lifeboats before sinking it.

The EAST INDIAN was the U-181's first victim on this patrol. In the January 15, 1943, U.S.Navy official report of the incident (see Appendix II E 9), it is stated:
Five minutes after the vessel sank, the submarine surfaced about fifty yards from the lifeboat and questioned the third mate, who was the ranking survivor: What is the name of the ship? EAST INDIAN. What flag? American. What cargo? 10,000 tons iron ore. Where from? India via Capetown. Where to? New York...What course from India? Through Mozambique Channel close to shore.

154

Ironically, then, while the sailors at sea and the officials at various Allied headquarters were worrying about spies ashore (as illustrated by both official and unofficial accounts in this book), a survivor of the sunken ship guilelessly provided the U-boat with the most vital intelligence it could hope for: where it could find other ships to sink.

Indeed, the sinking locations reported via radio back to U-boat headquarters by the U-181 proceeded like links of a chain around the Cape and up the African coast of the Indian Ocean. Five days after it sank the EAST INDIAN, the U-181 claimed its second victim off the coast of Port Elizabeth. On November 10, the third went down off East London. Three days later, the fourth was sunk between East London and Durban. Then the U-181 settled in off the coast of what was then called Lorenco Marques (today's Maputo), capital of Mozambique, where the Mozambique Channel opens up south of Barra Point. There, in a very small area around 25°S-34°N, it sank seven more ships between November 19 and December 2.

The following spring, Luth and the U-181 returned again to the same exact area, but with slightly less success — three sinkings off of Lorenco Marques between May 11 and June 7, 1943. Then, after moving several hundred miles out into the Indian Ocean east of Madagascar, four more between July 2 and August 4. Fortunately these were the last kills credited to the U-181.

Her subsequent voyages and ignominious end could be the subject of another book. Luth was reassigned to shore duty by 1944 and turned over the U-181 to another captain. Ordered to work with the Japanese in the Indian Ocean, the U-181 and her crew eventually found themselves cut off from proper supplies and virtually marooned far from their "Fatherland" by the Allies' more successful pursuit of anti-submarine warfare beginning in 1943. When Germany surrendered in May 1945, the U-181 was in Java, Dutch East Indies, where she evidently was taken over by the Japanese Navy. Four months later, when Japan also surrendered, she was scuttled in the Singapore harbor.

In another irony of war, Luth survived submarine combat unscathed but, just before the German surrender in the spring of 1945, was killed by a German sentry at his base on the Baltic when he gave the wrong password.[77]

B. Kilpatrick Correspondence (editor's files)
1.   **Ford inter-company buckslip: 1-21-82**
        Mike Davis — I am forwarding a letter from Rhonda Kilpatrick to see if some one in your department can help.
        I've included a section of Clare Snider's history of Ford Marine Dept that you may want to include in a reply to Miss Kilpatrick — John Nye

2. Letter from Ms. Rhonda I. Kilpatrick:

Route 3, Box 795
Jay, Florida 32565
January 6, 1982

Personnel Department
Ford Motor Company
The American Road
Dearborn, Michigan 48121

Dear Sirs:

My name is Rhonda Kilpatrick. I am hoping that you may provide me with information for my family history. My great uncle, John Sidney Kilpatrick, was chief engineer on the Ford-owned freighter, "M/S Lake Osweya" in World War II. My great grandmother, Mrs. Ella L. Kilpatrick, received a letter on July 21, 1945 from the Department of War Shipping Administration, stating the ship named above was torpedoed and sunk by the enemy on February 19, 1942. My great grandmother was presented a Mariner's Medal in commemoration of her son's service to his country.

John Sidney Kilpatrick was born September 14, 1905. The information I have gathered from my grandfather's records show that uncle began working at the Ford Motor Company in Detroit, Michigan in 1924 at the age of 19. At the time of his death, he was 37 years old and the ship "M/S Lake Osweya" was off the coast of Nova Scotia and Cape Cod. We have photographs of my great uncle taken with Edsel Ford and Henry Ford II on board one of the Ford-owned ships.

My family would greatly appreciate any information you could give us of the "M/S Lake Osweya," my great uncle, and his involvement with Ford Motor Company during his 18 years of service; including the circumstances surrounding his involvement in the war. If this information cannot be supplied by Ford Motor Company, could you please give me an address as to whom I might write to obtain this information?

Thank you very much.

Sincerely,
(s)
Rhonda I. Kilpatrick

3.   Ford reply (editor's files):
February 2, 1982
Ms. Rhonda I. Kilpatrick
Route 3, Box 7905
Jay, Florida 32565

Dear Ms. Kilpatrick:

This is in response to your letter of January 6 regarding your great uncle, John Sidney Kilpatrick.

We will keep looking for more information, but at the moment all we can come up with is the attached copy of a partial history of Ford's Marine Operations which covers the war period. The man who was writing this history died before it could be completed.

In the meantime, I suggest that you also contact the Navy Department in Washington. Since you are near the Navy installation at Pensacola, you may want to start there at the Public Information Office. Although there apparently was no contemporary information on what happened to your uncle's ship in 1942, it is possible captured German submarine records after the war might have shed some light on the matter.

Thank you for bringing this little-known bit of Ford history to our attention, and good luck on your research.

Sincerely,
(s)
Michael W. R. Davis[78]

C. LAKE OSWEYA Documents
1. 2-5-42 New York Port Director's Report (National Archives):

```
SERIAL P-0348
CONFIDENTIAL
NAME OF SHIP: S/S LAKE OSWEYA
OWNER: Ford Motor        OPERATOR OR AGENT: Navy Time Charter
ITINERARY: Sailing Date: 2/17/42   From: New York   To: Indigo 79

SHIP'S CREW
MASTER:    Karl O. PRINZ
OFFICERS:  Charles WAGNER
```

Deck Department		Engineering Dept.		Steward's Department	
Chief Mate	1	Ch. Engineer	1	Ch. Steward	1
2nd Mate	1	1st "	1	Ch. Cook	1
3rd Mate	1	2nd "	1	2nd Cook	1
Quartermaster	—	3rd "	1	3rd Cook	—
Boatswain	1	4th "	—	Messmen	4
Seaman — Able	6	Firemen	—	Electrician	1
Seaman — Ord.	2	Oilers	3		
Radio Operator	1	Wipers	1		

```
          PASSENGERS — Number on Board _____
```

```
U. S. NAVY PERSONNEL
Armed Guard Unit          Rating        Branch      Service #
Officer in Charge: FRENCH,Joseph L.ENSIGN USNR DDV(G)
Enlisted Men:
    BAILKEY,Harold          GM3c,V-6      USNR      305-18-87
    McMURRAY,William        AS, V-6       USNR      656-16-79
    SENN,Harold Anderson    AS, V-6       USNR      656-16-73
    BROWN,Charles James     AS, V-6       USNR      658-22-92
    BATSON,Charles Horace   AS, V-6       USNR      656-17-12
    FREEMAN,Wm Raymond Jr.  AS, V-6       USNR      658-17-40
Communications Group
    WHAYNE,Thomas Samuel    RM2c          USN       287-05-71
    BRASHER,Howard Jonnie   SM3c          USN       272-15-00
```

2. Crew beneficiary list (Ford Museum Archives):
M/S "LAKE OSWEYA"— Lost: Feb.19, 1942

NAME	RATING	NEXT OF KIN	ADDRESS
Karl E. Prinz	Master	Wife	29 Carstairs Road, Valley Stream, L.I., N.Y.
William Carroll	Chief Mate	Mother Mrs. M. Carroll	828 E.19th Street Paterson, N.J.
Alfred Abrahamson	2nd Mate	Mother Mrs. T. Abrahamson	2866 Randall Ave. Bronx, N.Y. City
Charles Kibbit	3rd Mate	Wife	1820 Market Street Galveston, TX

Name	Position	Next of Kin	Address
Fred G. Smith	Radio Clerk	Mother, Mrs. E. Smith	St. Cloud Hotel Jacksonville, Fla.
Herman Mathisen	Bos'n	Wife	713 Clouet St. New Orleans, La.
Winfred Sumner	Able Seaman	Mother Mrs. R. Sumner	Murfreesboro, N.C.
Herman L. Mathisen Jr.	Able Seaman	Mother, Mrs. A. Mathisen	713 Clouet St. New Orleans, La.
George Jacota	Able Seaman	Father, D. Jacota	222 E. Grixdale St. Detroit, Mich.
Ivor O. Johnson	Able Seaman	Uncle, O. Petersen	Turlock, California
Charles Phillips	Able Seaman	Mother, Mrs. D. Phillips	1073 W. 48th St. Norfolk, Va.
Buman C. Tolson, Jr.	Able Seaman	Mother, Mrs. A. Tolson	104 W. 32nd St. Norfolk, Va.
Donald Kerfoot	Ordinary Seaman	Wife	964 Amsterdam Ave. New York, N.Y.
George Murray	Ordinary Seaman	Aunt, Sarah Cudd	8 Johnson Street Millbury, Mass.
John Kilpatrick	Chief Engr.	Mother, Mrs. Ella Kilpatrick	Milton, Florida
Charles Wagner	1st Asst Engr.	Wife, Alice	1595 E. 48th Street Brooklyn, N.Y.
Thomas L. Evans	2nd Asst Engr.	Wife, Mrs. H. Evans	1211 Dukeland St. Baltimore, Md.
William T. O'Neal	3rd Asst	Wife, Mrs. K. O'Neal	Rt.4. Box 198A Norfolk, Va.
Bernard McMahon	Electrician	Wife, Mrs. J. McMahon	23 Harvard Ave. Staten Island, N.Y.
Joseph Vealie	Oiler	Mother, Mrs. H. Vealie	40 Highgate Terrace W. Englewood, N.J.
William Crosbie	Oiler	Mother Mrs. Eva Crosbie	Arichat, Nova Scotia
Leroy S. Pearce	Oiler	Mother, Mrs. A. Pearce	Richmond, Michigan
Samuel O. McDonald	Wiper	Mother, Mrs. Nan McDonald	509 E. 81st St. New York, N.Y.
Burtney Ruley	Steward	Sister, J. Ruley	700 Fullerton Parkway. Chicago, Ill.
George Roemer	1st Cook	Friend Oresto Compagnini	26 W. Delaware Ave. Marcus Hook, Pa.
Paul Kirwan	2nd Cook	Aunt, Mrs. H.	108D 4th St. Towanda, Pa.
Russell R. Carthy	Messman	Mother, Mrs. I. Riley	89 Virginia Ave. Welch, W. Va.
John Krieger	Messman	Mother, Mrs. Rose Krieger	175 Southern Blvd. Bronx, N.Y.
George Zies	Messman	Mother, Mrs. M.Zies	Smock, Pa.
Adam Robert Fass	Messman	Mother, Mrs. E. Fass	121 Simonson Ave.

D. ONONDAGA Official Report (National Archives):

NAVY DEPARTMENT
OFFICE OF THE CHIEF OF NAVAL OPERATIONS
WASHINGTON

Op-16-B-5   August 14, 1942
CONFIDENTIAL

MEMORANDUM FOR FILE

SUBJECT: SUMMARY OF STATEMENTS BY SURVIVORS OF S/S "ONONDAGA" U. S. FREIGHTER, 2310 G.T., OWNER: FORD MOTOR COMPANY, CHARTERED TO U. S. MARITIME COMMISSION.

1.   The "ONONDAGA" was torpedoed without warning at 1630 EWT, July 23, 1942, at 22°40' N — 78°44'W, while enroute from Nuevitas to Havana with a full cargo of Magnesium ore; draft 20' even keel. The vessel sank within a minute.

2.   The ship's course is not known but she was following the 100 fathom curve, speed 8.3 knots, radio silent, not zigzagging, 2 lookouts stationed; 1 on the bridge, 1 on the monkey island. The weather was fair, visibility good, wind NE force 2, daylight attack; several small fishing boats in sight.

3.   The explosion occurred amidship on the port side and presumably was caused by a torpedo fired from a sub off the port beam. Certain of the survivors state that immediately following the first explosion, a second torpedo hit aft on the starboard side. Extent damage is unknown; but ship quickly sank. There was no time to send distress signals. Confidential codes sank with the ship.

4.   It is not certain whether there were 32 or 33 on board; but only 14 survived and the others are missing and believed lost. The ship sank so quickly no lifeboats were launched and the survivors jumped overboard, reached 2 floating liferafts and were picked up by the Cuban fishing boat "LAVENTINA" on July 24, 1942, and landed at Punta San Juan.

5.   The submarine was not seen, nor was the wake of the torpedo.

NOTE: The U. S. Vice Counsel at Nuevitas expresses the opinion that due to carelessness of the ship's crew during the 3 days shore leave, enjoyed prior to ship's departure, practically everyone in Nueviatas knew the ship's destination and time of departure.

                                        E. D. Henderson
                                        Ensign, U. S. N. R.

CC: ONI B-8, 16-Z, (4 copies), F-10, Cominch, Cominch F-21D22, F-252, F-353, F-37 (C & R), Op-20-G-M, Op-23-L, Op-28, Op-30, Op-39, BuShips, BuOrdnance (Ensign P. L. Vissat), BuOrdnance, Atlantic Fleet Anti-Submarine Unit, BuPers-6.

E. The EAST INDIAN Mystery:

    1.   **5-1-42 crew list** (Ford Museum Archives):

<u>CREW LIST OF M S EAST INDIAN</u>   5-1-42

<u>NAME</u> MARRIED [80]	<u>CAPACITY</u>	<u>FULL ADDRESS</u>	<u>AGE</u>	
CAPT. O. L. Ste Marie	Master	18 Main St Springfield NJ	not listed	Yes
Clayton Hammond*	1st Mate	Matthews Va	31	No
Lemuel Marchant	2nd Mate	1102 Hancock St Chester Pa	38	Yes
Patrick Keenan*	3rd Mate	244 Ridley Ave Crum Lynn Pa	35	No
Archibald McHugh	Purser	1148 Fifth Ave New York NY	48	No
Arthur Esner**	Radio Opr	611 B West 8th St Chester Pa	43	Yes
Nils Peterson*	Carpenter	79 Dock St Yonkers NY	50	No
Marion Capers*	Boatswain	Bohannon Va	38	No
Raymond Edwards*	A.B.	Woods Cross Rds Gloucester, Va	27	No
Curtis Hudgins	A.B.	Gwynne P. O. Matthews Va	30	No
Vernon Davis	A.B.	Matthews Va	26	No
Martin Posti	A.B.	Rousseau Mich	33	No
Basil Florentine*	A.B.	1932 Atlantic Av Brooklyn NY	45	No
Andrew Hancak*	A.B.	3869 E 91 St Cleveland Ohio	34	No
Thomas Miranda*	O. S.	101 Kane St Brooklyn NY	21	No
Walter Pierson	O. S.	Grimstead P.O. Matthews Va	21	No
Andrew Dennis	O. S.	323 Commerce St Alexandria Va	33	No
Joseph O'Brien	O. S.	188-26 119 Rd St.Albans LI	35	Yes
Charles Branish*	O. S.	2420 Coral St Philadelphia Pa	24	No
Wilson Forrest	O. S.	Matthews Va	24	No
Bert Doyle	Ch. Engr.	309 9th St Upland Pa	66	Yes
Ernest Larson	1st Engr.	99 Warren St Brockton Mass	50	Yes
John Gillon	2nd Engr.	144 Belmont Ave Millmont Pk Pa	31	Yes
Walter Halback	3rd Engr.	137-34 Southgate St Springfield Gardens LI	37	No
James Smith*	Dk. Engr.	1726 B St SE Washington DC	33	No

Edward B. Hawlley	Elect.	131 223rd St Laurelton LI	32	No
William Ford	Oiler	14 Hudson Ave Edgewater NJ	22	No
Rollin Troublefield	Oiler	61 Cypress St Charleston SC	19	No
Herman Michaelsen	Oiler	9062 Palisade Ave Hudson Hts NJ	22	No
John Gregory	Oiler	5421 Woodcrest Ave Philadelphia Pa	42	Yes
Gregory Regolizio	Oiler	34 S Russell St Boston Mass	38	No
Walter Fraser*	Oiler	208 LaFayette St Salem Mass	22	No
Norman Louderback	Wiper	1208 Mt Ephraim St Camden NJ	25	Yes
George Gleason*	Wiper	529 N 7 St Camden NJ	25	No
Louis Lippert	Wiper	415 Fullerton Pkwy Chicago Ill	52	No
Murdock MacLean*	Steward	1150 26 Av N St. Petersburg Fla	57	Yes
Leo Kubey	Cook	739 Gov. Nichols St. New Orleans La	44	Yes
George Lloyd	2nd Cook	Cape May C H Cape May NJ	22	No
Archibald Bailey	Waiter	2672 Sacramento St San Francisco Cal	43	No
Matthew Duffy	Messman	1505 Leland Ave Bronx NY	41	No
Max Hassin	Messman	1332 55 St Brooklyn NY	38	No
Manuel Rodriguez	Messman	751 E 155 St Bronx NY	37	Yes
Owen Sweeney	Messman	4340 N Aldene Philadelphia Pa	29	No
John Gallwits	Messman	7041 Ohio Ave Cincinnati Ohio	33	No
Otto Petrigligone	Messman	171 Van Buren Ave Brooklyn NY	34	No
Walter Geiger	Messman	113 Van Wagener Ave Jersey City NY [81]	33	No

TOTAL NUMBER IN CREW 45 - NOT INCLUDING THE MASTER
* saved
** died from exposure after being saved

2.   **5-8-42 New York Port Director's Report** (National Archives):

PORT DIRECTOR'S REPORT ARMING MERCHANT VESSELS

CONFIDENTIAL

SERIAL PD NY0131   NAME OF SHIP: <u>S/S EAST INDIAN</u>
OWNER: <u>Ford Motor Co.</u>   OPERATOR or AGENT: <u>Same</u>
REGISTRY:<u> U. S.</u>   CLASS SHIP:<u> Cargo</u>

ITINERARY: Sailing Date: <u>5/8/42</u>   From:<u> New York</u>   To:<u> Persian Gulf</u>

SHIP'S CREW

MASTER: <u>BURKE, J. M.</u>

<u>Deck Department</u> :		<u>Engineering Dept.</u>:		<u>Steward's Department</u>:	
Chief Mate	1	Ch. Engineer	1	Ch. Steward	1
2nd Mate	1	1st "	1	Ch. Cook	1
3rd Mate	1	2nd "	1	2nd Cook	1
Quartermaster	–	3rd "	1	3rd Cook	—
Boatswain	1	4th "	—	Messmen	5
Seaman — Able	6	Firemen	—		
Seaman — Ord	3	Oilers	6		
Maintenance	3	Deck Engr	1		
Carpenter	1				
Purser	1				

Total Crew Including Master:<u> 42</u>

PASSENGERS — Number on Board: _____

U.S.NAVY PERSONNEL

<u>Armed Guard Unit</u>	<u>Rating</u>	<u>Branch</u>	<u>Service #</u>
Officer in Charge:AXTELL,Harold A.			
	Ensign	USNR	D-V(G)
Enlisted Men:			
FLEMING, James Roy	AS,V-6	USNR	624-21-45
JACQUES, Raymond Zackary	Sea1c,O-1	USNR	409-91-40
JONES, Paul Howard	AS, V-6	USNR	602-11-18
KING, Frank	AS, V-6	USNR	636-29-69
LEWIS, Burruss Blond	AS, V-6	USNR	602-11-02
LEWIS, James	Sea2c,O-1	USNR	405-88-96
MOORE, Charles Joseph, Jr.	Sea1c,O-1	USNR	406-20-97
OLIPHANT, Hugh Boyer, Jr.	AS, V-6	USNR	551-52-24
RIGGON, Jack Lewis	AS, V-6	USNR	656-24-05
ROBINSON, John Henry	AS, V-6	USNR	646-28-54

3. **11-18-42 letter, War Shipping to Ford** (Ford Museum Archives):

WAR SHIPPING ADMINISTRATION
WASHINGTON

November 18, 1942

REGISTERED MAIL — SECRET

Mr. W. C. Dierolf
Marine Export Manager
Ford Motor Company
Edgewater, New Jersey

— S/S EAST INDIAN —

Dear Mr. Dierolf:

We regret to inform you of advices received from the Navy Department indicating the loss of your S/S EAST INDIAN as a result of enemy action.

We are advised that the EAST INDIAN was struck by two torpedoes and sunk at 1556, November 3rd, in position 37 degrees 23 minutes south — 13 degrees 34 minutes east. It is further reported that the chief officer and 16 persons were landed at Capetown, South Africa. We have not as yet received word regarding the balance of the crew on board this vessel but should additional advices be submitted to this office we will be pleased to inform you.

In the event of any loss of life occurring as a result of this attack Mr. C. W. Sanders of the Coast Guard will attend to the notification of next of kin.

In notifying cargo interests, etc. please omit any reference to the manner and location of attack.

Very truly yours,
(s)
J. C. Outler
Director, Division of
Security and Communication

4.   11-19-42 cable, State Dept. to Navy (National Archives):

```
SD 5 SD WASHN DC NOV 19 1942              NCR 1958

FROM: STATE DEPT
FOR:  OPNAV

FOLLOWING RECD NOV 18 1942 439 PM FROM CAPETOWN NO 462 DATED NOV 18,
1942 3PM THE CAPT AND 21 OTHER PERSONS LOST THEIR LIVES IN THE SINKING
OF THE EAST INDIAN, AMERICAN, ON NOV 3RD, THE 21 PERSONS LOST INCLUDED
7 PASSENGERS THE SINKING OCCURED ABOUT 300 MILES SOUTHWEST OF THE CAPE
OF GOOD HOPE. COMPLETE DETAILS WILL BE SENT IN A LATER MESSAGE. YESTER-
DAY 17 PERSONS FROM THIS SHIP WERE BROUGHT INTO CAPETOWN. THEY INCLUDED
2 PASSENGERS, 2 ARMED GUARDS, 12 MEMBERS OF THE CREW AND THE CHIEF OF-
FICER CLAYTON HAMMOND. THEY WERE PICKED UP FROM A LIFEBOAT ON MONDAY.
ARTHUR ESNER, THE RADIO OPERATOR DIED LAST NIGHT IN THE HOSPITAL. THERE
IS SOME HOPE THAT AT LEAST SOME OF A GROUP OF 34 PERSONS WHO WERE LAST
SEEN AT 7 PM ON NOV 3RD ON FOUR LIFE RAFTS WILL BE PICKED UP.
16.....ACT.
13....10/11.....COMINCH....20G....F-37....20OP....FILE....A--
BUPERS....23....39...
NCR 1958

C O N F I D E N T I A L
```

5.   11-23-42 Ford transmittal (Ford Museum Archives):

Ford Motor Company
TELEGRAM

```
M A I L G R A M
Edgewater NJ   Nov.23, 1942.
VIA AIR MAIL
Capt. O. A. Johnson,
Marine Department,
Dearborn.

Attached hereto is copy of letter just received from the War Shipping
Administration in connection with the M/S "EAST INDIAN", which we are
forwarding to you promptly by airmail.

We also attach hereto information received from the Isthmian S. S.
Line, who were berth sub-agents for the M/S "EAST INDIAN", which
gives information with reference to survivors landed at Capetown thus
far.

As soon as we get any information with reference to the 34 persons
last seen on four life-boats, we will promptly notify you.

W.C.DIEROLF.
```

6.   11-19-42 letter (Ford Museum Archives):

WAR SHIPPING ADMINISTRATION
WASHINGTON

November 19, 1942.

SECRET

Mr W C Dierolf
Marine Export Manager
Ford Motor Company
Edgewater, New Jersey.

S. S. EAST INDIAN

Dear Mr. Dierolf:
        Supplementing our letter dated November 18th, regarding the
loss of your S/S EAST INDIAN we now quote below message received from
Capetown with further reference to the crew:

"The Captain and 21 other persons lost their lives in the sinking of
the EAST INDIAN on November 3rd. Included with those lost were seven
passengers. Complete details will be sent in a later message. 17 persons from this ship were brought into Capetown yesterday and they included two passengers, two Armed Guard, 12 members of the crew and
Chief Officer Hammond. They were picked up from a lifeboat on Monday.
Arthur Esner, Radio Operator, died last night in the hospital. There
is some hope that the remainder of the group of 34 persons who were
last seen in four lifeboats at 7 p.m. on the November 3rd will be
picked up."

        We will keep you advised of any additional information received
by this office relative to any further survivors being rescued.
        When the identity of the passengers who were lost as a result
of this attack is known it is requested that your office arrange to
notify the next of kin inasmuch as Mr. C W Sanders has no record in
his office of passenger next of kin.

                                    Very truly yours,

                                    (SGD) J C Outler
                                    Director, Division of
                                    Security and Communications

c o p y

7.   11-20-42 cable with list of survivors (Ford Museum Archives):

FOLLOWING CABLE   (UNDATED) RECEIVED TODAY (NOV.20, 1942)
FROM CAPETOWN BY ISTHMIAN S.S.LINE, PER TELEPHONE CALL MR.
MARVIN, THRU PORT DIRECTOR.

Following survivors of the M/S EAST INDIAN has been landed at
Capetown, S.A.:

Clayton Hammond   1st Mate
Patrick Keenan   3rd Mate
Marion Capers   Boatswain
Raymond Edwards   A.B.
Basil Florentine   A.B.
Andrew Hancak   A.B.
James Smith   Deck Engineer
Walter Fraser   Oiler
Nils Peterson   Carpenter
Charles Branish   O. S.
Thomas Miranda   O. S.
Arthur Esner   Radio Operator
      Died from exhaustion and exposure shortly after landing
Murdoch MacLean   Steward
      Hospitalized;query: broken arm and left leg. Also
      exhaustion; progressing favorably.
_____ Ealson (Presume this is "George Gleason": Wiper. Cable
being confirmed).
_____ Barnes   Passenger
_____ Varney   "   "
_____ King   Naval Rating
_____ Grimstaff   "   "

No news others. Advise owners

8. **1-4-43 mailgram** (National Archives):

```
FROM: COMONE 021055 NCR 17080    4 JAN 43
ACTION:    VCNO
           COMINCH C&R
MAILGRAM
```

THE S/S EAST INDIAN 8000 GROSS TONS ARMED AMERICAN CARGO VESSEL
WAS TORPEDOED AND SUNK WITHOUT WARNING AT 1700 GMT NOVEMBER 3
1942 ABOUT 317 MILES SOUTH BY WEST OF CAPETOWN. 14 SURVIVORS INCLUD-
ING 13 AMERICAN ONE PUERTO RICAN LANDED AT HALIFAX BY THE CAPETOWN
CASTLE ON DECEMBER 31 1942 AND BROUGHT TO BOSTON BY TRAIN ARRIVING
JANUARY 2 1943. THE VESSEL WAS ENROUTE FROM CAPETOWN FOR NEW YORK
WITH 9600 TONS GENERAL CARGO. VESSEL WAS PROCEEDING ON UNKNOWN COURSE
AT UNKNOWN SPEED, NOT ZIGZAGGING WITH CHIPPY SEA, GOOD VISIBILITY,
WIND SOUTH FORCE 3. TWO TORPEDOES STRUCK STARBOARD SIDE ENGINE ROOM.
NO AVOIDING ACTION WAS TAKEN NOR ARMAMENT USED. VESSEL SANK STERN
FIRST IN APPROXIMATELY TWO MINUTES. SHIP WAS ABANDONED IN ORDERLY
MANNER IN LIFEBOATS AND RAFTS. NUMBER OF CASUALTIES UNKNOWN. SUBMA-
RINE SURFACED AFTER VESSEL SANK AND ASKED NAME OF SHIP TONNAGE,
CARGO, DESTINATION AND OTHER PARTICULARS. COMMANDER ALSO ASKED IF
FOOD WAS NEEDED AND GAVE COURSE AND DISTANCE TO NEAREST LAND. HE ALSO
INQUIRED "WHAT IS AMERICAN DOING HELPING THE BLACK RUSSIANS"? SUBMA-
RINE DESCRIBED AS GERMAN 270 FEET OVERALL WITH ONE GUN POSSIBLY 3
INCH MOUNTED FORWARD AND A 20 MM MOUNTED AFT. HULL PAINTED GREY WITH
NO RUST NOTICEABLE. CONNING TOWER HAD 3 PERISCOPES. SURVIVORS RESCUED
BY HMSA CORVETTE DURENDER 13 DAYS AFTER SINKING ABOUT 135 MILES SOUTH
OF CAPETOWN. CLASSIFIED PUBLICATIONS WENT DOWN WITH THE SHIP. PUBLIC
RELATIONS OFFICER ONE ND COGNIZANT.

```
COMINCH............ACTION
10/11.....16....20G....F37....39....OOR....20OP....BUPERS....
23....20S....20S1...20S2....20S3....FILE
```

9. **1-15-43 Official Report of Survivors** (National Archives):

Op-16-B-5
CONFIDENTIAL

NAVY DEPARTMENT
OFFICE OF THE CHIEF OF NAVAL OPERATIONS
WASHINGTON

January 15, 1943

MEMORANDUM FOR FILE

SUBJECT: Summary of Statements by Survivors S/S EAST INDIAN, American, 8159 G.T., freighter, owned by the Ford Motor Company, Maritime Commission; charterers - Isthmian SS Co., agents.

1.   The EAST INDIAN was torpedoed without warning at 1700 GMT on November 3, 1942, at 37° 23' S — 13° 34' E, approximately 317 miles SW of the Cape of Good Hope, while enroute from Capetown, S.A., via Punta Arenas to New York, N.Y. The cargo consisted of 3500 tons manganese ore, 500 tons of tea, and 5600 tons of general cargo. Draft 28' 6" forward, 29' 6" aft. The vessel sank by the stern, starboard list, in 1000 fathoms of water, about two minutes after the first hit.
2.   The course of the vessel at the time of the attack was unknown. She had been zigzagging at a speed of 11.5 knots since 0700; pattern unknown. The radio silent and not used at time of the attack. There were ten trained lookouts stationed on the bridge, forecastle head, poop deck, and in the crow's nest. Those on the bridge were equipped with binoculars. The weather was clear; sun about 25° above the horizon; the sea was choppy; the wind from South, force 3: visibility excellent; and no ships in sight.
3.   Two torpedoes struck midship starboard side at the after bulkhead of the engine room almost simultaneously, emitting a grayish yellow smoke having a strong odor of cordite. Fire broke out immediately. The extent of the damage was unknown since the ship was flooded at once. The engines were not secured and time did not permit using the radio or taking any counter-offensive. Confidentials went down with the ship.
4.   Of the 12 passengers and 62 crew and armed guard, 23 were lost in the explosion or by drowning. 17 survivors were in the lifeboat and 34 on liferafts. The 17 men in the lifeboat reached Capetown; radio operator died ashore, and up to the time of their departure from there on December 15, they had received no word of the 34 survivors on the rafts.
5.   The attack was made by an apparently new, gray, 700 T. submarine, about 300' long with one 4" gun forward and one A.A. gun, smaller than 3" aft of the conning tower. The ship was equipped with three periscopes, a pipe rail around conning tower deck, and 20 M.M. AA gun in after part of conning tower; and was last seen about 10 minutes after the attack traveling West.
6.   Five minutes after the vessel sank, the submarine surfaced about fifty yards from the lifeboat and questioned the third mate, who was the ranking survivor: What is the name of ship? EAST INDIAN. What flag? American. What cargo? 10,000 tons Iron Ore. Where from? India via Capetown. Where to? To New York. What are you doing so far Southwest? Route called for us to go SW 400 miles and then direct to New York.

168

What course from India? Through Mozambique Channel close to shore. Why did you zigzag. If you had not been zigzagging I would have gotten to you about 9.00 o'clock this a.m. and saved you 100 miles of rowing. Orders. Do you need water or provisions? No. Where is Captain and Chief Officer? Went down with ship. I am only surviving officer. Is ship single screw or does it have two screws? Two screws.

At finish of interrogation, submarine gave the course to Capetown 30° which, according to Mate was wrong. Then gave chronometer time. The submarine Commander had a note book in his hand and apparently was checking off the information supplied to him by the Third Mate; indicating that he had been advised of the name and destination of the ship beforehand. In reply to question by Third Mate, the submarine Commander stated that he had not received any previous advices on the location of the ship and the meeting was entirely accidental. Although the submarine Commander stated that the contact with the EAST INDIAN was entirely accidental, the mate was convinced by the trend of the interview that the Commander had previous knowledge of the ship's name and route. The submarine Commander was about 40 years old; had dark hair; heavy beard; weight 185 pounds, height 6'; wearing dull brown coat with sheepskin lining and sheepskin collar; had German Navy cap with Swastika in red and white; spoke good English with only trace of German accent. Four other men in same type of coat took moving pictures of survivors, some of whom were still in water. Third Mate requested several times during the conversation that he be allowed to proceed and pick up other survivors who were still in water, but this was not permitted.

It was learned that one source of information operating for the Axis is a Nazi controlled vice ring in Capetown, through the medium of which merchant seamen, under the influence of intoxicants, reveal ship movements. In fact, a member of the crew, who perished, was accurately informed before sailing, the position and time of the ship's sinking by a member of the above mentioned vice ring.

The survivors remarked about the complete absence of sea or air patrols, and also added that, as a result of the lack of patrols, submarines in this zone were very effective.

H. V. STEBBINS
Lieut., U. S. N. R.

CC: ONI-B-8, 16-C (Ensign Judd), 16DZ (4 copies), F-10, Cominch, Cominch, F-21-22, F-252, F-353, F-37 (C&R), Op-20-G-M, Op-23-L, Op-28, Op-30, Op-39, BuShips, BuOrd (Re-6-B), BuOrd, Atlantic Fleet Anti-Sub Unit, BuPers-222-23322, CG, -IO 1,3,4,5,6,7 (3 copies), 8,10 (4 copies), 11 (3 copies), 12, 13, 14 (4 copies), 15 ND's . BuAero PL-7.

10. **Undated list in Ford Motor Company records of persons lost** (Ford Museum Archives):

List of persons lost M/S "East Indian"[82]

O L Ste Marie	Master
Bert Doyle	Chief Eng
Ernest Larson	1st Asst Eng
Lemuel Marchant	2nd Mate
Walter Halbach	3rd Engr
Vernon Davis	A B
Martin Pasti	A B
Joseph O'Brien	Maintenance Man
John Gillian	2nd Engr
Archibald McHugh	Purser
Henry Helsley	A B
Walter Pierson	O S
Andrew Dennis	O S
Wilson Forrest	Maintenance Man
James Smith	Deck Engr
Edward Hawley	Electrical
Owen Sweeney	Messman
William Ford	Oiler
John Gregory	Oiler
Gregory Regalizio	Oiler
Leo Kubey	Cook
Manuel Rodriguez	Messman
Otto Petriglione	Messman
Walter Geiger	Messman
Arthur Esner	Radio Operator — (died from exposure at Capetown SA)
Rollin Troublefield Jr.	Oiler
Norman Louderback	Wiper
George Gleason	Wiper
Louis Lippert	Wiper
George Lloyd	2nd Cook
Archibald Bailey	Waiter
Matthew Duffy	Messman
Max Hassin	Messman
John Gallitts	Messman

Passengers: Mike Kane F G Lamb M C Stanley T N Smith J E McGright

A Settineri E T Nowlin A Napolitano R A Thomas C Cornfield

Naval Crew: Understand two men saved and 11 men lost however we have no information on these two men as they were under Naval Control.

11.   6-29-43 New York Times (3:2) report:

RAFT'S SAIL DESCRIBES EAST INDIAN'S SINKING
Story of Torpedoing Written by Seaman — His Body Beside It

MACEIO, Brazil, June 28 (UP) — The last dramatic moments aboard the 8,000-ton American merchant ship EAST INDIAN, torpedoed in mid-Atlantic last year, and the agony and despair of countless days without food or water in a storm-beaten open raft were recorded by an unidentified young blond seaman whose body was found on a raft grounded near here today.

The record was written on a sail. Large parts of it were unreadable.

"I can't forget these terrible moments," the seaman wrote. "Our ship was cut...embarking water rapidly. We were en route to pick up meat and food for our brothers at war. Never had the EAST INDIAN made a better voyage. No submarines were in sight. Kenney made jokes about Hitler.

"All of us tried to forget the danger of German ambushes and thought more of seeing our people again and about the presents we would bring them.

"Suddenly it happened...a terrible sound and the shaking ship tried to rise out of the water...crazy...we were running all around, despite many drills to meet this situation.

"I threw myself into the water and tried to swim away from the ship. Suddenly water covered me and when I came up only three rafts remained of what had been our EAST INDIAN.

"Kenney's raft picked me up and little by little we lost sight of the other two. There were six men in our raft: Kenney, two stokemen, one messboy, Earfield, an officer, and myself. As there were only four oars each of us rowed a little. Kenney took command and directed us toward where he believed there was land.

"The morning finally came, sunny and hot. Kenney suggested we pool our money and wrap it in a canvas. There was plenty of food and water. We could easily wait ten days.

"The tenth day is Tuesday...our hopes dwindle...help never comes, day after day, hour after hour, no ship, no plane. Kenney says it is because we don't pray at night...I believe so..."

12.   6-29-43 Washington Daily News report (Ford Museum Archives):[83]

IT'S BECAUSE WE DON'T PRAY
Rambling Log Scrawled on a Sail Pictures Horror at Sea

MACEIO, Brazil, June 29 — Words scrawled on a canvas sail by a young seaman as he waited for death told today of the last hours aboard a torpedoed U. S. merchantman and the futile effort of the survivors to reach land.

The body of the seaman was found on a raft grounded near here. His ship was the 8150-ton EAST INDIAN. Nothing was known of the five companions his written record said were originally on the raft with him.

Large parts of the story had been washed out but he wrote of a pal named Kenney.

"We were en route to pick up meat and food for our brothers at war," he wrote. "Never had the EAST INDIAN made a better voyage. No submarines in sight. Kenney made jokes about Hitler; with a little mustache he went around imitating the crazy dictator."

He then told of his son, Robert, and someone named Janet, apparently his wife, and said his fellows talked of the presents they'd take home from the voyage.

"Yesterday, Nov. 1, Kenney said was All Saints Day and that we should pray for victory. It was nightfall and he had already left the messroom. Suddenly it happened...a terrible sound and the shaking ship tried to rise out of the water...Crazy...We were all running around...I ran to my berth to get a picture of the family taken when little Bobbie was born.

"Yells of pain...Many were caught down below. I threw myself into the water and tried to swim away from the ship. I never knew swimming could be so hard. Suddenly water covered

me and when I came up only three rafts remained of what had been our EAST INDIAN.

"Kenney's raft picked me up and little by little we lost sight of the other two. There were six men on our raft - Kenney, two stokemen, one messboy, Earfield, an officer and myself. As there were only four oars.

"Kenney's raft picked me up and little by little we lost sight of the other two. There were six men on our raft - Kenney, two stokemen, one messboy, Earfield, an officer and myself. As there were only four oars each of us rowed a little. Kenney took command and directed us towards where he believed there was land."

The record started trailing off.

"The morning finally came," he went on. "Sunny and hot. Kenney suggested we pool our money and wrap it in canvas. There was plenty of food and water. We could easily wait 10 days.

"The 10th day is Tuesday...Our hopes dwindle...Help never comes, day after day, hour after hour...no ship, no plane...Kenney says it is because we don't pray at night...I believe so..."

13. 7-1-43 Axtell letter (Ford Museum Archives):

212 Tulip Avenue
Takoma Park, D.C.

July 1, 1943

Mr. O. A. Johnson,
Traffic Department,
Ford Motor Company,
Dearborn, Michigan.

Dear Sir:

I am writing to request some information in regard to your ship EAST INDIAN which was torpedoed and sunk early in November, 1942.

My son, Lieutenant Harold A. Axtell, Jr., was officer of the armed guard gun crew on the ship at the time of the sinking and is now reported missing in action by the Navy Department.

I understand that some of the crew who were in a life boat made their way back to Cape Town, South Africa, and have since arrived in this country. Undoubtedly some of the crew made a report to your company and am wondering if you can give any information from the report.

The Washington Daily News of June 29, 1943, carried a story which I am enclosing. One of the rafts from the East Indian has been found near Maceio, Brazil. One of the crew left a rambling log on a sail. He stated that there were six men on the raft, and would like to inquire if the Earfield mentioned was mess boy or one of the ship's officers. If Earfield was a mess boy it is possible that the officer mentioned was my son.

As you may readily understand, I am anxious to gather all the information possible in regard to the incident and would be deeply appreciative of any information that you may be in a position to give.

Thanking you in advance, I am
Yours truly,
(s)
Harold A. Axtell [84]

14. **7-5-43 Ford reply** (Ford Museum Archives):

July 5, 1943

Mr. Harold A. Axtell,
212 Tulip Avenue,
Takoma Park, D.C.

Dear Mr. Axtell:

We have your letter of the 1st and note that your son was an officer in the armed guard on the M/S EAST INDIAN at the time the vessel was lost.

We read this same article in a local newspaper. We have no record of either a party named "Earfield" or "Kenney" as being aboard this vessel at the time it was lost. Neither of these men were members of the crew of the vessel, according to our records, nor were they passengers on the ship. It is possible they were members of the armed guard crew. We have no knowledge of the names of the men in the armed guard as they were all naval men and the Government has not supplied us with their names.

We are very sorry we cannot give you further information but the vessel was operating in Government service at the time and the information we, ourselves, have is very meager.

Yours very truly,
FORD MOTOR COMPANY

O A Johnson:a

15. **8-6-43 McHugh letter** (Ford Museum Archives):

729 Greenwich Street
New York, 14 NY

August 6, 1943

Mr. Henry Ford
Ford Motor Works
Detroit, Michigan

Dear Mr. Ford:

I have thought of writing you for some few weeks past concerning the raft from the "East Indian" which came ashore at Maceio, Brazil. It was I who made a personal visit to the United Press Offices and obtained the complete story which I re-wrote when reaching home and sent over to your Edgewater plant. And now, after repeated calls, it is disheartening to hear that they have no further news. It seems to me that all the next of kin of those 34 raftees have a right to know all we can about the man on that particular raft to set our minds at rest. You, having experienced a great grief over the death of your only son, can appreciate the anguish of having your favorite brother left to die on a raft hundreds of miles from land, and I wish to offer you my sympathy, but you cannot possibly know, Mr. Ford, the anguish of never learning positively the mortal end of someone left to die like that.

It is for this reason and because I know positively that a man on the spot (any spot) can learn more than any arm of the Government will take the trouble to tell us, I ask that you give deep consideration to the request I make of sending your Rio representative to the spot to see the paper diary, as well as the sail and get all the details he can. I know there are some of the survivors who feel the whole thing is a hoax, but men don't make hoaxes who are left to die that way.....and it means less than nothing to me that certain of the survivors do not recall any of the men described, or their names. The United Press told me they are dependent, largely, upon Portuguese legmen in that area, and considering the fact that the paper diary was and is largely undecipherable the names could be very easily a grand mixup; furthermore, your Edgewater plant informed me they have checked even Lloyd's registry and there is no other ship registered with the name "East Indian." Furthermore, a check of the calendar shows no other month but November to have a Friday the 13th or a Sunday the 15th. Even supposing, as some do, the men to have come from another ship and to have transferred themselves from their own to the raft from the "East Indian" this, too, is ridiculous else, why would the writer mention the "East Indian" so frequently?

I must confess to amazement that the Ford Company seems to have made no extraordinary move in the matter. I should think, as this seems to be the only evidence left of any of your ships, that the Company would be avid to get all the facts it can.

May I hear Mr. Ford that you will accede to this request? My brother was the purser for the last two trips the "East Indian" made.....furthermore, he was a Veteran of the last war and now his Regiment is requesting all information possible regarding his later life and his death. Naturally, I would like to give them this, but more than anyone else, I want the information for myself. It has been a long and very weary time for me; I heard the news over the New York City broadcasting station, just four days after the torpedoing, and having knowledge of the worth of the German claims did not fool myself that it was not true. Then, there was the long wait before any word of the lifeboat came through......the Navy got that well mixed up and as I know of other errors the Navy personnel has made, I don't trust their information any too much, I assure you; therefore, again my request of you to send someone to Maceio to ferret out all he can.

Sincerely yours,
(s)
(Miss) Isabelle H. McHugh

P.S. I do not know if the Edgewater plant sent you the full story as I got it from the United Press, word for word, but if not, I hope you will get it for it is a marvelous story of patience, resignation, and bravery.....and most amazing of all, contains no single word of bitterness or complaint. [85]

16.   8-16-43 Ford reply (Ford Museum Archives):

August 16, 1943

Miss Isabelle H. McHugh
729 Greenwich Street
New York 14, N.Y.
Dear Miss McHugh:

Your letter of August 6th, addressed to Mr. Henry Ford, has been referred to me for attention.

Prior to receipt of your letter, we had been informed of the finding of this raft and immediately made an investigation of the matter, so far as was possible. As you know, the vessel was in the service of the U. S. Government at the time the sinking occurred and the information we have been able to obtain has been very meager.

We have no record of either a party named "Garfield" or Kenny" as being aboard the vessel at the time it was lost and in discussing the matter with a survivor, we are informed positively that no parties of these names were aboard the vessel.

There were a number of old and valued Ford employes lost on this vessel and you may be sure every effort has been made to determine if there have been any more survivors. I assure you if we receive any further definite information which might be of interest, we shall be glad to write you further.

Yours very truly,
FORD MOTOR COMPANY
(s)
O. A. Johnson
Director of Traffic

OAJ:as

17.   **8-17-43 Ford transmittal of translation** (Ford Museum Archives):

Ford Motor Company

From: Edgewater Branch N J   Date   August 17, 1943
To: Marine   Dept   Dearborn
Attention Captain O. A. Johnson

Attached hereto is copy of translation from the June 29th, 1943 edition of the Portuguese newspaper "Diario de Noite" of Rio de Janeiro regarding the East Indian's raft which landed on the Brazilian coast. [86]

There are a lot of discrepancies between the facts as shown in the diary and the true facts about the East Indian. This paper was brought back from Rio by the former electrician of the East Indian who happened to be in Rio at the time it was published.

If any more details come to our attention about this matter we shall keep you informed.

(s) J. M. Vealie [87]
Marine Traffic Department

wv/des

18.   **8-20-43 Ford hoax memo** (Ford Museum Archives):

DEPARTMENTAL COMMUNICATION

To: Capt. Johnson   8-20-43

Attached is copy of translation of article in the Brazilian paper regarding finding of the raft supposedly from the M/S East Indian.
There are several discrepancies in the article:
1. Mention is made that ship was going to load meat. This would indicate the vessel was "light" and apparently sailing to Argentina to load meat. The East Indian had a full cargo — mostly ore for the U.S.A.
2. There was no one by the name of "Keney" listed in the crew and MacLean says none of the Navy men on the vessel was named Keney.

3. Reference is made to "Maysie — the dog mascot" aboard the E. Indian. MacLean says they had no dog on the vessel.

4. The writer says his boat carried six men, including the Chief Mate Garfield. The Chief Mate of the E. Indian was Clayton Hammond, who was saved and was in charge of MacLean's lifeboat. There was no member in the E. Indian crew by name of Garfield.

NJA

19.   1-25-44 letter, Ford to War Shipping Administration (National Archives)

FORD MOTOR COMPANY
EDGEWATER, N.J.

January 25, 1944

Mr. J.C. Outler
Director Division of Security
          and Communications,
War Shipping Administration,
Washington, 25, D.C.

Dear Sir:

We have just received communication from Foley Bros., 86 Trinity Place, New York City, stating that they were advised by one of their men returning from South Africa that eight members of the ' EAST INDIAN " crew were washed ashore near Capetown, South Africa, and were buried by the American Consul. They state that there was in particular one A. Napolitano, who was one of thei men traveling back to the States as a passenger on this vessel, and that his statue was of such a nature it was easily identified as his body.

We have had several requests regarding various persons who were left on the rafts from the sinking of this vessel. Any information you may be able to give us would be greatly appreciated.

Yours very truly,
FORD MOTOR COMPANY,
/s/ J. W. Vealie
Marine Traffic

JWV:M

20.   1-28-44 letter, War Shipping Administration to State Dept. (National Archives)

WAR SHIPPING ADMINISTRATION
WASHINGTON 25, D.C.
January 28, 1944

RESTRICTED

Attention Miss Dailor
Shipping Division
State Department
Washington, D.C.

M/S EAST INDIAN

Dear Miss Dialor:

Please find attached the letter from the Ford Motor Company, which is self-explanitory. Our understanding is that you have no information concerning the alleged eight members, but the you will persue the matter further with the American Consul at Capetown, in order to obtain the desired information. We shall appreciate your advices in this connection.

Very truly yours,
(s)
J. C. Outler,
Director, Division of
Security and Communications

21.   5-15-44 letter, Cape Town Consulate to State Dept. (National Archives)

```
AIRMAIL
No. 96.
CONFIDENTIAL
AMERICAN CONSULATE GENERAL,
     Cape Town, South Africa,                May 15, 1944.

SUBJECT:    Fate of the Crew members and passengers of the
            S.S. EAST INDIAN.

THE HONORABLE
     THE SECRETARY OF STATE
          WASHINGTON.

SIR:

     I have the honor to refer to the Department's Confidential
instruction of February 7, 1944, transmitting an enquiry of the
Ford Motor Company of Edgewater, New Jersey, regarding the re-
ported washing ashore and burial of eight members of the crew of
the EAST INDIAN (195.7 EAST INDIAN, S.S.).
     In this connection I beg leave to refer to the Consulate
General's despatch of December 22, 1942, entitled "Transmitting
```

twenty three Reports of Death of members of the crew and passengers of the S. S. EAST INDIAN", as well as the telegrams mentioned in the department's instruction, and to my reply of May 15, 1944, to the Department's instruction of January 28, 1944 (300.113 Napolitano, Pasquale).

No further information is available beyond that reported in the Consulate General's despatch of December 22, 1942, referred to above, and there is no foundation for the report that eight bodies of crew members or passengers were washed ashore and buried at or near Cape Town.

I regret that there is nothing I can add to my despatches of December 22, 1942 and of May 15, 1944 referred to above.

Respectfully yours,
(s)
Irving N. Linnell
American Consul General

File 885.
RKB/ame.

22.   Was the Brazilian Lifeboat a Hoax?

As indicated in the Ford interoffice correspondence of August 17, 1943 (#17) and August 20, 1943 (#18), the Marine Department staff and management believed that the reports of the Brazilian lifeboat were a hoax.

Today after the passage of nearly a half century, it is easy to examine the evidence far from the emotions and tensions of wartime and conclude that they were probably wrong. I believe that the lifeboat was from the EAST INDIAN, and it is possible that further research in the United States and perhaps Brazil could prove this beyond any doubt.

Ford's reasons for doubting the authenticity of the lifeboat tale were contained in the August 20 memo:
1. In translation, the diary reported that the ship was bound to pick up a cargo of meat, whereas it already was loaded with cargo, mainly manganese ore.
2. The names in the story, as translated in both the Brazilian newspaper and the United Press report, did not coincide with available crew lists and memories of a survivor.
3. The diary referred to the crew having a dog, Maysie, and a survivor denied that such a mascot was aboard.
4. The diary as reported in the Brazilian newspaper obtained by Ford referred to a "Chief Mate Garfield" as being on the raft, whereas Ford knew that the EAST INDIAN's mate had a different name and in fact survived.

Three of these doubts can be explained readily by the evidence.

Generally, one has to recognize that, in the first place, the diary was described as being written in "poor English," in pencil, and on a piece of sailcloth. Initially it was translated out of English into Portuguese (the language of Brazil) by a local medical officer in a remote provincial coastal city; this was the version printed in the Rio de Janeiro newspaper. Then it was translated back into English by a Ford translator.

The proof that there were translation discrepancies can be found by comparing the translated Brazilian newspaper version of the tale with the United Press version printed in U. S. newspapers. Many words are different — for example, liferaft versus lifeboat, fireman versus stoker, Keney versus Kenney, Garfield versus Earfield. It is unclear whether the United Press version originated with a correspondent in Maceio who made an independent translation of the diary on the scene, or is a re-translation from a Brazilian newspaper story.

There is no question that Ford personnel in 1943 made an effort to judge the authenticity of the report. In the EAST INDIAN file in the Ford Archives at Henry Ford Museum and Greenfield Village, there is a maritime map of the South Atlantic showing prevailing winds and ocean currents, with the intended course of the ship marked in pencil. It is easy to see from this map that a lifeboat from the point where the ship was sunk could have drifted in time to the point on the Brazilian coast where reportedly it washed ashore.

Ford's mistake was in being too literal-minded and having too much faith in the translation. Miss McHugh was right — the company should have examined the original diary from Maceio.

Let's consider each point. First, the ship was carrying metal (manganese ore), not meat. It is conceivable the sailor writing the diary spelled it wrong ("meatal"?), or the translator made an error. As to whether the ship was headed to load or already loaded, again a translation error or simply undecipherable words may be the explanation.

Second, the names reported. While there was no "Keney" or "Kenney" on the roster, there was a "Kubey," the ship's cook. MacLean's account hints the cook went down with the ship but we have to remember he was seriously injured and relying on memory of a very confusing event after surviving a terrible ordeal. "Kubey" could easily have been read as one of the other names as transcribed in the largely unreadable diary.

Third, the mascot. The survivor who denied its existence was an officer, Steward M. Stanley MacLean. It does not seem unreasonable that young sailors would have such a pet and playfully keep its presence secret from the ship's officers. And, naturally, stuffy management personnel (then or now) would never consider the possibility of a violation of "company rules." Or MacLean might not have wanted to admit such a violation to his bosses in the era of authoritarian Harry Bennett management.

Fourth, the name "Garfield" or "Earfield." One of the passengers was named "Cornfield," and this is clearly the person referred to. The identification of Garfield/Earfield/Cornfield as an "officer" or "mate" (translations differ) could indeed be correct, as these are licensed titles, but refer to a position on a different ship than the EAST INDIAN since Cornfield is known to have been a passenger. It was not unusual for crew from lost or damaged ships to be passengers on other vessels, as indeed the EAST INDIAN survivors so returned to North America. This interpretation is reinforced by all three published versions of the diary which reported "Kenney took command" (UP) and "Keney was the one at the rudder and the one who gave instructions." If Kenney/Keney/Kubey took command, then it was as an officer (Cook) of the EAST INDIAN, in which case he would have outranked an officer from another ship who was merely a passenger.

Many details about the EAST INDIAN were correct in either of the translations, especially as to timing of the sinking and dates, and would have been unlikely to have been known in an obscure Brazilian city. On the other hand, there do remain some puzzling discrepancies, such as the number of liferafts (three in the diary version, four in MacLean's account); the diary states the liferaft/boat had oars, but the fact the rafts did not have oars was the reason that MacLean's lifeboat set off for help. Finally, if 34 men were left behind on four rafts (MacLean's account), that would have been eight or nine per raft; but the Brazilian diary reports on six men on the boat or raft washed ashore. Some of these discrepancies may be due to translation or readability problems.

Perhaps more important is Ford's whole supposition of a hoax, which was based on wartime hysteria about spies, plots, saboteurs, etc. Why ever would such a hoax be perpetrated, by Nazi spies or anyone else? No conceivable reason whatsoever.

Now, how can the authenticity of the lifeboat story be proven unquestionably? First, by checking records for the next-of-kin of those married seaman lost on the EAST INDIAN. We know that the diary writer was blond, wore glasses, was married to a woman named Janet, and had a son named Robert. We know that "Keney" was married to a woman named Mary. Very few (eight) of the civilian crew who failed to survive the attack were married. (The marital status of the lost Navy personnel and passengers, as well as their homes, is unknown.) Research in city directories for matching names, or newspaper obituaries about the known lost men, might make it possible to identify the last two to live on that lifeboat 50 years ago. Below the eight are listed with their home addresses as of May 1, 1942:

> Lemuel Marchant, 2nd Mate, 38, 1102 Hancock St., Chester, Pa.
> Joseph O'Brien, O S, 35, 188-26 119 Rd., St Albans, L.I., N.Y.
> Ernest Larson, 1st Engr, 50, 99 Warren St., Brockton, Mass.
> John Gillon, 2nd Engr, 31, 144 Belmont Ave., Millmont Park, Pa.
> John Gregory, oiler, 42, 5421 Woodcrest Ave., Philadelphia, Pa
> Norman Louderback, wiper, 25, 1208 Mt Ephraim St., Camden, N.J.
> Leo Kubey, cook, 44, 739 Gov Nichols St., New Orleans, La.*
> Manuel Rodriguez, messman, 37, 751 E 155 St., Bronx, N.Y.

> * Likely the other person ("Keney" or "Kenney") in the diary

Second, the possibility exists that Brazilian authorities kept a copy of the diary when the body of the young seaman found in the boat was interred. If the incident of the boat was not a hoax but did indeed happen, then there presumably would have been a coroner's inquest with the report filed in the municipal records of Maceio, Brazil. Miss McHugh asked Ford to undertake such an investigation in 1943, but the request apparently was never considered seriously under wartime conditions, even though the company then (as now) had personnel in Brazil and, of course, also the possible aid of the dealer network.

Third, research in Brazilian newspaper archives could produce one or more original stories which could be re-translated with scholarly accuracy to see if any of the discrepancies can be resolved. Clearly, these are beyond the scope of this book. But the Brazilian Lifeboat Story will remain a mystery until some of these steps, or others, are taken, even 50 years late for the survivors.

APPENDIX III - TABLES

TABLE I   **Laker-type Ships Operated by Ford**

	Name	Design	Year	Builder	Location
1.	LAKE ALLEN				
	(ex WAR TRUMPET)	1144	1918	GLE	Ecorse
2.	LAKE BENBOW	1020A	1918	DSC	Wyandotte
3.	LAKE CRYSTAL				
	(ex WAR SPINX)	1144	1918	GLE	Ecorse
4.	LAKE FARGE	1093	1918	ASC	Cleveland
5.	LAKE FOLCROFT	1093	1918	DSC	Wyandotte
6.	LAKE FREELAND	1093	1918	ASC	Lorain
7.	LAKE FRUGALITY	1093	1920	ASC	Lorain
8.	LAKE FRUMET	1093	1919	ASC	Lorain
9.	LAKE GORIN	1020A	1918	DSC	Wyandotte
10.	LAKE HEMLOCK				
	(ex WAR NAIAD)	1144	1918	GLE	Ecorse
11.	LAKE INAHA				
	(ex LAKE FRESNO)	1093	1919	ASC	Lorain
12.	LAKE KYTTLE	1044	1918	MSC	Manitowoc
13.	LAKE LOUISE				
	(ex WAR DRUM)	1144	1918	GLE	Ashtabula
14.	LAKE ORMOC	1020A	1918	DSC	Wyandotte
15.	LAKE OSWEYA	1020B	1918	SSC	Saginaw
16.	LAKE PLEASANT				
	(ex WAR SPRITE)	1144	1918	GLE	Ashtabula
17.	LAKE SAPOR	1093	1918	DSC	Wyandotte
18.	ONEIDA	NA	1920	DSC	Wyandotte
19.	ONONDAGA	NA	1920	DSC	Wyandotte

ASC = American Shipbuilding Company
DSC = Detroit Shipbuilding Company
GLE = Great Lakes Engineering Works
MSC = Manitowoc Shipbuilding Company
SSC = Saginaw Shipbuilding Company

TABLE II Ford Motor Company Fleet - 1941

Vessel	Official Number	Built*	LOA	Beam	Depth	Gr Tons	Net Tons	Cap @ 21 ft.	Crew	Fuel	H.P.	Engines	Avg RPM	Kph @ Avg RPM
M/S BENSON FORD	223909	1924	612'	62'2"	32'	8626	6393	14500 NT	36	Diesel	3000	Sun Dxfrd	82	12.5
M/S HENRY FORD II	223980	1924	611'	62'2"	32'	8877	7074	15200 NT	36	"	3000	"	80.9	12.5
M/S LAKE ORMOC	216716	1918/1928	261'	43'6"	24'2"	2422	1469	3500 NT	27	"	1000	Bsch Slzr	145	9.7
M/S LAKE OSWEYA	216914	1918/1930	261'	43'6"	24'2"	2398	1461	3500 NT	27	"	1000	Sun Dxfrd	98.1	10.9
M/S EAST INDIAN	216802	1918/1925	461'	58'	40'	8159	5160	10700 NT	40	"	5000	"	82.5	12.7
M/S GREEN ISLAND	236370	1937	300'	43'	20'	1946	1603	3000 NT**	20	"	1200	Cooper	200	11.5
M/S NORFOLK	236397	1937	300'	43'	20'	1946	1603	3000 NT**	20	"	1200	Bessemer	200	11.5
M/S CHESTER	230959	1931	300'	43'	20'	1819	1129	2800 NT**	22	"	1600	Wsthnghs	200	11.3
M/S EDGEWATER	230960	1931	300'	43'	20'	1819	1129	2800 NT**	22	"	1600	"	200	11.3
S/S ONEIDA	220779	1920	261'	43'6"	24'2"	2309	1440	3500 NT	29	Oil	1200	Amer Ship	83.5	9.5
S/S ONONDAGA	220782	1920	261'	43'6"	24'2"	2309	1440	3500 NT	29	"	1200	"	83.5	9.5
Tug BARLOW	217888	1919	142'	27'7"	14'8"	422	234		20	"	850	Beth Ship	99	12.8
Tug BARRALLTON	218009	1919	142'	27'7"	14'8"	426	200		20	"	850	"	99	12.8
Tug BUTTERCUP	218243	1919	142'	27'7"	14'8"	418	200		20	"	850	"	99	12.8
Tug HUMRICK	218072	1919	142'	27'7"	14'8"	418	190		20	"	850	"	99	12.8
Tug DEARBORN	231780	1932	85'	21'	13'	109	65		8	Diesel	660	CprBsmr	115	13.8
Tug SANTAREM (1)	NA	NA	45'	14'	5'	16	11		NA	"	60	"	NA	NA
Bge LAKE ALLEN	216194	1918/1927	261'	43'8"	20'4"	2015	1883	4300 NT	10	"				
Bge LAKE CRYSTAL	216168	1918/1927	261'	43'8"	22'6"	2015	1883	4300 NT	10	"				
Bge LAKE FARGE	217237	1918/1928	261'	43'6"	28'2"	2419	2231	3200 NT	10	"				
Bge LAKE FOLCROFT	217658	1918/1929	323'	43'6"	28'2"	3183	3040	5450 NT	13	Oil				
Bge LAKE FREELAND	217764	1918/1929	323'	43'6"	28'2"	3183	3040	5450 NT	13	"				
Bge LAKE FRUGALITY	218499	1920/1929	323'	43'6"	28'2"	3183	3040	5450 NT	13	"				
Bge LAKE FRUMET	218616	1919/1928	261'	43'6"	28'2"	2419	2231	3200 NT	10	Diesel				
Bge LAKE HEMLOCK	216261	1918/1927	261'	43'6"	22'6"	2015	1883	4300 NT	10	"				
Bge LAKE INAHA	217971	1919/1930	323'	43'6"	28'2"	3160	3018	5450 NT	13	Oil				
Bge LAKE KYTTLE	217087	1918/1927	257'	43'8"	22'6"	1991	1855	4300 NT	10	Diesel				
Bge LAKE LOUISE	216406	1918/1927	261'	43'6"	22'6"	2023	1890	4300 NT	10	"				
Bge LAKE PLEASANT	216738	1918/1930	324'	43'6"	22'6"	2644	2496	5900 NT	13	Oil				
Bge LAKE SAPOR	217657	1918/1930	323'	43'6"	28'2"	3159	3017	5450 NT	13	"				
Lighter NO.5		1913	100"	33'	8'9"			400 NT (Used at Edgewater)						

* Where two dates are shown, second is for reconditioning

** Tonnages shown for canal vessels is at 12'5" draft

(1 This vessel is at South America)

182

TABLE III Ford Vessel Statistics - 1975

	S/S WM CLAY FORD	S/S JOHN DYKSTRA	S/S ERNEST R. BREECH	M/S HENRY FORD II (SELF-UNLOADER)	M/S BENSON FORD
YEAR BUILT:	1953	1953	1952	1924 1974	1924
TO SELF-UNLOADER:	--	--			--
BUILT AT:	GREAT LAKES ENGINEERING WORKS River Rouge, Mich.	DEFOE SHIP BUILDING CO. Bay City, Mich.	DEFOE SHIP BUILDING CO. Bay City, Mich.	AMERICAN SHIP BUILDING CO. Lorain, Ohio	GREAT LAKES ENGNRG WORKS River Rouge, Mich.
VESSEL REGISTER NO.:	266029	265808	264317	223980	223909
HULL NUMBER:	300	424	422	788	245
GROSS REG. TONNAGE:	11,590	10,606	11,076	8,798	8,193
NET REG. TONNAGE:	8,590	8,083	8,472	5,934	5,193
TYPE POWER:	STEAM TURBINE	STEAM TURBINE	STEAM TURBINE	DIESEL	DIESEL
MAKE:	WESTINGHOUSE	DE LAVAL	BETHLEHEM	SUN-DOXFORD	SUN-DOXFORD
ENGINE HP:	7000	5000	4000	3000	3000
TYPE FUEL USED:	BUNKER C OIL	BUNKER C OIL	BUNKER C OIL	DIESEL OIL	DIESEL OIL
FUEL CAPACITY:	150,000 GALS	120,000 GALS	110,000 GALS	84,000 GALS	92,000 GALS
NORMAL FUEL CONS:	400 GALS PER HR	350 GALS PER HR	325 GALS PER HR	160 GALS PER HR	160 GALS PER HR
SPEED - LIGHT:	18 MPH	18 MPH	16.5 MPH	13.5 MPH	13.5 MPH
- LOADED:	16 MPH	16 MPH	15.5 MPH	12.5 MPH	12.5 MPH
CARGO CAPACITY:	20,400 G.T.	18,600 G.T.	18,700 G.T.	13,400 G.T.	13,400 G.T.
AT FEET OF DRAFT:	26' 1½ "	25' 2½ "	25' 4¾ "	22' 4"	22'
OVER ALL LENGTH:	647'	644'	642'	612'	612'
LENGTH BETWEEN PERPENDICULARS:	629'	618'	624'	590'	586'
BEAM:	70'	67'	67'	62'	62'
MOULDED DEPTH:	36'	35'	35'	32'	32'
NO. COMPARTMENTS:	3	4	4	2	3
NUMBER HATCHES:	19	19	19	17	18
SIZE HATCHES:	11' X 46'	11' X 43'	11' X 43'	12' X 40'	12' X 40'
NUMBER OF OFFICERS:	10	9	10	9	9
UNLICENSED CREW:	19	20	19	24	20
PASS QTRS FOR:	4	6	8	2	4
ELECTRIC POWER:	440-110 V.AC	440 V.AC	230-115 V.DC	220 V.DC	220 V.DC
BOW THRUSTER H.P.:	800	900	800	500	500
TYPE DIESEL ENGINE:	CATERPILLAR	CATERPILLAR	CATERPILLAR	CUMMINS	CUMMINS

BIBLIOGRAPHY

Books and Periodicals

Baut, Donald V., "A Salute to the Ford Motor Company Fleet," *The Dearborn Historian* , Vol.15 No.1: Winter, 1975.

Beall, Irl V., "The Yacht SIALIA and her Unique Engines, *Inland Seas*, Fall 1972.

Bennett, Harry, with Marcus, Paul, *We Never Called Him Henry*, Gold Medal Books, Greenwich, Connecticut, 1951.

Bryan, Ford R., *Beyond the Model T - The Other Ventures of Henry Ford* , Wayne State University Press, Detroit, 1990.

Dowling, Rev. Edward J., *The "Lakers" of World War I* , University of Detroit Press, Detroit, 1967.

Farago, Ladislas, *The Tenth Fleet* , Ivan Obolensky, Inc., New York, 1962.

_____, *The Game of the Foxes: The Untold Story of German Espionage in the United States and Great Britain During World War II*, David McKay Company, Inc., New York, 1971.

"Ford Motor Company," (5-part series), *The Detroit Marine Historian*, Vol.43, Nos.6, 7, 8, 9, 10: February through June, 1990.

Ford News, Feb.15, Dec.8, 1923; March 22, May 8, May 22, June 8, June 24, July 1, Aug.22, Oct.1, 1924; Jan.3, Feb.15, May 1, July 1, July 15, 1925; Jan.1, Feb.1, June 1, Aug.1, 1926; Feb.1, Oct.1, 1927; March 15, May 15, Aug.1, Aug.15, Sept.1, Sept.15, Oct.1, Oct.15, Nov.1, Nov.15, Dec.1, Dec.15, 1928; Jan.2, Jan.15, Feb.1, Feb.15, March 1, March 15, April 1, April 15, May 1, May 15, June 1, June 15, July 1, July 15, Aug.1, Aug.15, Sept.2, Sept.16, Oct.1, 1929; May 1, June 16, July 1, July 15, 1930; June, August, December, 1931; August 1937; June 1938; March 1939, June 1941.

Gannon, Michael, *Operation Drumbeat*, Harper & Row, New York, 1990.

Garrett, Wayne, "Scrapping The Surplus World War I Lakers," (3-part series), *The Detroit Marine Historian*, Vol.43, Nos.3, 4, 5: November, December 1989; January 1990.

Greenwood, John O., *Namesakes, 1930-1955, A Quarter Century of Lake Ships*, Freshwater Press, Cleveland, 1978.

Hill, Frank Ernest, and Wilkins, Mira, *American Business Abroad: Ford on Six Continents*, Wayne State University Press, Detroit, 1964.

"Lakes Shipping Company," The *Detroit Marine Historian* , Vol.43, No.2: October 1989.

MacLean, M. Stanley, *13 Days Adrift* , privately printed, St. Petersburg, Florida, 1943.

Morison, Samuel Eliot, *History of United States Naval Operations in World War II*, Vol.I, *The Battle of the Atlantic, Sept 1939-May 1943*, Little, Brown and Company, Boston, 1947.

_____, Vol.X, <u>The Atlantic Battle Won,</u> May 1943-May 1945, Little, Brown and Company, Boston, 1960.

Nevins, Allan, *Ford: The Times, The Man, The Company*, Charles Scribner's Son's, New York, 1954.

_____, and Hill, Frank Ernest *Ford, Expansion and Challenge*, 1915-1933, Charles Scribners Son's, New York, 1957.

_____, *Ford: Decline and Rebirth, 1933-1962*, Charles Scribners Son's, New York, 1962.

Pitt, Barrie, and the editors of Time-Life Books, *The Battle of the Atlantic*, Time-Life Books, Inc., Alexandria, Va., 1977.

Pope, Stephen, Taylor, James and Wheal, Elizabeth-Anne, *The Meridian Encyclopedia of the Second World War*, Penguin Books, New York, 1992.

Ratigan, William, *Great Lakes Shipwrecks & Survivors*, Eerdmans Publishing Company, Grand Rapids, Second Ed., 1971.

Rohwer, Jurgen, *Axis Submarine Successes*, Naval Institute Press, Annapolis, 1983.

Sorensen, Charles E., with Williamson, Samuel T., *My Forty Years With Ford*, W. W. Norton & Company Inc, New York, 1956.

Ford Archives

Just as the Nevins-Hill "official histories" of Ford Motor Company are exceedingly sparse in their mention of the Ford Fleet, so are the company records and memoirs maintained at the Henry Ford Museum and Greenfield Village.

Nevertheless, the following Accessions, including some not yet released by the company for public review, may contain irregular records of Ford's marine activities. Those in **boldface** were principal sources at the Archives for the supporting research of this book:

Accession 37-1 (re-numbered 263), Boxes 1, 2, 3; **Accession 38, Box 66**; **Accession 119**, Box 24, **35, 36, 37, 54**; Accession 235, Box 35; **Accession 264, Box 1**; **Accession 319, Box 1**; Accession 364; **Accession 390, Box 68, 69**; Accession 545, Box 3, 10; Accession 546; Accession 571; Accession 628; **Accession 675, Box 2**, 6, 7, 8, 9; Accession 685; **Accession 730, Box 8, 10**; Accession 742, Box 17, 39; Accession 748.

FOOTNOTES

1. Snider's original 1981 text read "shall never be separated," not anticipating the sale of Ford's fleet ten years later. Also note his respectful reference to the founder of Ford Motor Company (and other executives) throughout this memoir as "Mr.", rather than such more familiar terms as Henry, Old Henry or even just Ford.

2. Sorensen, <u>My Forty Years with Ford</u>, 170.

3. There is no authority for this perhaps apocryphal tale.

4. "Eagle's Nest on the Rouge," <u>Beyond the Model T</u>, Ford R. Bryan.

5. Obviously the high-level Interstate-75 bridge between Fort and Jefferson, completed in 1967, was not counted by Snider in this memoir, and in any event presents no impediment to navigation.

6. <u>Ford News</u>, May 8, 1924.

7. <u>Ford News</u>, June 1, 1924.

8. Snider's memoir does not mention the prices Ford paid for these two ships. However, a document in the Ford Archives shows depreciated "book value" in 1926 of $1,618,670 for the HENRY and $1,720,863 for the BENSON, indicting somewhat higher costs when new; the difference in 1926 values between the two nearly identical ships probably re flected varying equipment.

9. <u>Ford News</u>, August 22, 1924.

10. Irl V. Beall to C. J. Snider, September 25, 1972.

11. Not used

12. The after staterooms, however, were steam-heated.

13. The SIALIA continued serving as a private yacht under two or three owners over the next decade. In 1939, its name was changed to YANKEE CLIPPER and it went into charter service out of Philadelphia. In 1940 it was re-acquired by the Navy as USS CORAL but decommissioned in 1943. The former SIALIA was finally scrapped in 1947 ("The Yacht SIALIA and Her Unique Engines," <u>Inland Seas</u>, Fall 1972, Irl V. Beall).

14. <u>Ford News</u>, September 15, 1928.

15. <u>Ford News</u>, January 3, 1925. Early in 1925, the two lakers received new paint jobs, in which huge Ford script signs were highly visible, black against the side of the white cabin areas.

16. In 1926, the EAST INDIAN was assigned a book value of $1,293,784, indicating about $1.2 million had been spent on her refurbishing.

17. As a result of the Florida land boom.

18. Beall's memory may have been a bit hazy. The <u>Ford News</u> for June 1, 1926, reported the EAST INDIAN's first European voyage for Ford carried 3,984 cars and trucks plus 205 Fordson tractors. The tractors, 200 trucks, 415 touring cars, 4 roadsters and 65 chassis were unloaded at Trieste; 500 touring cars, 80 Tudors, 20 Fordors and 300 trucks at Barcelona; 1000 touring cars, 200 Tudors and 400 trucks in Copenhagen, and 200 touring cars, 200 Tudors and 400 trucks in Antwerp.

19. Beall to Snider, September 25, 1972

20. "Destruction of 199 Ships," <u>Beyond the Model T</u> , Ford R. Bryan. There is a discrepancy between the $8,530 amount Bryan reported and the cost per ship calculated by Ford Motor Company after World War II when it was attempting to settle loss claims with the Government. The claims discussion (Accession 730, Folder 48 in the Ford Archives) attributed a Government figure of from $16,883 to $18,530 per Laker, whereas Ford calculated $30,022 each (which included Ford's costs to transport them to Dearborn). However, the original purchase agreement Ford had with the Government was based on the scrap value of the ships; any which Ford wished to convert to use as barges or ships would require higher payments, and this may account for the differences. In any case, they were great bargains.

21. In 1937, the GORIN and the BENBOW were sold for $60,000 each to a Norwegian company and renamed NIDARDAL and NIDAROS. NIDARDAL is listed in most available accounts as having "foundered" December 16, 1941, location and cause unknown. She is not listed as the victim of an Axis submarine attack but could have been sunk by other enemy action. On the other hand, several Lakers came into Axis hands either before or during the war and several (especially those flying the Japanese flag) are known to have been sunk by Allied forces. Or she could have been the victim of inept seamanship or weather, as became the fate of so many Lakers in the postwar period. NIDAROS survived the war, was renamed EASTERN TRADER in 1946 under Panamanian registry and SANTA DOLORES in 1956. She was scrapped in Hong Kong in 1959-60.

22. SANTAREM was still at the Brazilian plantations when the U. S. entered World War II.

23. The HEBARD was in service for Ford as early as June 8, 1924, moving barges of lumber between Ford's Pequaming and L'Anse mills in Northern Michigan.

24. BALLCAMP went to Cumco Company, New York City, in 1933, and BAYMEAD and BATHALUM to the Soviet government in 1934, all three for $25,000 each.

25. In 1990 dollars, the barge captain's pay annualized would amount to $26,921, and the lowest-paid ordinary seaman, $11,747. The higher-ranking positions were paid scarcely more than in 1926, but the lower ranks had increased substantially, perhaps thanks to unionization. The 1942 wage for an ordinary seaman was 60% higher than in 1926, whereas a master was paid only 2% more, while a chief engineer had no increase. Ford's seamen belonged to the National Maritime Union. In 1988, Rouge Steel Company's agreement with the National Maritime Union called for Ordinary Seaman base rates of about $11 an hour, or about $1900 a month at straight time — and most of them worked substantial overtime during the sailing season.

26. This possessive use of the company name was common for many Detroiters, especially from factory or lower-level white-collar ranks. It reflected the fact that for more than 50 years, the company was owned by Henry Ford and his family. The same appellation — "Dodge's" — existed for the Dodge Plant, and for somewhat the same reason: it was owned by the Dodge brothers and their families until the formation of Chrysler Corporation.

27. The expression "girls" may not be correct in the 1990s, but it was the language used with no disrespect by men of Snider's generation.

28. Operation Drumbeat , Michael Gannon; The Tenth Fleet , Ladislas Farago; History of United States Naval Operations in World War II: Volume I, The Battle of the Atlantic ; Volume X, The Atlantic Battle Won, Samuel Eliot Morison.

29. Ironically, this later led to a trivial but lengthy dispute between Ford and the Government. On September 12, 1941, while in Halifax, Nova Scotia, the Navy ensign in charge of the team ordered the ship's captain to obtain an extra set of signal flags. The ship-supply company in Halifax sent Ford the bill for $152.50 in May of 1942, which Ford paid. But when Ford sought reimbursement from the Government in 1947 as part of general "settling up," the Government auditor demurred, demanding supporting receipts or affidavits. It took 16 exchanges of correspondence over a 14-month period before payment was finally approved! (Archives and Library, Henry Ford Museum & Greenfield Village.)

30. The company's rubber plantation in Brazil never succeeded in producing enough to supply the Rouge tire plant.

31. National Archives; Operations Archives Branch, Naval Historical Center. Postwar research in German Naval records showed the culprit was the U-96. Its Captain was Heinrich Lehmann-Willenbrock, one of Germany's top ten U-boat aces, credited with sinking 22 Allied ships (The Battle of the Atlantic, Time-Life Books). Nazi submarines radioed regular action reports back to their headquarters in Europe. The location of the sinking was recorded by the U. S. Navy as 33° N, but this obviously is a typographical error, since that would have placed it east of South Carolina in the middle of the Atlantic, hardly the route to a convoy for the USSR. The U-96 was sunk almost at war's end during an Army Air Force raid of the Wilhelmshaven German Naval Base on the North Sea, March 30, 1945.

32. As noted in the editor's introduction, it was an inquiry in 1982 from a niece of LAKE OSWEYA chief engineer John Kilpatrick that resulted in this book being brought to publication.

33. The same date that the U. S. suffered its last major Pacific Ocean defeat, surrender of Corregidor in the Philippines, while also achieving its first victory — in the Battle of the Coral Sea.

34. This sub was the U-125. For more about her voyage and compassionate but doomed captain, see *Appendix II A.*

35. Curiously, no official records on the GREEN ISLAND sinking could be located either in the National Archives or the Ford Archives. The account is wholly from secondary sources, including whatever notations Clare Snider may have made at the time or recalled.

36. Just how unsafe these waters were in 1942 is illustrated by the sinkings chalked up by the U-125, as related in *Appendix II A.*

37. German records showed the ONEIDA was sunk by the German submarine U-166, which itself had barely two more weeks of life. A Coast Guard airplane flying out of Houma, Louisiana, sank the U-166 with all hands in the Gulf of Mexico on August 1, one of the very few Nazi subs sunk by Americans in 1942.

38. Eastern War Time. As we have seen, there was no consistency in the way time (GCT, Z, GMT, EWT) was reported in those early days of the war. 1630 hours July 23 would be eight hours earlier than 0030 July 24, about right for the time zone differences, considering special war hours in effect then. The location difference probably can be accounted for by an Intelligence intercept of the submarine's report or the resulting Nazi propaganda announcement, which became the basis of the War Shipping notification, sent before the official U. S. Navy report was prepared.

39. German records revealed that the ONONDAGA had been sunk by the submarine U-129. This submarine was "placed out of service" in July 1944 at the Nazi submarine base at Lorient, Brittany, Occupied France, and was reported by the U. S. Navy as scuttled in May 1945. Presumably it had suffered either operational or bomb damage before being trapped helpless by the Allied invasion of Normandy to the north the month before.

40. In those days, a favorite wartime warning was "Loose lips sink ships." Whether the concern was justified by actual Nazi spy operations is unknown. Naval histories do not address the issue.

41. At the Robins Drydock, Brooklyn, from April 13 to 26 for "defensing."

42. According to postwar settlements, the EAST INDIAN officers and crew demanded a 15% war bonus before signing over because of the obvious hazards. Ford readily agreed but when it tried to obtain reimbursement from the Government in 1945 for the added $5,268 paid from May 8 to November 3, 1942, the claim was denied because of the nature and language of the time charter being imposed at the time.

43. Capt. Ste. Marie had been master of the ONONDAGA before the war.

44. Inhibited no doubt by wartime secrecy restraints, MacLean made no reference to the cargo, but it most likely was war supplies for the Soviet Union. The route there through the Persian Gulf and Iran was not only all-weather but much safer than the northern route to Murmansk.

45. There appear to be discrepancies as to how many were lost and how many survived. The official Marine Casualty Report filed February 15, 1943, put the losses at 34 crew, 7 passengers and 11 Navy Armed Guard. Those listed as having survived (more reliable than those lost since there may have been some "unknowns" given wartime circumstances) were 13 crew, 2 passengers and 2 Navy personnel (one crewman who died after being rescued is not included). Together those add to only 69. An undated list (in the Ford Archives) of persons lost on the EAST INDIAN includes names of 10 passengers (not 7 as in the Casualty Report) and 34 crew — but 2 of the crew listed as lost indeed were among those saved. In addition the original May 8, 1942, Navy personnel roster for the ship has 11 listed, and if no others joined the ship after the roster was made up or its sailing from New York, that means only 9 Navy were lost, since 2 were saved. On the other hand, MacLean's account reports 13 in the Navy crew ("a navy crew of 12 stalwart young men who were commanded by our Ensign Mr. Axtell").

46. The ship's cook was Leo Kubey, 44, of New Orleans, Louisiana. However, there is a possibility he did not "go down with the ship" but survived to die on one of the liferafts. See *Appendix II E 22.*

47. Presumably Second Cook George Lloyd, 22, of Cape May, New Jersey.

48. Second Engineer John Gillon (also spelled Gillian in one list), 31, of Millmont Park, Pennsylvania. Both he and George Lloyd were lost. Bernard probably was Edward Bernard Hawlley, 32, the ship's electrician, of Laurelton, Long Island, New York. He was listed on the crew list as unmarried, but a daughter, Mary Eleanor Hawlley of the same address, was granted his life insurance and pay benefits.

49. Patrick Keenan, 35, of Crum Lynn, Pennsylvania.
50. For more information on the U-181 and the consequences of the mate's answers, see *Appendix II A*.
51. A 31-year-old from Matthews, Virginia, near Norfolk, the listed hometown of four other crewmen.
52. The count was either taken before MacLean transferred to the lifeboat, or was mistaken, since ultimately 18 on the lifeboat reached safety, one to die later from exposure. See also *footnote 45*.
53. Marion Capers, 38, of Bohannon, Virginia, near Matthews and Norfolk, another of the survivors.
54. Probably Martin Posti, 33, of Rousseau, Michigan, southwest of Houghton.
55. Joseph O'Brien, 35, of St. Albans, Long Island, New York.
56. Bert Doyle, 66, of Upland, Pennsylvania.
57. Archibald McHugh, 48, of New York City. His sister later wrote to Ford seeking more information on his death.
58. Jack Lewis Riggon, a U. S. Navy able seaman.
59. Sparks was Arthur Esner, 43, of Chester, Pennsylvania.
60. Flip was either Basil Florentine, 45, or Thomas Miranda, 29. Both were from Brooklyn, and survived.
61. Identity unknown. No EAST INDIAN crewman listed a Texas hometown, and those of passengers and Navy personnel are unknown.
62. Walter Fraser, 22, of Salem, Massachusetts, an oiler on the EAST INDIAN.
63. The first U. S. Navy report from interviews with survivors, dated January 4, 1943, identified the rescue ship as "HMSA Corvette DURENDER." (HMSA meant "His Majesty's South African.")
64. As noted elsewhere, such rumors were rampant during the war years, and even found their way into official Navy reports. There is no evidence, however, that they were true.
65. This editor disputes the 1943 Ford belief in a hoax. Plausible explanations can be found for the main reasons of their probably erroneous finding. See *Appendix II E 22*.
66. Previously published accounts erroneously attribute the ALLEN's loss to enemy action.
67. Some accounts give a different date in April, and a slightly different location.
68. Actually, it was Bennett who hired Bugas shortly after Henry Ford II returned from the Navy. But "Young Henry" knew quality when he saw it and quickly utilized Bugas's skills.
69. Schanbeck indeed was well connected in Grosse Pointe, but in a tolerant way rather than as an equal of the elite, for his father had been the village policeman for many years.
70. Actually, records were found in the Ford Archives documenting operating profits for the ships as early as 1926 and for the Ford Navigation Company as recent as 1941. Snider would have had no knowledge of these and undoubtedly by 1947 a more professional analysis was needed, which he initiated.
71. In recent years, the MEBA and the MM&P merged with the NMU. Ken Gerasimos, a former Ford licensed and unlicensed Marine employee, and son of Capt. Michael Gerasimos of the Ford Fleet, is a high ranking officer of this union.
72. The BENSON's cost in 1924 had been around $1.8 million, or about $2.6 million in 1953 dollars. So the CLAY was quite a step upward in terms of equipment costs.
73. Ratigan, Great Lakes Shipwrecks & Survivors.
74. Rohwer, Axis Submarine Successes.
75. Gannon, Morison.
76. Time-Life, The Battle of the Atlantic.
77. Time-Life; Rohrer.
78. A follow-up inquiry was sent to Ms. Kilpatrick at the above address early in 1992, ten years later, as this book project was getting under way. It was returned as undeliverable. Were it not for her inquiry, this book would never have been published.
79. This was a typographical error. It should have read Indiga.
80. There was also a column for "nationality;" however, all were listed as "American."
81. Probably a typographical error: "NJ" intended.
82. Two of those listed, James Smith and George Gleason, were among those reported November 20, 1942, as safe at Capetown after the MacLean lifeboat was rescued. One, Henry Helsley, was not on the May 1, 1942, original crew list.
83. The slightly different wording of the stories as published in the New York Times and the Washington Daily News probably are merely the customarily different versions for a morning newspaper (Times) and an afternoon paper of the same day (News) as prepared by the United Press. An identical story to that in the Washington paper appeared on page one of The Detroit News the same day. None of them recognized that the EAST INDIAN was a Ford ship.
84. Evidently Mr. Axtell's son had been promoted subsequent to his listing as an ensign in the May 6, 1942, Port Director's Report. MacLean identified young Axtell as an Annapolis graduate who had just completed a convoy to Murmansk, USSR, at the time he took over command of the EAST INDIAN gun crew.
85. In the last paragraph of Miss McHugh's letter, there is confirmation that the Nazi propaganda machine utilized the sinking reports routinely radioed back to U-boat headquarters, and that these were reported in the U. S., albeit with skepticism. The curious aspect is that she (and presumably other "next-of-kin") became aware of the sinking long before it became "official." It is common in warfare for successes to be exaggerated and losses to be underplayed, sometimes even with the best of intentions to be forthright, due to confusion and excitement of witnesses. However, if the Allies had reacted to the Nazi submarine reports, which they evidently brushed off as false propaganda, they might have significantly reduced the losses. The German submarines apparently stayed put without interference for several days where they had good hunting, as shown in the cases of the U-125 in the Caribbean and the U-181 in the Indian Ocean.
86. Incorporated in the text as Chapter 12, The Brazilian Lifeboat Story
87. Note that the last name is the same as that of an oiler, Joseph Vealie, lost on the LAKE OSWEYA.

VESSEL INDEX